FORTRESSES AND TREASURES OF
ROMAN WALES

A Roman Auxiliary in battle dress, as depicted by a member of the Ermine Street Guard who perform each year at Caerleon. (By kind permission of the National Museum of Wales, Cardiff.)

FORTRESSES AND TREASURES OF

ROMAN WALES

SARAH SYMONS

First published in Great Britain in 2009 by
The Breedon Books Publishing Company Limited
Breedon House, 3 The Parker Centre,
Derby, DE21 4SZ.

By the same author
The Wonders of Dan yr Ogof
(The National Showcave Centre for Wales)

ISBN 978-1-85983-699-6

Printed and bound by TJ International Ltd., Padstow, Cornwall.

CONTENTS

ACKNOWLEDGEMENTS

I would like to express my sincere thanks to the National Museum of Wales, to the Museums of Brecon, Caerleon, Carmarthen and Segontium, Caernarfon, for allowing me to take photographs of their exhibits, and to the National Museum, Cardiff, and the Museums of Abergavenny, Carmarthen and Swansea for providing me with excellent photographs of those items relevant to the book.

I would also like to thank Swansea, Brecon, Neath, Carmarthen and Cardiff Central Library for allowing me to view their archives, and also to the Shropshire County Library for their valuable assistance.

I would also like to extend my grateful thanks to the Glamorgan and Gwent Archaeological Trust, Swansea, and to Dyfed Archaeological Trust, Llandeilo, for their kind hospitality by allowing me to view their archives and for the valuable contribution of photographs, and to the Achaelogia Cambrensis and Cadw for allowing me to use their photographs. And to Mr Eric Jones of Gaer Farm, Brecon.

INTRODUCTION

The mighty force of Rome swept across Western Europe until it came to the furthermost point on the French coast, but, not in the least deterred by the expanse of sea confronting them, the Roman army launched their invasion fleet on Britannia, with four legions, and landed on the shores of Kent in AD 43. Despite opposition from the native tribes across southern England, the Roman army reached the River Severn and the boundaries of the land we now call Wales by AD 48. The Roman legions also invaded Wales along its eastern borders in AD 47, and, in the campaigns led by Ostorius Scapula, overthrew the Cornovii and consolidated their hold on the territory with a further network of military installations.

According to the Roman historian Tacitus, the Emperor Claudius had instructed the army to 'secure' this south-west region, which included south and south-east Wales, so by the mid-50s the Romans had pushed forward to the River Usk and established their might in the form of a strongly defended legionary fortress at Usk itself, thereby beginning an occupation that lasted over 300 years.

There were several ruling tribes in Wales at the time of the Roman invasion: the **Silures**, who dominated the entire region of the south, from the Wye to the Gower peninsular; the **Demetae** in the south west; the **Cornovii** and **Dobuni** in the east; the **Ordovices** in the mountainous area of central Wales which extended into Snowdonia and the eastern boundaries of Roman Wales; and the **Deceangli** in the far north, whose lands also stretched eastwards to where the Romans had established another legionary fortress at Chester.

To enforce their grip on the territory, the Romans then built a long line of forts that extended along the entire length of Wales. These stations not only guarded the military roads that they had constructed to link the garrisons, but also guarded their approaches. However, the Romans encountered severe resistance from the Silures, in whose territory the greatest number of forts had been built. This Celtic tribe, described by Tacitus as the most fierce and courageous of all, waged guerrilla-like warfare on the invaders at every opportunity and inflicted losses among their forces. It is said that they even defeated an entire legion in AD 52.

Wars and battles produce their own heroes, and in the case of the Silures they had a great champion in Caractacus. He was the son of Cunobelinus, a powerful king of south-east England, but after falling foul to the Romans at the onset of the invasion he had fled to South Wales and formed a rebel army to fight the Romans. Tacitus stated that the success of the campaigns against the Romans made Caractacus pre-eminent among British chieftains, and he was regarded as Wales's greatest hero. However, after a fierce battle in AD 51, in which he was defeated, Caractacus escaped north but was betrayed by the queen of the Brigantes. She handed him over to the Romans, and Caractacus was subsequently taken to Rome where he was paraded through the streets before being brought before the Emperor Claudius. However, so impressed was

Claudius by Caractacus's bearing and oratory, that he spared his life and granted him freedom so that he and his wife could live in honourable captivity.

However, under Julius Frontinus the Silures were finally subdued during the years AD 74–78, thus ending 30 years of fierce and often bloody confrontations. The near annihilation of the Ordovices in the north by the next govenor and general, Julius Agricola, was quickly followed with the occupation of Anglesey, and the final conquest of Wales occurred during the following year.

Following the final conquest, Emperor Severus was anxious that the Roman way of life should be introduced into the country, with emphasis on law and order. Accordingly, Julius Agricola, who also conquered the north, instructed his troops to begin treating the defeated Celts 'with justice and moderation'. So, after the brutality of the invasion the populace began experiencing a more peaceful era, with a gradual integration into Roman customs and culture, with many Roman soldiers marrying native women and setting up homes in the province. The Romans also gave the Celts an opportunity to govern themselves, and set up administrative centres with their own law courts. This gave the people a sense of citizenship and the management of their own affairs. Soon, the Roman way of life became an integral part of their lives, and they even adopted the Roman style of dress and learned to read and write. Into this equation the Romans also introduced the monetary system and, of course, the Latin language, which was widely used by the Church for many centuries afterwards. Moreover, much of the Roman vocabulary found its way into the Welsh language. Those who won favour with the Romans or held high office lived in luxurious villas, a number of which have been discovered around the country, with a concentration along the Vale of Glamorgan at Llantwit Major and Barry.

With the retreat of the Roman troops back to Rome in the fifth century, the forts were soon abandoned, left to become ruins upon the landscape until most of their stonework was eventually plundered by mediaeval builders. In some places only their bare foundations have survived. Others have been covered over by centuries of earth and grass, leaving their discovery to the good fortune of being ploughed up in modern times.

These discoveries have provided us with the means of looking back to the Roman period, and by sifting through the remains, archaeologists have been able to tell us what these noble structures once looked like and about the precision with which they were built. The archaeologists have also been able to identify the various buildings around the forts and the function they served all those centuries ago. Even the discovery of soldiers' personal effects and cooking utensils, etc., have given us an insight into their daily regimes.

The fortresses of Wales have certainly yielded a good supply of treasures from the Roman period and have provided us with an excellent opportunity to study the artistry of the Roman potter and metal worker. Their craft has lived on despite being buried for 18 centuries, and it is also to the archaeologists' credit that many of these treasures have been restored to their former beauty, to be admired and enjoyed for all time.

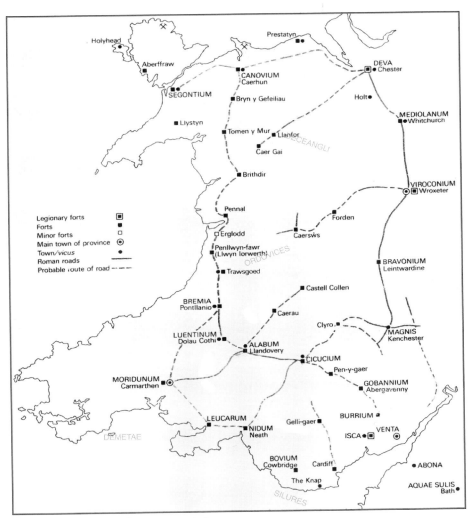

A map of Wales during the Roman period.

USK (BURRIUM)

Having experienced such fierce opposition from the Silures, the Romans began building forts inside their territory, starting with the one at Usk around AD 55, to bring such concerted opposition to an end and gain control of the area.

The legion to whom this awesome task was assigned was the 20th, which had come up to the 'front line' from Gloucester where they had been based upon arriving in the West Country. The legion had originally come from Neuss in the Rhineland of Germany and comprised over 5,300 heavily armed infantrymen, all of whom were Roman citizens as opposed to their auxiliary comrades who had been drawn from the conquered provinces of the Empire and who occupied all the auxiliary fortresses. The legionaries were also better paid than auxiliaries and occupied positions of greater trust within the army.

The campaign for the conquest of Siluria was long and bloody, and fraught with disaster. The Romans had underestimated the fighting prowess of the Silures, whose resistance lasted over 30 years.

The Roman historian Tacitus recorded that 'as the army was experiencing difficulties, a station was planned in the land of the Silures'. This may have referred to Usk. The siting of a legionary fortress here was also of great strategic importance, as it commanded all routes of communication along the Usk Valley and was therefore in a position to repel any opposition from the Silurian tribe. However, the siting of the fortress on the eastern bank of the river was not ideal. It was already the start of winter when building commenced, but the Romans, not familiar with the wintry conditions, built their fortress on the flood plain which, thereafter, caused many problems whenever the level of the river rose.

The existence of a Roman fort on this site was recorded by the Egyptian geographer Ptolemy (AD 100–170), who referred to it as Bulleaum; although it was mentioned as Burrium in the *Antonine Itinerary* – the Roman travel guide, compiled in the second century – and identified as being on *Iter XIII* (Route 13). The *Itinerary* also placed Burrium centrally between Caerleon and Monmouth, which it is. The renowned antiquarian William Camden intimated as far back as the 16th century that he was certain there were Roman remains at Usk, and historian John Horsley confirmed that the Bulleaum mentioned by Ptolemy and the Burrium of the *Itinerary* were one and the same.

Physical evidence that a Roman fort existed here came during the 19th century when, like in other locations throughout Wales, Roman artefacts began to appear in large quantities on the surface.

It was during the construction of the gaol in 1841 that a paved street was discovered and later identified as Roman. Excavations were then carried out there by archaeologist A.D. Berrington during the winter months of 1877–78. An interesting find from these excavations was a fragment of an extremely rare type of Roman glassware. The vessel was a thin, blown flask of a deep royal blue colour that had been covered with white globules. Also among the finds were a few pieces of clay cones, which were used for separating pots being fired in a kiln. This suggested that one was in the vicinity. Final confirmation regarding the existence of the fort came with the discovery of 70–80 Roman coins at the courthouse site.

In 1878, also in the vicinity of the courthouse, a pit was discovered that was 'extraordinarily large' and filled with broken pieces of pottery, illustrating the type of pots used by the Roman soldiers for drinking, eating and cooking. Among them was a straight-sided jar made of smooth red-coloured pottery called Samian. This pottery, which comprises high-class tableware, is also referred to as *Terra Sigillata*, and is decorated with various pictorial scenes and patterns in high relief. Samian ware sometimes displays the maker's name stamped somewhere on the article. This highly glossed pottery was imported to these shores from factories in Gaul and was widely distributed throughout Europe to supply the Roman army wherever it went. It was mainly used by the officers, but civilians in the Roman settlements were also known to grace their tables with it. Also on the site of the courthouse, a large fragment of a tombstone was found commemorating the death of a young child belonging to a serving soldier. This had been taken from the legion's cemetery and re-used as a building block.

A little to the east, a gravel bank was found that was 35ft wide and 9ft high with its direction running parallel with a ditch, which suggested it was part of the fort's outer defences.

The remains of wooden huts were also found, but there was evidence that these had been burnt down during Roman times. The evidence suggested that after the aforementioned ditch had been filled in the area had been occupied by stone buildings, among whose foundations lay the base of a furnace used for iron smelting. As works such as furnaces were usually located close to the defences for fire-safety purposes, it was more than probable that the excavators had found the *Via Sagularis* which skirted the perimeter of each fort, so named after the *segum* – a cloak worn by the soldiers who assembled there for duty.

The rampart itself had been almost completely levelled in the past, but sufficient remained to reveal that it had consisted mainly of turf and had been about 10ft high. Closer scrutiny revealed that in digging one of the ditches the Romans had had to cut into the underlying gravel to attain the height they wanted and had created a *berm*, an area 6ft across which separated the rampart and ditch. This space often served as an extra area of defence.

The rest of the fortress was not discovered until 1965, when its south-eastern corner and outer defences containing a single bank and 15ft-wide ditch were found lying under Usk's Maryport Street. At one point, the ditch had been cut across the cold plunge bath of the legion's bathhouse, which was similar in style to modern-day Turkish baths and contained a cold bath room (*frigidarium*); a warm bath room (*tepidarium*); and a hot water bath (*caldarium*). Unfortunately, excavation of this building could not proceed as it was obstructed by modern buildings.

As this area was designated to become the site for the new local government headquarters, a rescue operation was requested before further building work obliterated all trace of the Roman remains. This was carried out during 1973–74 by Professor W.H. Manning, on behalf of the Department of the Environment and the Department of Archaeology of University College, Cardiff.

It was soon discovered that the fortress was of a considerable size. Its length, north to south, extended in the region of 1,558ft, and its width measured 1,124ft, thus giving a total area exceeding 48 acres. The fortress was also found to have had four symmetrically placed entrances with double portals 45ft wide to carry a double carriageway. These had been flanked by timbered twin towers, 10ft deep. There was also a bridge crossing the ditch in front of the east gate which led directly into the interior. The south-east gate, the *porta principalis sinistra*, was also uncovered to show that it was similar in plan to the north-east and north-west gates, all of which were considered to be the most elaborate to have been found in Britain. However, only one complete internal tower and parts of three others were uncovered. It was not possible to excavate the southern defences either, but a geophysical survey in 1973 showed them to be of a similar plan to the others. The defences on the northern side were located in a sewer trench, and the rampart there was found to have a depth of 8.5ft and was just over 16ft wide. The ditch was 6ft deep, over 17ft wide and cut into a deep V-shape with a flat bottom. These enormous ditches would have provided the fortress with an adequate defence system, and any intruder caught in the middle would also have been in the sights of the archers, whose range usually extended as far as the defences.

All Roman forts were built to the same military plan, so that whenever the troops were moved from one to the other they knew precisely where each individual building was in the event of an attack. For instance, behind the rampart was the *intervallum*. This was a narrow strip of land that surrounded the inside perimeter of each fortress, and in the event of an attack it gave unhindered access to all points along the ramparts. At Usk, a series of nine ovens had been cut into the outer ditch. They covered a length of 70ft, which extended to the edge of the wooden bridge. It was common practice for the Roman army to place their ovens up against the ramparts. This not only protected them from the wind, but also avoided accidental fires from breaking out and threatening the internal buildings, especially if they had been made of timber, as was normally the case. Another interesting discovery along the *intervallum* were some kilns and semi-circular hearths with clay bases. Among the debris was some lead sheeting which had been left with nails still attached.

The *Via Sagularis* skirting the perimeter was 26ft 3in wide and constructed with pebbles and Llanbadoc rock, which had been quarried on the west bank of the river almost opposite the fortress. This road also served the granaries, with each one large enough to store a year's supply of grain for 500 men. In a fortress of this size, therefore, at least 10 granaries would have been required to feed an entire legion.

The granaries were long, narrow structures with massive walls strengthened with external buttresses to withstand the weight of the grain and to support the roofs. The floors rested on wooden stilts a few feet above the ground to keep the grain well ventilated and protected from rodents. There were also loading bays and an area of hard-standing in front of each building where carts delivering the grain could manoeuvre back and forth. Loading platforms, too, built to the same height as the vehicles, enabled the grain to be transported straight into the granary.

The entire granary site was successfully exposed during the excavation and revealed the numerous post holes into which the stilts had been driven. The buildings had been laid out in pairs, suggesting that five of the granaries had been split into two halves with a roof that ran the entire length of each building. The pitch of the roofs was set at 30–35 degrees to ensure that water or snow would run off freely and prevent water from seeping under the edges of the timber shingles lining the roof. Like tiling, the shingles, made of rectangular slips of wood, were nailed onto the roof. The design of the smaller granaries appeared to allow ventilation under the shelter of a central roof which also extended over the loading bay. Apart from this group of small granaries, there was also a group of three much larger ones. One, measuring 119ft x 42ft, had a pit cut through its trenches and contained fragments of Flavian pottery (AD 69–117), which suggested that the granaries were among the first to have been built. Some cobbling was found in front of their western ends that had provided an area of hardstanding for the wagons.

It was estimated that the large granaries at Usk had been capable of storing rations for 2,826 men and that the smaller ones had stored rations for 1,625. After their decline, supposedly when the fort was later abandoned, nothing else had occupied their site until well into the second century.

The major road within this and any other fortress was the *Via Principalis*. This ran east to west across the centre of the fort and usually split it into two unequal parts. Along its route were the principal buildings that included the *Principia* itself – the headquarters

The excavation of the Granaries at Usk. (By kind permission of the Glamorgan & Gwent Archaeological Trust.)

building – containing all the administrative offices and ceremonial items like the regimental standards, religious objects and the regimental funds. For security reasons this building was always located in the central position with the *Praetorium* – the residence of the commandant – standing next to it on the adjoining *Via Praetoria*. Being the main street and carrying all the heavy wheeled traffic, the *Via Principalis* was built to the highest standards with the best materials available. Straddling the roadway to the south were the eight houses accommodating the senior officers and the legion's workshops and stores, but as the remains of these were lying immediately beneath the town's cattle market they could not be excavated.

However, the foundations of the *Praetorium* were found, showing that the house had consisted of a small range of rooms on its western side, which were separated from the main block by a narrow corridor and had been built around a large central courtyard. Among the rooms would have been offices for the commandant's military staff who used them during the day before returning to their own quarters when not on duty. The house was usually built to the commandant's personal requirements, as befitted his rank, and was styled on a Mediterranean villa similar to the one he would have had back home. It was usually embellished with features such as colonnades and a covered verandah overlooking a central courtyard with a stone-built well for his own private water supply. Some of his rooms would also have been heated with a hypocaust. This was a system whereby heat from an outside furnace was conveyed into the building under floors that were raised on brick or tiled pillars. The heat was also conveyed through vents in the walls. This method was the Roman central heating system and was a forerunner of our own.

The hypocaust would also have provided the commandant with hot water for his own private bathing suite. Attending him were many servants who were not necessarily military, but were probably slaves drawn from the locality.

The other major discoveries to be fully excavated were the six barrack blocks built against the defences in the north-east corner, in the upper part of the fortress called the *retentura*.

As was usual, the barracks were laid out in pairs facing inwards on to a common street with 12 rows of cubicles, also arranged in pairs for the recruits. Each cubicle accommodated eight men. This derived from the time when eight men shared a single tent while on manoeuvres. The centurions' quarters were much larger and were located at the end of each block, which took up at least one-third of the entire building. As their quarters comprised more rooms, sometimes as many as 10, they were also far wider than the rest. Some of these rooms were used as offices, with the smaller ones, no larger than walk-in cupboards, being used for storing armour, etc.

One barrack block had an unusual internal arrangement of pits and recesses in the walls, where remnants of hay and oat seeds were found. This suggested that fodder had been stored there for horses and that the building had been a combination of a barrack and stable block with quarters for the grooms. It is, of course, possible that when the fortress was abandoned the barracks were converted to accommodate horses. This conversion in a Roman fortress is, so far, unparalleled among others in Britain, although combined structures for men and horses have been found in Roman forts on the Continent.

The presence of a cavalry unit in a legionary fortress was not considered unusual, since 120 mounted troops were attached to each legion. These units would have given the legion's scouts greater access to the mountainous regions to police the area, and given despatch riders swift communication between the individual forts, which were built only a day's march from one another in order to summon help whenever attacked.

It was found that one of the barracks had been repeatedly repaired. Circular post holes showed where timber uprights had supported a verandah, 31ft wide, and this would have given the barrack block some protection from the weather. The presence of clay hearths in two rooms indicated that the occupants, unaccustomed to the British winter, had built fires there to keep themselves warm. One block showed that it had been deliberately dismantled, with any re-usable timbers removed and what had not been required burnt on the spot.

Large pits and numerous holes indicated the whereabouts of the communal latrines. These wooden structures consisted of walls made of wattle and daub with panels that had not entirely reached the roof. This allowed light and ventilation to enter under the eaves. The roofs were also covered with wooden shingles. Inside, the toilet facilities were very basic, with no partitions or individual cubicles. The men were obliged to sit together on wooden seats over a drain, either in a straight row or an L-shaped arrangement. Afterwards, they washed themselves with sponges on top of sticks that had been dipped in vinegar. These were then rinsed in a water-filled gutter.

Excavations also showed that the pits had been cleaned out from time to time, but they were found to contain numerous fragments of discarded Samian ware. These were dated to the mid-first century, when the fort was built. The pits had been dug down to a depth of 10ft, and as their area was also quite extensive it was no wonder that the soldiers had used them for throwing away broken and unwanted items. From the quantities of glass fragments also recovered in the area, it was possible to reconstruct a number of bottles and large jars back to their original state. These marvellous examples in pale green glass can be seen in the Caerleon Legionary Museum. There are also several reconstructed buff-coloured storage jars on display alongside the glass.

As some coins of Claudius and Nero were discovered throughout the fortress, they confirmed its establishment was around the year AD 55. More specifically, the chance discovery of a small disc with a charging boar in high relief confirmed that the 20th Legion had occupied the fortress. This animal had become the official insignia of the legion and had probably broken off a piece of ceremonial armour.

About 20 years after its founding, the fortress was abandoned, probably as a result of the flooding, and a new legionary fort was established seven miles down river at Caerleon, where supplies could be brought in directly from the sea. A much smaller fort was then built inside Usk's north-eastern quarter and was probably maintained as a works depot with a much reduced garrison. This was the time when the granaries fell into decline as less grain was required.

The bulk of the 20th Legion was transferred north to Deva (Chester) to take control of a legionary fortress there. But, with the need to maintain military control over this part of Siluria, the army built another fortress at nearby Abergavenny, which was manned by auxiliary troops.

ABERGAVENNY (GOBANNIUM)

This fort is the Gobannium mentioned in the *Antonine Itinerary*, and it was established on the banks of the River Usk to play a vital role in supporting the legionary fort at Usk before the military headquarters was transferred to Caerleon. It also protected the borders of what was becoming the new Roman province. In this respect, it then became one of a long chain of forts established throughout the region we now call Wales.

The name Gobannium is said to have derived from the Celtic word 'Gobann', meaning ironsmith, which suggested that there was an earlier Iron Age settlement here. The name of the River Gefenni, once called Gobannia, means 'river of the ironsmith'. The modern name of Abergavenny literally means 'the mouth of the Gefenni'.

The fort, classed as an auxiliary one, was built soon after the legionary fortress at Usk, in about AD 57, on level ground close to the river, for a more permanent role. The garrison consisted of auxiliaries from the Second Augustan Legion. The fort was also linked to Caerleon in the south-west by means of the Roman road that also ran southwards to the fortress at Usk. At Abergavenny the Roman road continued towards the other strategically placed fort at Brecon in the north-east.

A display showing examples of Roman pottery found at Gobannium, inculuding an oil jar and the neck of an amphora. (By kind permission of the Abergavenny Museum.)

Evidence that a possible Roman fort existed here surfaced in 1848, when cremation burials were found on the site of an old cemetery along the Hereford road to the west of Bailey Park on the outskirts of the town. The burials were enclosed in ancient stone coffins, inside which were found Roman Samian and other domestic vessels. A small hoard of silver coins was also found by a workman who confessed that he had traded them in for one shilling and sixpence and a pint of beer. The Dan-y-Bryn site at Abergavenny is almost certainly a Roman burial ground, and as these were usually sited alongside roadways near settlements it may indicate the line of the Roman road to Kenchester, near Hereford. A brick stamped LEG II AVG, referring to the Second Augustan Legion, was found near the castle. It told us the name of the garrison, and, most probably, the brick had come from the legion's bathhouse, which was at its usual location outside the fort near the river bank where it discharged its excess water.

Another significant find a century ago was a gold *aureus* coin from the reign of Otho (AD 69), found in the vicinity of the Abergavenny Castle. Coins of this value were considered extremely valuable and were not often in circulation. They usually appeared in soldiers' pay packets, and were equivalent to 25 *denarii*. The *aureus* was the only gold coin in the Roman currency. It was lighter in weight than an English sovereign, but had the same purity. In AD 64, Nero, in his wisdom, called in all the *aurei* in circulation for the purpose of melting them down and re-issuing them at a slightly lower standard.

It was not until over 100 years later, in 1964, that a ditch and the north-west gate of the long sought after fort were discovered by workmen making the foundations for the new post office in present-day Flannel Street. There, a complete half of a Samian bowl was recovered. A rescue operation then got underway to excavate the area before further development took place. The ditch, which was one of the fort's outer defences, was 25ft wide and at least 6ft deep, and it ran roughly along the line of the western end of Flannel Street. The ditch produced a variety of finds ranging from the Claudian period (AD 41–54) to the mid-second century. One of the finds was a bronze buckle with its hinged terminal intact. Investigation also revealed that the ditch had been filled in about AD 150, either prior to abandonment or due to a reduction in the size of the fort. More bricks stamped LEG II AVG also emerged to confirm the garrison's name. The finding of scraps of bronze in the Flannel Street area indicated the presence of the metal workshops there.

In 1972 the excavation of Orchard Street revealed a section of the south-west turf and timber rampart with the timber slots of a granary. The abnormal alignment of the granary suggested that in Roman times the loop of the river had eroded the bank on this side and that this had caused the defect.

After locating the ramparts, the archaeologists were able to trace the fort running roughly along the line of the old mediaeval town wall. Excavations here uncovered one gateway and two sides of the fort. Meanwhile, excavations in the town brought to light two decorated Samian bowls from the Claudian period and around two dozen plain vessels from the reign of Nero, regarded as an extremely high number to be found at any one fort for that period. An interesting find in Cross Street was a small, pot-bellied

*A cinerary urn with cremated remains
visible inside. This is now displayed at
the National Museum.*
*(By kind permission of the National Museum of Wales,
Cardiff.)*

bottle that had once contained oil for covering the body after bathing. Further interesting finds were the two broken bronze fastenings from a soldier's armour. They had fastened the breastplate to the back one. It was strange how these particular pieces were found, as one had come from the ditch in Flannel Street, and the other from the river bank. A large rubbish dump that was discovered by the river contained many Roman items, and it was thought that a number of them had been washed up there.

Among the items were a ridge-shaped bowl with a pink waxy gloss bearing the maker's name, which identified it to the Nero-Vespasian era in the mid-first century; a 'dolphin' brooch with a slender bow, of Claudian date; an enamelled pendant and several broken Samian dishes and bowls dated to the early first century. One part of an *amphora* was regarded as having come from the legion's kilns at Usk. The 15 shards of orange-coloured pottery, belonging to different domestic utensils, were thought to have been imitations of the *mortaria* imported from south-east England. Domestic items of this range were also being produced locally and in the Severn Valley.

Owing to the extensive development in the town, further excavations were not possible, but it was thought that Gobannium had been occupied well into the third century, although there is little evidence to suggest that the garrison had been continuously in residence until then.

A few miles to the east lies the ancient town of Monmouth, once thought to have been the site of a Roman military station called Blestium, but despite various searches no Roman fort or remains were ever found, apart from a few coins. However, a Romano-British settlement did establish itself there.

CAERLEON (ISCA SILURUM)

Having moved out of Usk, the military strategists decided to site their new headquarters for the south-west region at Caerleon, about seven miles from Newport on the South Wales coast, where they could not only have the advantage of being near the sea, but could also support Julius Frontinus's campaigns against the Silures.

At such an idyllic site, with the high banks of the River Usk providing some kind of a defence, they proceeded to build their new legionary fortress on an elevated plateau overlooking the broad sweep of the river. This also provided an excellent anchorage for their galleons bringing supplies to the garrison.

The Romans called it Isca Silurum, after the river and the territory, and the fortress was to become one of the most important military sites in Europe. It was mentioned in the *Antonine Itinerary* as Isca Legua Augusta (Isca of the Augustan Legion), and continued to be occupied for nearly 400 years. There were only three legionary fortresses in Roman Britain: Caerleon, Chester and York, all of which were bases for an entire legion. At Caerleon there were an estimated 6,000 men, all elite troops of the Second Augustan Legion.

The legion had performed duties in Germany before joining the invasion of Britain in AD 43, and was personally commanded by the Emperor Vespasian (AD 69–79) during the initial phases of the conquest of southern Britain when still a young general. The legion was the proud creation of the first Roman Emperor, Augustus, (63 BC–AD 14), after whom it was named, and had been formed out of the remnants of another Second Legion. Later, the Emperor Antonius bestowed the title of *Antoniniana* upon it, causing the legion to be known as 'Caracalla's Own', after a nickname the Emperor had acquired from wearing a hooded garment called a *caracalla*. Prior to arriving in Caerleon, the legion had been stationed at Exeter, Devon.

The fortress of Isca Silurum was of the usual rectangular military shape with rounded corners, 540yds long and 450yds broad covering 50 acres. Although the River Usk and its tributary the Afon Llwyd provided a moderate defence, militarily, the fortress was initially defended by a deep ditch, 10ft broad with a well-guarded palisaded clay and turf bank 30ft wide. The turfs would have been cut to a regular size so that they could be easily carried by the soldiers and laid in carefully built-up layers until the required height was achieved. So compact were these earthen banks that during excavations nearly 2,000 years later they were still intact. Oak logs, used as foundations, were found against a primary bank and were dated to AD 70, confirming when this great fortress was constructed. Other defences included five internal turrets, watch towers and guard rooms all placed at intervals along the rampart wall, which would have been patrolled at all times. Entry was through imposing gateways placed at the four points of the compass and flanked by strong guard towers that were 25ft square. The main street of the fortress, the *Via Principalis*, along which the main buildings were located including the *Principia* itself, was found to be running beneath the modern streets of Backhall Street, Museum Street and The Broadway, while the *Via Praetoria* and the *Via Decumana* were running beneath the High Street, both leading from the centre of the fortress to the two end gateways.

The fortress had the space and amenities to accommodate the entire legion of 10 cohorts, each with six centuries comprising 80 men and commanded by a centurion. The accommodation included several large barrack blocks situated around the fortress, with quarters for senior and junior officers and a luxurious house for the commandant. Among the other buildings was an elaborate, if not monumental, bathhouse, granaries, workshops, stores and a hospital. It also had its own kilns for making pottery, which was called 'Caerleon ware'.

The fortress underwent several phases of construction during its long history. During Trajan's reign, around AD 100, the clay bank was reinforced with a heavily fortified stone wall, 20ft high, and all the timber defences were rebuilt in stone, as were all internal buildings. After this reconstruction, there followed a period of inactivity at the fortress when seven cohorts of the legion were transferred north to build Hadrian's Wall around AD 122. Occupation continued well into the third century.

Even several hundred years after its construction, the fortress attracted numerous visitors. In the 12th century, Gerald Cambrensis (known also as Gerald of Wales) described the fortress as being 'an imposing ruin upon the landscape', and for years legend had it that King Arthur held his court here. In 1405 the French Expeditionary Force, recruited to support Owain Glyndwr, took time off to visit the ruined fortress. But the mediaeval builders had already been at work and dismantled much of the stonework to build their houses in the town, even taking some of the masonry to build the castle. In 1603 a 'centurial stone' was found, on which the centurion Valerius Maximus of the 8th Cohort was mentioned. For a long time afterwards, Caerleon became a romantic centre for poets and writers. Even Lord Tennyson was inspired to write some of his poems while staying in the town at the Hanbury Arms overlooking the river. His poem *Enid* contains several references to Guinevere.

Throughout the 18th and 19th centuries, travellers and scholars began finding Roman coins and other artefacts, together with countless tiles stamped LEG II AVG., the insignia of the Second Augustan Legion. Most of the finds were sold to visitors and were lost. Even stone tablets, bearing Latin inscriptions to describe work that had been carried out on the fort, were used for mending roads without realising their historical value. One such stone to have survived was an altar dedicated to 'Salus Regina' by 'P. Sallienius Thalamus', a prefect of the legion, found in the churchyard in 1846. Also found in the churchyard was a large section of a richly patterned mosaic floor. As the *Principia* is known to lie under the churchyard, this mosaic could well have formed one of the building's ornamental floors. A stone head of Mithras and several bronze surgical instruments with flattened ends were also found there. These and the other relics were taken to the newly erected museum for safekeeping. This building was initiated by the 19th-century Hull businessman turned antiquarian John Edward Lee in 1841. The museum was opened in 1850 and is situated in the High Street.

An exhibit at the Caerleon Legionary Museum showing a storage jar and amphorae.

In the Spring of 1877 workmen engaged in laying a sewer in Backhall Street uncovered a large fragment of another mosaic floor that had been supported by the pillars of a hypocaust and had collapsed into the cavity beneath. The mosaic had formed the floor of a second heated changing room in the cold bath hall in the

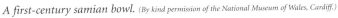

A first-century samian bowl. (By kind permission of the National Museum of Wales, Cardiff.)

An exhibit of mosaic floor discovered in the headquaters building at Isca Silurum as displayed by the Caerleon Legionary Museum. The motif shows a Cantharus, a Greek vessel for mixing wines.

fortress's bathhouse. Following its rescue and cleaning, the mosaic can now be seen on the wall of the *frigidarium* inside the specially erected building that exhibits the baths, and it is displayed only a few feet from where it was found.

The fortress baths were fully excavated in 1964 and 1981 and were found to have been built around AD 75 on a grand scale, with an enormous exercise hall, an aisle and a large courtyard which provided a dramatic entrance. Within the courtyard was a long, narrow open-air swimming pool (*natatio*), which had an overall length of 135ft. This would have held 80,250 gallons of water fed through lead piping. The surface area of the pool makes it larger than the one at Bath. The excavated remains of the swimming pool are also on display, along with parts of the *frigidarium* and the heated changing room (*apodyterium*). A complete excavation of these halls could not be made because they were obstructed by modern buildings. A viewing gallery enables the visitor to see the excavated halls, and, in the case of the swimming pool, the visitor can see the wall that had been built in AD 130 to shorten its length to 86ft. This was probably done when the garrison had been reduced in size.

In AD 220 further alterations were made to its depth which then rendered the pool too shallow to use. The visitor's attention is also drawn to the fact that the pool actually extends another 36ft beyond the wall of the exhibition building, but since this extension lies beneath neighbouring buildings it too could not be excavated.

An ornate Fountain House had once stood at the shallow end of the pool with water cascading down steps made of Purbeck marble. These too have survived and are on show, as are the foundations of the Fountain House apse. During excavation, fragments of painted wall plaster were found which showed that the interior had been richly decorated. In AD 150 the Fountain House became unsafe through subsidence and was demolished. However, a carved head of a dolphin that had formed part of the fountain's water feature survived and was rescued by the excavators.

The bath building itself was a very impressive one, with each of the bathing rooms and hallways having high, vaulted ceilings. The remains of the *frigidarium* and *apodyterium* are shown at right angles to the swimming pool. The *apodyterium* was where the bathers undressed and stored their clothes. This is identified by the large area of small, square-brick pillars that supported its heated floor. Many of the under-floor heating channels and the deep drains of the baths are among the interesting features to be seen. To the right of the changing room is the cold plunge bath with its mosaic floor proudly mounted on a neighbouring wall. The bathers had their own sequence for bathing, whereby they would pass into the cold bath hall from the *apodyterium*. When first built, this hall had a pair of alcoves in which there were circular basins on pedestals where the men would splash themselves down. After dousing themselves, they would cover their bodies with oil to remove any dirt before scraping it off with long-handled strigils. These were curved to make the procedure easier. Later, the alcoves in the *frigidarium* were found to have been turned into additional cold bathing pools. The plaster linings and half-rounded mouldings of

Part of the Mosiac floor discovered inside the baths, and now to be displayed hanging beside the excavated bathing rooms at the Caerleon Legionary Museum. (By kind permission of the National Museum of Wales, Cardiff.)

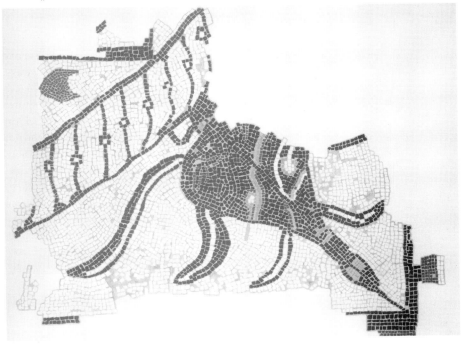

The excavated swimming pool at Caerleon, which clearly shows the wall built to shorten its length, on display at the Caerleon Exhibition Hall. (By kind permission of CADW.)

these pools have also survived remarkably intact and are also on show. They give the visitor some idea of what the hall had once looked like.

It is interesting to note that the exhibition represents only one-sixth of the entire bathing complex. If the other parts could have been excavated, then it would have shown what magnificent examples of Roman architecture they were, and the extent of the luxury bestowed upon the Roman soldier in carrying out his bathing ritual. With an overall length of some 360ft, the baths are equal in size to Wells Cathedral, and in Roman times their lofty roofs would have dominated the skyline. It is said that the structure and vaulting of the *frigidarium* may have resembled one of the surviving Cluny Baths in Paris. At other forts, the fortress

A silver and gold inlaid Strigil with oil bottle, which were found in the fortress baths. These are now on display at the Caerleon Legionary Museum. (By kind permission of the National Museum of Wales, Cardiff.)

baths have always been located outside the defences, but at Caerleon they were built in a central area next to the hospital.

The baths underwent drastic changes during their lifetime. In AD 110–111 modifications were carried out to combat flooding by raising all the floors throughout the complex. Then, following further alterations, particularly to the swimming pool, there followed a period of neglect, although the baths remained operational until the year AD 240. They survived as a ruined shell as late as the 18th century, when an Italian artist portrayed them in an engraving showing their vaulted halls with some of their ceilings, but, despite crumbling from neglect, they still provided a dramatic picture and portrayed their past grandeur. Had the mediaeval builders not stolen so much of the stonework, then part of them might have survived intact like the one found in Paris.

Full-scale excavations of the fortress were begun in 1908 by the Liverpool Committee in co-operation with the Monmouthshire and Caerleon Antiquarian Association, with assistance supplied by the land owner Colonel Sir Arthur Mackworth. At the time, land for the extension of the churchyard was being prepared and, as Roman artefacts had begun to appear on the site, it was decided to halt further building developments until the excavations had been completed. On the initiative of the distinguished archaeologist R.E. Mortimer Wheeler (Later Sir Mortimer Wheeler), then director of the National Museum of Wales, a local Excavation Committee was set up, but the task of recording and preserving the artefacts was taken over by the National Museum of Wales in 1931. It was they who then conducted all future excavations on behalf of the Ministry of Works, the forerunner of Cadw.

Excavations revealed temporary cookhouses had been built behind one of the earlier ramparts before they were made more secure in stone. These had left behind quantities of charcoal in which was discovered a small hoard of *denarii*, comprising eight of Hadrian, three of Faustina and one of Antoninus Pius, which indicated they had functioned until the middle of the second century.

Among the other finds were fragments of jars, various cooking pots and pie dishes. One of the defensive ditches had become silted up with various refuse and yielded many fragments of soldiers' sandals, all of which had been perfectly preserved.

The *Via Quintana*, the road extending across the fortress and almost dividing it in half, revealed a single building with a block of rooms facing a courtyard, surrounded by paved corridors. Charcoal deposits and iron slag found in the courtyard suggested that the building may have been a legionary workshop with the arrangement of rooms serving as accommodation for the workforce. This workshop appeared to have continued in use throughout the second century and possibly later. Another large structure with multiple rooms was also located nearby. It was thought to be a storehouse as it was found in the vicinity of several others.

Three more large buildings were found facing the *Via Quintana*, one of which had a sunken courtyard, 32.5ft wide. For this area the Romans had laid paving stones on top of the natural clay and had used natural materials such as river cobbles for the walls dividing a corridor from the verandah. The middle rooms measured 19.5 x 15.5ft and fronted the corridor that was 6.5ft wide. From the layout it was suspected that this had been the commandant's residence.

In 1926 the area known as Jenkins Field, at the junction of modern Church Street and Norman Street, was excavated. This revealed foundations of a stone building of some size which had replaced an earlier timber one and was thought to have been a hospital. A series of rooms were found to have had concrete floors with passages on either side and corridors that had been flagged. Red clay roofing tiles littered the floor, many of which bore the legend LEG II AVG, and showed that the building had been roofed with them. Interestingly, one tile had been trodden on by one of the soldiers before it had set, which left the marks of his hob-nailed sandal. Dogs too had left imprints of their paws as they had walked across the wet clay. Other finds included pieces of window glass and many examples of first-century pottery which included flagons, bowls and a *mortarium* – a bowl whose interior was heavily gritted with sharp particles to grind or mash up food. From the various fragments of coloured wall plaster lying around, it was obvious

This is a photograph of Prysg Field at Caerleon, which shows the barracks with a latrine and north west gate in the background.

The foundations of a latrine alongside Prysg Field barracks.

that special attention had been given to some rooms and clearly showed the Roman taste in interior decoration at that point in their history. Traces of red lines and a pattern of yellow flowers on a red background decorated some, while others had floral patterns in green, yellow and black. There were also designs of red panels edged with green and yellow lines on a white background. These valuable finds helped to recreate the past and turned cold stones into reality. It was thought that the building had been occupied around the second half of the first century, and it remained in use until AD 200 when the building ceased to function.

In 1927 the piece of land known as Prysg Field came on the market, and under the supervision of Mr V.E. Nash Williams, the new director of the National Museum of Wales, excavations revealed the discovery of four barrack blocks lying side by side and just inside the *intervallum* in the north-western corner of the fortress. Each block measured up to 250ft long and 35–40ft wide. They comprised the same layout as those at Usk, with rooms for the centurion at one end, followed by 12 double cubicles arranged in strict pairs, side by side, for the recruits. The barracks were also grouped in blocks of two with each pair facing inwards onto a common street, 20ft wide with a cobbled surface. The whole range of barracks here accommodated an exact complement of two cohorts. As at Usk, each cubicle in a block accommodated eight men who slept on bunk beds placed around the walls and had a central table for eating. Each block had been covered with a verandah running down the inner side of the building. Vast quantities of window glass were found as well as fragments of white wall plaster. The floors consisted mainly of beaten clay, though some had been floored

A bronze plaque of winged Victory, on display at the Caerleon Legionary Museum. (By kind permission of the National Museum of Wales, Cardiff.)

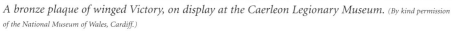

with concrete. In one cubicle, a heavy *olla* was found intact and half sunk into the floor. This had probably contained a drinking supply for the soldiers. Another room contained a pit or recess in the floor with a single upright slab and an outlet to the verandah outside. This crude structure had served as a latrine. As drains were found in the end rooms it was thought that they might have been used for ablutions. One even had a stone trough in the corner which suggested that this was where the centurion had washed himself.

Excavations of the barracks revealed masses of stratified pottery and coins, which showed that they had been built during the late first century and were occupied well into the third. Among the pottery were cooking pots and *ollae* – square-shaped dishes used for stews. There was also an abundance of triangular tile antefixes of various designs that had been nailed onto the eaves as some kind of decoration. The most common design was that of the sun with an eight-spoked wheel above. One barrack yielded a small hoard of second-century coins, including a second brass of Vespasian and a *denarius* of Hadrian (AD 117–138). One wonders if this had been the savings of a soldier who had died before reaping the benefit of his endeavours. A *denarius* was just over a day's pay for a second-century legionary soldier. Another significant find in one of the centurion's quarters was a bronze plaque showing the winged female figure of Victory with a standard in one hand. This was thought to have come from a ceremonial piece of equipment or part of a private shrine. The plaque is now on display at the Legionary Museum in the High Street.

At Caerleon, the entire excavated barracks in Prysg Field are open to visitors who can see their exact layout at leisure. At the back of the barracks are the remains of a communal latrine consisting of a rectangular chamber, 29ft long and 15ft wide. This had also been built close to the back entrances of the barracks and lay parallel to the *intervallum*. It was discovered that the structure had been roughly constructed with rubble and sandstone and had been bound together with poor quality mortar. Inside, it had a stone floor and an open channel 1.5ft wide and sunk 2ft below floor level. The entire latrine system can be seen, as can the remnants of the north-west guardhouse which stands almost next to it. The circular outlines of the ovens alongside the *intervallum* can also be clearly seen, giving a clear picture of the soldiers' lives in this part of the fortress.

In 1939, at a property known as Myrtle Cottage Orchard, excavations brought to light a complete complement of nine barracks in which were found second-century coins from the reign of Commodus (AD 180–192). Many of the rooms held a surprising amount of rubbish including window glass and pieces of broken pottery dating from the fourth century. But the most significant discovery on this site was a hoard of five gold *aurei*, covering several reigns, hidden under the floor and revealing themselves in a hollow at the side of the excavation trench. It appeared that they had been in mint condition when hidden away. Two of the coins showed the face of Nero and one showed Agrippa, with the reverse showing an unusual picture of a chariot with four elephants. The other Emperors represented were: Vespasian (AD 72), and Domitian (AD 73), soldiers were encouraged to save their pay and their savings were

The hoard of five aurei found on the Myrtle Cottage site. They are on display at the Caerleon Legionary Museum. (By kind permission of the National Museum of Wales, Cardiff.)

usually kept in the regimental safe in the *Sacellum* of the headquarters, but this particular soldier had obviously preferred to have had his money close at hand. The soldiers were also encouraged to pay towards the cost of their funerals through an army fund. More personal items included small bronze and enamelled objects, such as discs, which had been either studs or buttons. There was also a fine collection of inlaid bronze and enamel buckles. All of these items are on display at the Legionary Museum.

Another significant find in the barracks was the statuette of a *Genius Paterfamilias*, which had probably been used as a personal good luck charm. Traditionally, the *Genius* or father figure was venerated as a personal guardian that brought protection to the household; a kind of Roman St Christopher. This particular *Genius*, clad in a flowing toga with his head covered in the drapery and holding a scroll in one hand, had probably been given to the soldier by his family for his safety and well-being. At least half of these figures found in Britain can be dated to the third century or later, but only two others have been recovered from military sites; one from Shields and the other from Richborough.

Chance finds have also given us the names of at least two centurions who lived in the barracks. They came from two leaden dies, marked respectively VIBI SEVE (Vibius Severus) and SEN PAVILLIN, with each name preceded by a back-to-front 'C', the special mark to denote the man's rank as a centurion. Sometimes the mark was written in a more exaggerated form, similar to the mathematical symbol for 'more than'.

While excavating outside the fortress, at the foot of the castle mound, a surprising find was an inscribed tablet, which informed us that the barracks had been rebuilt during the joint reigns of Gallienus and Valerian, during AD 254–260, probably after falling into disrepair. The last few words of the inscription states that the work was carried out under the direction of the centurions of the Seventh Cohort of the Second Legion. The latin inscription reads:

IMPP VALERIANVS ET GALLIENVS AVGG ET
VALERIANVS NOBILISSIMVS CAES COHORTI VII
CENTVRIAS A SOLO...LEG II AVG...

The tablet calls Gallienus and Valerianus 'noble Caesars' and the phrase '*a solo*' means that the work was completed 'from the ground up'. It is also interesting to note that more than half of the inscribed stones discovered in Wales have come from

The statuette of the Genuis Paterfamilias found at Isca Silurum, which is now exhibited at the Caerleon Legionary Museum. (By kind permission of the Glamorgan & Gwent Archaeological Trust.)

Caerleon. It was usual for the soldiers to get involved with rebuilding and maintenance work in all the forts. Work was precise, and if a soldier's work was not to his centurion's satisfaction, he was punished.

The demise of the fortress began in around AD 250, when the need for a military presence in the area had diminished and after the bulk of the legion had been withdrawn, possibly to Richborough in Kent. This withdrawal meant that the fortress was to be occupied by a 'caretaker garrison'. However, the fortress continued to function until the end of the third century, when the main buildings were finally demolished. But the native population made use of what they could, by taking away stonework for their own use and turning the baths' courtyard into a cattle pen.

A display at the Caerleon Legionary Museum which shows examples of enamelled buckles found outside the fortress. (By kind permission of the National Museum of Wales, Cardiff.)

The Amphitheatre

The most notable surviving structure from the Roman period in Caerleon is without doubt the great amphitheatre, built just 50ft beyond the fortress's south-west wall where a civilian settlement had become established. The amphitheatre, which had attracted visitors since the Middle Ages, was successfully excavated by Mortimer Wheeler and his wife Tess in 1926–27 and is the most fully excavated amphitheatre in Europe. Evidence showed that the building was erected during the reign of Vespasian around the year AD 75, at the time when he was building the Colosseum in Rome.

Oval in shape, it measures 267 x 222ft overall, and is also regarded as the only other major Roman structure of any significance to exist south of Hadrian's Wall. At the outset, Mortimer Wheeler contacted *The Daily Mail* for support in the cost of the excavations, and they in turn responded by canvassing for contributions, the most notable coming from an organisation known as The Loyal Knights of the Round Table of America. *The Daily Mail* then purchased the site and generously presented it to the nation. It is now a national monument under the care of Cadw.

Throughout the ages, the amphitheatre was seen as simply a depression in the ground surrounded by individual grass-covered mounds, which the local inhabitants, in ignorance of its true identity, called 'King Arthur's Round Table', a belief that was handed down for several generations to became part of the local folklore.

In its original form, the central arena was surrounded by a seating bank, enclosed between stone walls and lined with tiers of wooden seats to provide accommodation for 6,000 spectators. The upper part of the structure, where the spectators sat, was probably an open-framed timber grandstand. Access to the seats was by vaulted passages, and the

The Amphitheatre at Caerleon.

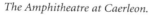

staircases were entered through arched doorways. There were eight entrances in all, placed symmetrically around the arena, with two for processional events and the other six for spectators. There were separate entrances into the arena for the animals and gladiators, with small brick-built chambers where they could wait their turn before going in. An external wall, 32ft high, surrounded the entire structure, and during excavations a trench cut through the side of the mound revealed that the outer retaining wall was 5.5ft thick with heavy buttresses inside and out. These withstood the pressure from the surrounding banks of earth and some of them can still be seen today. However, the wall dividing the arena from the spectators has been extensively robbed in the past.

During excavations, hinges from the gates allowing the gladiators into the arena were found, as were the sockets for their posts. A coin of Vespasian (AD 77–80), verifying the date of the amphitheatre's construction, was found embedded in the mortar. The arena itself was paved with large river cobbles on a bed of fine sand 2ft deep, and a drain 2.5ft wide ran from the main north entrance straight down the middle to discharge the excess rain water into the river. Even after 18 centuries, this system was found to be operating as efficiently as it ever had.

The amphitheatre also produced eight whole or broken stone inscriptions. Some of them were found built into the arena wall and recorded the work of rebuilding carried out by the Second Augustan Legion. A curious find among the debris filling the northern half of the arena was a scratched message on a thin piece of lead, just 3ins square. The message constituted a curse written by a gladiator to Nemesis, the goddess of fate and vengeance, for having had his property stolen. On it he had written:

DOMNA NII/MIISIS DO TI/ BI PALLIIVM/ IIT GALLICVLAS/ QVI TVLIT NON/ RIIDIMAT N../....SANGVINI/SVI.

(The obliques show where the message was separated.)

It was translated as: 'Lady Nemesis, I give thee this cloak and these boots. Let no man take them except at the peril of his life/or red chestnut.' The translation of 'Sangvini' is thought to have come from the word *Sanguineus* which is one of the terms applied to a horse's colour, and 'svi' or 'sui' to the owner of a horse, suggesting that it might have referred to one of the mounted *Venatores* who hunted wild beasts in the arena. The strokes 'II' is the Roman cursive form of 'E', so the gladiator wrote Nemesis as NII/MIISIS, which displays the force of his anger. Shrines to Nemesis have also been found at other amphitheatres, with one at Chester.

The last phase of the building was assigned to the second decade of the third century, following which there was a period of neglect when the walls either crumbled or fell down. The amphitheatre had to be rebuilt and strengthened in places by the addition of more solid buttresses. At this time, the surface of the arena was made up with gravel, broken bricks and stone slabs. The latest of these repairs appeared to have blocked a stone gutter, as well as the main drain which was 290ft long. During the present-day excavations it was found partially filled up with sand, into which a glass beaker, a gaming disc and a handled jug had found their way. After being cleaned out,

The shrine dedicated to the Goddess of Good Fortune, Minerva, found in the civic baths outside the fortress. It is now on display at the Caerleon Legionary Museum

the drain was then able to function as well as ever. The glass beaker was said to have been produced during the first century by the Rheinish glass factories and had been engraved with the scene of a chariot race. Also among the debris of the third century were two beautifully enamelled pendants, one of which had a pattern on both sides.

When all the repairs had been concluded, the amphitheatre continued in use until the end of the third century, as indicated by the 19 coins, AD 254–296, recovered from the repaired road surfaces. There were also bricks, which had been used for rebuilding the walls, found bearing the stamp LEG II AVG ANTO. '*Anto*' represented Antoninus, the Emperor, who had bestowed the high honour upon the legion for its distinguished services.

Evidence suggested that after the third century the structure fell into irreversible decay, and, just like its neighbours in the fortress, it began to slowly disintegrate at the hands of stone robbers. However, a substantial destruction took place in the 14th century, indicated by coins from the reigns of Edward I and II found on site. Even 50 coins from the reigns of George I and II were recovered, implying that stone robbing was still rife in the 18th century.

There was strong evidence that a large civilian settlement had established itself outside the fort's defences, which included many major buildings as well as houses. One of these was the communal baths, which lay to the west of the amphitheatre. This building had occupied its site long before the amphitheatre was built, and was discovered during present-day excavations because its hypocaust system had been laid too close to the site of the amphitheatre and had been destroyed in order to make way for one of its entrances. As such, when the amphitheatre was excavated, the remains of the hypocaust led to the discovery of the baths. The hypocaust had been subsequently rebuilt, but only a small portion of the bath building has survived. Nevertheless, it still managed to produce a coin of Vespasian, which had been lost by someone when in mint condition.

While excavating close to the amphitheatre, the porticos of two large buildings were also uncovered, one of which had a courtyard. This latter building was probably an inn.

To the south east of the fortress walls a second bath building was discovered. It had a new complex of bathing rooms added at a later date, including a colonnaded courtyard.

Both bath buildings provided a social centre where people gathered and talked over the events of the day. The separate bathing suites would have had separate entrances, with separate bathing times for the men and women. A number of gaming counters were recovered as well as dice, which indicated that besides rooms for bathing, massage and rest, there were also those set aside for gambling. Among the interesting finds were two sculptured stone tablets, one dedicated to the goddess Fortune and the other with the head of Medusa. Another significant discovery was a tall stone carved with the figures of a man and a woman standing beneath an archway. A Latin inscription beneath the figures records that the man, Cornelius Castus, and his wife, Julia Belismiscus, were offering a dedication to the goddess Fortune for the safety of the bathers. The words *Bono Eventus*, meaning 'good luck', were also added. But the most valuable find was a bronze strigil, beautifully engraved with silver and gold that must have been lost by a wealthy citizen. A pot-bellied bottle which had contained oil was another worthy find left behind by a Roman bather.

The area around the mediaeval castle revealed the presence of a luxurious Roman villa, which had been completely buried by the mediaeval workmen digging out the moat. A pleasing discovery was a quantity of wall plaster with all its colours brightly preserved. Channels for conveying heat were also found running across its walls, and the bricks which had supported the hypocaust were still intact and stamped with LEG II AVG. Several column bases supported the theory that the courtyard had been colonnaded. A water tank was also found, which had probably provided the owner with his bath water. Such elaborate designs suggest that the villa had probably belonged to someone of importance. Several pieces of high-quality domestic ware were also recovered, including some Samian depicting gladiators in combat against various wild animals. Parts of an ornamental buckle with inlaid enamel, several ornamental bosses, brass pins and needles, and even keys were also found. These items are now on display at the Legionary Museum.

In an excavation east of Mill Street, where two of the fortress's main roads crossed, a complete neighbourhood of 22 dwellings was discovered alongside the walls of additional buildings. All the dwellings were long, narrow and crudely constructed with coarse rubble masonry, and all fronted the main north–south road. Although they had been crudely constructed, they all had the luxury of being roofed with terracotta tiles, and many had flooring made of cobbles and clay. The internal layouts were all different and probably determined their use – either domestic or industrial. Metalworking was thought to have taken place there, judging from the deposits of slag. Other trades were indicated by the presence of carpenters', masons', and plasterers' tools found among the debris. Cart and horse harnesses, a reaping hook and the blade of a scythe also emerged, to indicate that agriculture had sustained this tiny community.

Traces of two other Romano-British civilian sites were also found around the fortress. At one of the sites the home of what appeared to be a wealthy person was found. It was a corridor-type house with rooms flanked by colonnades and with projecting wings on either side. When these communities had established themselves they were known to have traded with the Romans and had provided them with fresh home-grown produce, even offering their labour. Under the new regime, people began to adopt the Roman way of life and, as seen at the communal baths, they had also adopted the Roman culture. The civilian population also became familiar with new types of vegetables imported into the country, including olive oil from the Mediterranean which the local people used for cooking.

One of the sites produced a vast quantity of fine Samian ware, showing that the people had used good quality pottery. Over 2,000 shards of *mortaria* were also found, ranging in date from the first to the fourth century. The *mortarium* was a popular kitchen utensil that was used when food had to be ground or pulverized, which was often the case in Roman times. The acidic soil in the area had severely affected the preservation of many of these bowls, but the harder fired fabrics such as the 'Oxford whites' appeared to have been less affected by the conditions. This pottery which was manufactured around AD 100 had a granular, sandy texture and was off-white in colour with a pink core.

While work was being carried out on the proposed South Wales railway at the end of the 19th century, a Roman cemetery was discovered and two stone coffins were unearthed. One of which, although partly filled with clay, contained a bottle of greenish-coloured glass that was later identified as a perfume bottle and considered to have been a 'grave gift'. A large urn, also of a greenish colour, was found a third full of cremated bone fragments. Although cremation was the popular way for disposing of their dead, the Romans also carried out the older ritual of burial. Other finds at the cemetery were: a figure of a goat cast in bronze, a bronze lamp and, curiously, a bronze ruler that extended to 1ft. The latter was a compact instrument with two notches to receive the studs which extended the ruler to its fullest extent. A similar bronze ruler was found in a merchant's shop in Pompeii, but as no other specimen has been found in Britain this ruler is considered extremely rare.

In 1603 an inscribed tablet was found that commemorated the restoration of the Temple of Diana in AD 250 by the legion's commanding officer, Postumius Varus. However, this temple was never located. Inscriptions were also found during the present excavations implying that a Temple of Mithras might also have been present in the vicinity. This was another place where people worshipped and gathered to socialize but, as is the case with the Temple of Diana, its location has also never been found.

There have been very few Mithraic Temples discovered in Roman Britain. One was discovered outside the fortress of Segontium at Caernarfon, which added to the five already discovered, and it was thought that one had also existed at the Roman settlement of Moridunum (Carmarthen). Therefore, finding one at Caerleon would have been a coup. Both this and the Temple of Diana would have been splendid additions to the town. Judging from the grandeur of the Roman architecture, Caerleon must have been an opulent-looking settlement.

Another place that grew into a sophisticated Romano-British settlement was nearby Venta Silurum (Caerwent). Here, the Silures were allowed self government, and Venta became their capital, hence the name. Here, too, the citizens had the luxury of living in Roman-styled, stone-built houses with colourful plastered walls, ceilings and mosaic floors. There was also a temple complex, and the walled town had its own debating chamber in a grand forum that was surrounded on three sides by shops and an enormous area that doubled as a market place. Venta went on to flourish until the late fourth century.

The fourth century also witnessed a sinister episode at Caerleon when the reigning Emperor ordered two Christians to be killed in the amphitheatre.

As the fortress continued to decay, the town of Caerleon went on to flourish, but it too fell victim to the invading Danes who plundered it on many occasions before finally destroying it in AD 976.

The Norman Conquest then brought a new and much different era when rebuilding took place using stonework from the fortress. Even the castle was built entirely from Roman masonry.

Thereafter, Caerleon continued to grow into a busy town, attracting travellers throughout the centuries, which it continues to do in the present day.

CARDIFF (CAERDYDD)

The momentous discovery that a first-century Roman fort existed on the present site of the Norman castle in the centre of the city came in 1889, when the late Third Marquis of Bute, in his attempts to connect the castle gardens with Cathays Park by means of a bridge, uncovered a massive 10ft wall which extended along the west and south sides. This was identified as Roman stonework and ended years of speculation after Roman objects had began appearing to suggest that a Roman structure was somewhere in the immediate vicinity.

In 1763 the Revd W. Harris, a canon of Llandaff, got in touch with the Society of Antiquaries regarding the question of a Roman settlement being present within the town after a quantity of Roman coins had been found in the castle precinct under The Green. The Revd Harris also mentioned that Cardiff was located on the *Via Julia*, which was a major Roman road running along the south-west coast to Carmarthen. Also, a letter from a man who signed himself 'Siluris' had written to say that, as a boy, he had come across a hypocaust in the south-west corner of the castle. His descriptions were very explicit, but despite this information nothing was done until 100 years later when the wall was found and confirmed as being Roman by Mr J. Storrie, who was then curator of the Cardiff Museum.

Excavations got underway immediately, in 1899, during which the walls and bastions of the north-east and south sides were exposed, as well as the north gateway of the fort. At the foot of the wall were found some fragments of pottery and bone, plus the interesting

This photograph shows the excavated Guard Chamber. It was first published in the Archaeologia Cambrensis. *(By kind permission of the* Archaeologia Cambrensis.*)*

discovery of a copper bracelet and some glass beads. Coins bearing the names of Faustina, Gallicius and Carausius were helpful in dating the wall to the first century. The remains of the north gateway were found to have survived to a height of 4ft 9in and were 8–9ft thick. There had been guard chambers on either side, projecting both internally and externally, which had the same polygonal form as the bastions. Access to the gateway had been by way of a ladder from the rampart.

It is interesting to note that the Marquis reconstructed the northern gateway from documented evidence of other Roman gateways of that period, and this is the gateway visitors are able to see in the castle grounds today. The Roman foundations lie immediately underneath.

The Romans thought it was important to establish a military station here because of its great strategic location, situated as it was on the left bank of the River Taff, only 12 miles from its confluence with the Bristol Channel and within marching distance of their legionary fortress at Caerleon. It was also a benefit that it was on the coast because Cardiff's large bay not only provided a safe anchorage for its fleet, but it also offered greater mobility in ferrying troops to different sites along the coast of Wales instead of crossing the mountainous terrain inland, which was rife with rebellious tribesmen. It also ensured swift delivery of supplies to other fortresses along the coast.

Clues that a Roman fortress existed here lie in the city's Welsh name – Caerdydd, ie. Caer Taff – 'Fort on the Taff'. Caer-taf or Caer-daf eventually became Cardiff and Caerdydd.

The arrival of the Normans to the area in 1081 brought about the complete destruction of the fort when they utilised whatever materials they could to build their castle on the same site, thus obliterating all traces of the Roman walls. It is this castle, credited to the Norman lord Robert Fitzhubert, that is present on the Roman site today.

In building their castle upon Roman foundations, the Normans also enlarged the Roman ditches for their own defences. It was while they were doing this work that they threw up large banks of earth which eventually buried many of the Roman walls, preserving the remains until their discovery 900 years later.

Evidence suggested that the Roman fort was first established on the banks of the Taff around AD 55, during Nero's reign, and at about the same time as Usk, at the time when the Romans began infiltrating into Silurian territory.

During its long history, spanning 300 years, the fort had been reduced in size on three different occasions, so that four separate forts were subsequently built inside the original enclosure. Evidence for this was revealed during the progress of the excavations, the first of which occurred at the beginning of the 20th century, overseen by the late Sir Mortimer Wheeler. It was discovered that the original fort had exceeded 30 acres and been built from timber, it was defended by a high bank made of turf and had a deep ditch. The remains of the timber buildings were found beneath the north-eastern part of the present Castle Green. One of these was an extremely large building, measuring some 138ft long and 78ft wide, and was thought to have been the headquarters. The original fort would have needed to be this large in order to accommodate the number of troops introduced into the south-west to suppress the activities of the Silures. Tacitus mentions in his *Annals* that extra auxiliaries were ordered into the area by the governor Ostorius Scapula, showing us that Cardiff played as important a role as Usk in trying to establish military control in the area.

After a period of about 30 years, probably when there had been a lull in the fighting, the fort was reduced in size with a clay and turf rampart, which was surmounted by a timber palisade and fronted by a single V-shaped ditch. Excavations revealed that the north–south road used by the first fort was still in use and had been resurfaced.

During this second phase there were signs that a civilian settlement had been established outside the southern defences in the vicinity of the modern High Street. The Roman boundary was found on the site of Lloyds Bank during its construction in 1892, along with fragments of Samian and coarse ware. The settlement was made up of several dwellings set in long rows. These were found to have been built over the site of the commandant's house from the previous fort. Several examples of first-century pottery were found, including large quantities of glossy Samian ware. A flattish dish was marked with the stamp of the potter, 'PRIMUS'. Overfired roof tiles appear to suggest that they were produced from the fort's own kilns.

When the fort was reduced for the second time the southern defences remained the same as before. Only the ditch was altered to suit its new role. This reduction was probably to accommodate a smaller garrison between the years AD 75–78 as at that time, with the conquest of the Silures achieved and with troops moved to deal with the uprising in Scotland, the need for a larger garrison had diminished. During this phase the civilian settlement was still flourishing, and judging from the large quantities of slag uncovered metalworking had taken place, including smithing and bronze working.

The fourth fort was, however, twice as large as both the second and the third one but was still very much smaller than the original first-century enclosure. When built, its northern defences extended well into those of its predecessor but had retained the same western boundary. The fort followed the same rectangular plan with rounded corners and measured 641 x 602ft, covering about 10 acres. A central gate, with flanking guard towers, was incorporated into the north and south walls to give access to the fort, and it had the extra protection of polygonal bastions situated at each corner, which could be used for artillery, comprising enormous catapults and ballistae. The bastions were massive structures, varying in thickness from 18–19ft and projecting about 10ft away from the main wall. The surfaces of the roads were also found at this point. Each of the gateways was 42ft wide overall, from back to front, and projected 9ft from the wall with a pair of towers at each end. A coin found beneath the kerb of the southern gateway indicated that this fourth, more powerful encampment was built around AD 260. In mediaeval times, this gateway was replaced by the existing Black Tower. Interestingly, the masonry of the west guard chamber and the gateway were still standing several feet high. These guard chambers were entered by narrow doorways in their back walls with archways wide enough to take two doors. It also appeared that there had been two floor levels, with the upper one having openings to allow the defenders to repulse attacks. The flanking bastions would also have had similar chambers on the same level. They had been added to an already existing wall, and the workmanship appeared to have been of two separate periods. Coins which dated from the Victorius period to the Julian,

(268–363), found in the north gateway, suggest that the fort remained a permanent structure until the end of the fourth century.

The walls around the fort were robustly built to a thickness of 10.5ft, with a rubble core made of large rounded stones gathered from the river bed and then faced on both sides with lias limestone, which had been brought from either Leckwith Hill or Lavernock Point. These walls were then backed by an earthen bank.

Further evidence of the third-century fort came to light during alterations to the castle's clock tower in 1912, when another stretch of Roman masonry, 7.5ft high, was

The Roman wall and frieze at Cardiff Castle.

exposed. It was of the same style as the other wall, with foundations resting on natural gravel, and was found to be passing through the residential buildings of the castle. During alterations to the castle's kitchen, the west wall of the fort was also uncovered. Drainage works then uncovered the Roman roadway crossing the interior of the fort from east to west. This was probably the *Via Principalis*.

Between 1974 and the 1980s annual excavations were carried out on the site by students of University College, but, owing to the dominance of the existing buildings and the extensive landscaping of the castle green by 'Capability Brown', no evidence of the fort's internal buildings could be found, except for a few timber buildings. However, several interesting items had been uncovered, including Roman bronze brooches and some Samian ware with an attractive leaf design around the rims of the bowls.

It became apparent that the castle's keep and moat were lying inside the fort's north-west corner and had thereby obliterated all Roman structures in that area. It was also evident that the Norman builders had incorporated part of the fortress wall into the castle's own, especially on the Duke Street side, which had retained its average height of 12ft.

The west gate of the castle had also been built on top of the fortress's wall, as had the Octagon and Herbert towers on either side of it. The clock tower, too, which stands at the south-west corner of the castle facing Castle Street, had its walls built upon the Roman foundations. The towers form an impressive frontage to the castle and are the public's first view of Cardiff's most historic landmark. Sections of the Roman wall, defined by their different colour to the main stonework, are clearly visible to the passer-by. These stones, the Roman jewellery, coins and pottery, along with a long stretch of the original Roman wall, are the only remaining proof of Cardiff's important role in the Roman era.

Bastioned fortresses such as Cardiff became part of the so-called 'Saxon Shore' type coastal fortresses that were distributed around the western and southern coasts of Britain in an effort to repulse sea-borne invaders who could have used rivers as highways to penetrate into the country. Thus, Cardiff entered a new era of being an effective defensive fortress. The last coins to be found on the site were those of Valentinian I (AD 364–375) and Gratian (AD 367–383), indicating that the fort had remained in occupation until almost the end of the fourth century. By the year AD 410, the Roman army had departed Britain's shores to deal with their own troubles in Rome.

The length of wall which generated so much interest at its discovery is now on public view inside the castle grounds, and it is protected in a specially built underground gallery which extends along the entire length of the wall. The wall, which is 10ft thick at the base, reduces to 8ft further along and is regarded as the best example of Roman masonry to be found in Wales.

Opposite the wall, and continuing along the entire length of the gallery, is an entertaining frieze showing life in the area during Roman times, with scenes from Silurian villages, the arrival of the Romans and subsequent clashes with the natives. The figures are life-sized and three dimensional, made of cement and plaster and coloured with metallic bronze paint. The frieze culminates in one enormous tableau showing a team of horses drawing a chariot through a busy street. This amazing frieze is the creation of local artist Mr Frank Abraham, who constructed it between 1981 and 1983.

CAERPHILLY

Caerphilly, situated about 10 miles north of Cardiff, was the chosen site for another auxiliary fortress in the area, and was situated at the point where the Roman road to the north was met by the route going west from the legionary fortress of Caerleon. This route may have been used by the Romans to reach the lead mining and smelting site of Machen, which was also sited on this road, five miles away.

It was thought that the fort was established around the year AD 78 and was strategically placed to command good views of the lines of approach down the Rhymney Valley to the east, up to the spur of Mynydd (Mountain) Eglwysilan to the north and from the western shoulder of Caerphilly Mountain to the south.

The fort was not discovered until 1963, when the outer defences of Caerphilly Castle were being examined. The discovery of Roman foundations came as a total surprise. No one had suspected that such an historically important structure like a Roman fort was lying hidden beneath the mediaeval building, although Roman pottery had surfaced when work to the castle was being carried out on behalf of the Marquis of Bute in the 1930s.

Parts of the fort's north-west and north-eastern defences came to light, including some internal walls, and from their position it was found that the entire castle was lying immediately over them. The western defences were lying close to the modern-day Nantgarw Road, with those on the east facing the North Lake.

The defences of the fort comprised a rampart of clay and turf on a bed of cobbles, which in turn lay on sandy soil and was fronted by two ditches with an overall width of 43ft. This had survived to a height of 2ft. The discovery of a post hole suggested that the rampart had been fronted by a timber palisade. The ditches were V-shaped and were about 7ft wide, and dug 3ft into the natural soil. Resting against the outer scarp of the inner ditch was a deposit of clay which had been reinforced with squared building blocks of varying sizes. Behind the rampart was a layer of road metalling 9–10ft wide. This could only have been the *intervallum* or rampart roadway.

A trench cut through the north-west defences revealed at least four different periods where rebuilding had taken place, but a large ditch dug during the time of the Civil War had destroyed the Roman levels for some distance. Beyond it were walls which defined a building 31ft wide, that were separated by a stony path. A second building was located and its layout suggested that the trench had cut across the north-eastern end of two barrack blocks.

The year of the fort's establishment was verified by the small amount of Samian ware and coarse pottery found there, dating back to the latter part of the first century. Fragments of glass bottles were found, dating from the first–second century, around the time when occupation ceased, believed to be around AD 130. At this time many forts were being abandoned, probably because the Silures were no longer considered a threat to the military occupation of the area.

The site of the Roman fort was later occupied by an enormous artillery battery for the defence of the castle during the Civil War.

GELLIGAER

The Roman remains at Gelligaer are those of two large encampments found side by side on the outskirts of a residential area there, situated among the beautiful mountains of Glamorgan, 13 miles from Cardiff and 780ft above sea level.

The site was probably chosen for its commanding position, with an extensive view of the surrounding countryside, and for being just nine miles from Pen-y-darren, the shortest distance between any two forts in Wales.

The main fortification was found to have had a parade ground where training took place, and although it had been designated as a practice camp excavations revealed that it had all the features and facilities of an auxiliary fortress, which had been garrisoned by a detachment from the Second Augustan Legion.

Gelligaer was first excavated by the Cardiff Naturalists' Society in 1899, which continued until 1901 when the entire complex was exposed and its ground plan recovered intact due to not having had modern buildings built on top. Excavations revealed an almost square enclosure measuring 346 x 386ft, an area of just under three acres. It was evident that the area had recently been ploughed, although, despite this disturbance, it was still defined by a broad bank that had formed its south-west boundary. The ramparts had been constructed from turf and clay placed on a bed of cobbles for stability and then faced on both sides with coarse masonry. Outside the ramparts was a 5ft berm and a ditch 19ft wide which provided an adequate defence. Deep depressions marked the sites of four spacious gateways. From the evidence provided, these had been arched and had a double roadway going through that had been flanked by guard towers. When the south-west and south-east gateways were

A plan of the Roman site, first published in the Archaeologia Cambrensis. *(By kind permission of the* Archaeologia Cambrensis.*)*

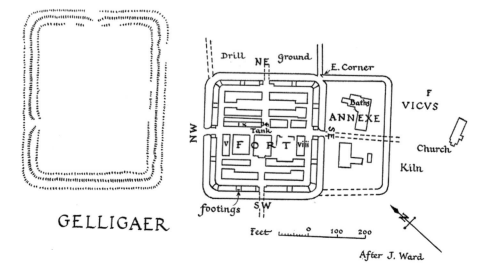

GELLIGAER

uncovered, their roadways revealed deep grooves which had been made by wheeled traffic, indicating that they had been well used. Even the sockets in which the pivots of the great doors had turned and the square holes into which the bolts had shot were in a remarkable state of preservation. Two moulded bases discovered in a ditch near the south-east gate suggested that the gates had incorporated massive columns, thus making the entrance into the enclosure a very impressive one. In addition, excavations revealed that 12 turrets had been set into the walls and had been placed symmetrically between the corners and the gateways. In all, Gelligaer must have looked an extremely imposing fortification upon the landscape.

Inside the fort, the walls of the buildings had not survived any higher than 3ft owing to fact that stone robbers had also been actively engaged here.

In the centre was the *Principia*. This measured 69 x 80ft but had the unusual feature of having two large rectangular areas within its walls. The one in the upper half of the building led into a suite of five rooms at the rear, one of which was the *Sacellum* situated right in their centre. To the right of the *Sacellum* was a room containing a sink with a drain, while the outer room contained a hearth. It was thought that these four rooms had been clerks' offices, which had the advantage of being heated, and were also possibly somewhere to prepare food and wash their hands. The lower courtyard had been much more elaborate, having been surrounded on three sides by colonnades with an entrance into the street. These would have given visitors a very pleasant impression upon entering what was considered a highly important building.

The next building along the *Via Principalis* was the *Praetoria*, with rooms grouped around a small central courtyard, similar to an Italian villa. Strangely, no hypocaust was found which would have been usual in the home of the highest-ranking officer. Its design puzzled the archaeologists, yet no other building on the site could be suggested for having been the commandant's residence. However, the debris showed that the building had the usual tiled roof and glazed windows.

To the north of this building stood a small granary with its floors resting on sleeper walls to prevent dampness from seeping through to the grain. Internally, these measured 54ft x 32ft wide. There was also a loading bay attached. Another small granary was found at the side of the *Principia*, but as it occupied only a small area it left a large open space with room for another building.

Six large pairs of barrack blocks were located to the east and west of the principal buildings. Each pair measured 136ft long x 28ft wide and benefitted from a wooden verandah. Ovens on which the recruits would have cooked their meals were located close by on the ground floors of the turrets. There were also double blocks of buildings fronting the street connecting the south-east and the north-west gates, but these were thought to have been stables.

Behind the barracks and next to the *Via Praetoria* was another long building that had been divided down the centre. Measuring 134ft long x 38ft wide, it had a water tank at the end which suggested that it might also have been a stable. Opposite were smaller buildings thought to have been storehouses and a magazine. Another building, 136ft x 31ft, had wings, suggesting that it had been a hospital.

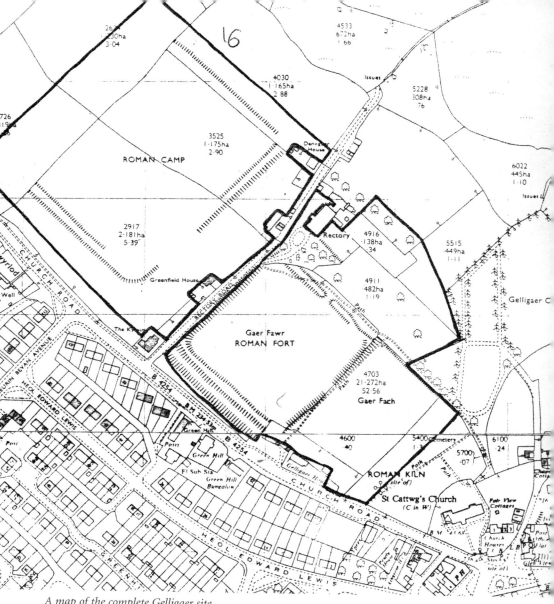

A map of the complete Gelligaer site.

A considerable amount of broken window glass was found. It was of an unusual type, being dull on one side with a blue-green hue and averaging from one-eighth of an inch thick to one-fifth. Many of the pieces were found to have a rounded edge.

Adjoining the fort on its eastern borders was a large annexe of about two acres, lying on land that had been called Gaer Fach (little fort). In the top half was an ample sized bathhouse measuring 140ft long and 60ft wide. It had been built on elaborate lines and included a circular *laconicum* or sweating chamber. It also had an extra-cold plunge bath. Some of the rooms had been decorated with painted wall plaster. To the west of the bathhouse was a large courtyard, 58ft long by 50ft wide, in which two

A photograph showing the excavation of the North Guard Chamber, which was first published in the Archaeologia Cambrensis. *(By kind permission of the* Archaeologia Cambrensis.*)*

ovens were found, which would have perhaps provided the bathers with a hot snack after their bath. With the exception of the luxurious baths at Caerleon, the bathhouse at Gelligaer was considered to have been the most elaborate found in Wales.

There was evidence that some remodelling had taken place to the building, due, it was thought, to the fact that the builders had misjudged the water level and had to increase the height of the foundations to avoid flooding. Among the small objects found were fragments of glass, some of which had broken off a bowl with an external moulding, and another from a white glass cup. Both vessels were said to have belonged to the earlier part of the second century. A coin of Hadrian was also found, as well as a coin of Nerva dated AD 96–98. Nothing of the annexe now remains, except for an inward-facing scarp. This area had also been well defended by a stone wall 3ft thick that had been backed with earth. There was also a berm 6–9ft wide and a shallow V-shaped ditch, 15ft wide. A small structure, 12ft x 9ft, just inside the north-eastern corner of the gate may have been a guard chamber.

In the lower south-western half of the annexe was another rectangular yard measuring 83ft x 41ft, with a building 42ft x 18ft wide attached to its south-eastern wall. The purpose of this structure is not certain, but it was probably an outside workshop or storage unit.

Just beyond the boundary of the annexe lies the churchyard of St Catwg's Church, and it was here that the most surprising discovery was made in 1913, when grave-diggers at work in the new churchyard extension came across Roman masonry and an area of hard, burnt earth. Then, 15in below the surface, they discovered a foundation of rough stones that had been cemented together, beneath which lay a number of flues. To their surprise they had unearthed a Roman kiln measuring 9ft square with

*This photograph records the discovery of Roman kilns in the churchyard. It was first published in
the* Archaeologia Cambrensis. *(By kind permission of the* Archaeologia Cambrensis.*)*

walls 2ft thick, consisting of a vaulted main central flue with six transverse flues on
either side. Fragments of roofing tiles and *mortaria*, all made with the same clay, were
found in and around the structure, suggesting that they had been the products of the
kiln which had been intended for use at the fort. A greenish-coloured glaze was
discovered on the side of the flues, a feature which had not been observed in any other
kilns of this period. It was abundant in the cross flues and had penetrated into the
fissures and gaps in the masonry. The glaze, which was exceedingly hard and brittle,
had apparently been produced through the reaction between the gaseous products of
the firing and the pennant sandstone used in the kiln.

Also in the south-eastern area were found Roman cinerary urns containing burnt
human bones, which implied that a cemetery had existed along the road leading away
from the fort.

The parade ground was located in the north-east corner on land adjoining the
rectory known as The Lawn. The area measured 348ft long by 147ft wide and had been
well gravelled to provide a sound surface for drilling purposes.

Of all the discoveries, the most interesting, historically, was the inscribed stone
found in the north-western gateway. This provided the most accurate description of
the fort by naming its garrison and period of occupancy. The largest surviving section
was restored and read:

Imp Caes[ari] divi / NER[vae] f[olio] Ner[vae] Triano / Aug[usto]
Germ[anico] Dac[ico] Pont[ifici] / Max[imo] Trib[unicia] P[otestate]
P[atri] Co[n]s[uli] V / Imp[erator] III I / Leg[io] II Avg[usta].

(The slashes denote where the words were separated on the tablet, and the brackets reveal the entire word which could not be written because of the restriction of the tablet's size.)

Translated, it refers to the fifth consularship of the Emperor Trajan, which occurred in AD 103, thus dating the building of the gateway to the beginning of the second century, with its construction carried out by the Second Augustan Legion. (Trajan died AD 117 and was succeeded by Hadrian.)

Three other fragments of Trajanic building inscriptions also came to light inside the fortress. Two were found in a back-filled ditch near the south-west gateway and a further portion of larger stone at about the same place, providing clear evidence that the troopers of the Second Augustan had carried out this important work. In fact, Gelligaer is considered to be the finest example of a stone fort to have been built in Wales, and it was shown through excavation that it had been built with stone right from the outset, with no reconstruction having taken place to the interior.

Coins are also a reliable source of information in dating various aspects of a fort's occupation, and at Gelligaer a *sesterius* of Hadrian was found in one of the barrack blocks. It had been minted between AD 119 and 138 and was almost new when the owner lost it. This was the last dateable object recorded at Gelligaer, although other dateable evidence of occupation came from a limited amount of pottery, including bowls, an *ovolo* with a wide beaded border and three black-fumed cooking pots with upstanding rims of second-century date. However, restoration of a flanged, conical bowl and *mortaria* suggests that there had been some form of occupation at Gelligaer from the late third to the fourth century, implying the possibility that a civilian settlement had established itself outside the annexe, which would have been an ideal location. Other coins found on the site are now in the possession of the National Museum of Wales.

It was estimated that the garrison was withdrawn sometime around AD 196, following which a period of desolation occurred, when the stone columns of the headquarters had been thrown into the ditch near the north-east gate and its well filled with pottery, tiles and stones. The south-east granary also suffered damage, as did the bath building, with fragments from its flagged floors found lying among the debris. After this period, it is thought the garrison returned and carried out repairs, which included the rebuilding of the bathhouse. Gelligaer is said to have fallen into final disuse when the conquest of Wales had been completed.

Following excavation, the site has returned to the pastoral land it had become, on which horses now graze. The only visible signs that a large fortress was ever sited there are the lines of its walls appearing as undulating mounds beneath the grass. Access to the site is possible along the lane leading in from the main road, which is signposted.

Gelligaer I

Alongside the fort in the adjoining field, separated by the lane, another encampment was found measuring 384ft wide and covering an area of six acres, double that of its neighbour.

At first, it presented itself as an enormous earthwork which, as a result of constant ploughing, only revealed parts of its defences. However, traces of two V-shaped ditches were located, each about 12ft wide, with large gaps in the banks to indicate the whereabouts of its entrances.

There were no signs of any internal buildings, and this may have been due to the fact that the encampment was never finished. It was probably constructed as a temporary measure, providing an area of accommodation for its builders while the main fort was being built.

Apart from the discoveries at Gelligaer, four other camps used for training recruits were found in the area, one of which measured 100ft square. These practice camps were designed to keep troops abreast of all the newest fighting techniques and improve their battle skills. They were built with the same precision and care as a fortress, with the soldiers becoming involved in their construction, many of whom had expertise in stone masonry, carpentry and other essential trades like metal working for repairing the armoury. One mile to the west of Gelligaer was another small group, with one camp measuring only 78 x 75ft. This programme of building practice camps even extended towards Bargoed, where another eight were found.

PEN-Y-DARREN

Continuing his chain of fortresses into south-eastern Wales, Julius Frontinus established another auxiliary fortress here on a spur of land overlooking the eastern side of the Afon Taf Valley outside Merthyr Tydfil, in Glamorganshire.

Evidence of Roman remains were first discovered here in 1786, when Roman blocks and a tesselated pavement were unearthed during the building of Pen-y-darren House, after which the site was named. The house has long been demolished. From 1902–05, more Roman items emerged when F. Treherne Davies investigated the site prior to levelling operations for the construction of a football ground. During this operation, a paved causeway or road and the foundations of a wall emerged, which turned out to have been the south-eastern rampart resting on a stone base and constructed with turfs and clay.

Another major discovery was the hypocaust of the external bathhouse, lying south-west of the fort. It had a concrete floor placed on nine rows of brick pillars. The furnace was located at the north end of the building and had a narrow walled entrance. Thirty feet to the east was another hypocaust which had a paved and walled culvert. A third hypocaust was discovered with a pile of collapsed voissoirs that had formed its archway. In all, the bath building covered an area 120ft long and 75ft wide.

It was not until 1957 that a full scale excavation of the fort was carried out, ably assisted by some young students from the local school. During excavations, it was found that the fort had undergone two periods of construction. Outside the defences lay a narrow berm and two ditches, 12ft and 9ft respectively, separated by an interval of 7ft. A large post hole for a timber-built tower was found in the stone core. A deep well was also found with brick-sided walls. Although much of the stonework had been robbed in the past, several stone buildings were located just south of Pen-y-darren House, the most significant of which was the buttressed granary. This structure was at least 55ft long and 27ft wide, with walls nearly 2ft thick, and buttressed externally at intervals of 9ft. Traverse sleeper walls, some 2ft thick and also spaced at intervals, carried the floor which, judging from the number of nails in the debris, had been a wooden one.

North-east of the bath building and nearer to the fort was a rectangular building, 45ft long and 16ft wide. It had been divided into two rooms by a cross wall and was separated by an alleyway. The purpose of this building was not clear, but among the small finds was the top half of a Gaulish clay statuette of Venus which might have been someone's good luck charm. A length of semi-circular roof tiling also emerged, as did a floor tile with the imprints of a dog's paws upon it.

Several cinerary urns were exposed to the north of the site, suggesting that a Roman cemetery was lying beside the north-bound road leading out of the fort. Two more urns appeared where Pen-y-darren House had once stood, which were blue in colour.

Among the pottery objects found were remnants of buff-coloured *amphorae*, of which only the handles had survived, as had the necks and tops of jugs and flagons. These objects are now on display at Cyfartha Castle, Merthyr Tydfil, as are the examples of red coarse pottery and several Samian bowls and dishes, many of which have been reconstructed to their original shapes. Miraculously, the rim of a Samian plate had survived intact, as had a Samian fruit bowl with an elaborate pattern of running dogs around the bottom. A bowl made of black burnished pottery is also on display. This type was made in Dorset, but as the Romans had abandoned the fort before its use had become widespread, very little of it was found at Pen-y-darren. Box-shaped flue tiles found in the bath building and scored with a criss-cross design are also shown at the castle, along with examples of glass objects ranging from window glass and bottle glass to the complete rim of a glass vase. It is obvious to the viewer that the pieces of window glass have a different, duller texture, which can be explained by the fact that the Romans made their glass in large flat moulds; therefore, the side facing the mould had a rougher surface and was less translucent.

The coins found on the site indicate that the fort was established around AD 74–78 during Frontinus's governorship, and examination of the pottery suggests that occupation continued until the first 30 years of the second century. The remains of the fort now lie buried beneath the sports stadium, and there are no visible signs of its once powerful presence upon the Silurian landscape.

PEN-Y-GAER

The auxiliary fortress at Pen-y-Gaer was established at about the same time as the one at Abergavenny, shortly after the Romans had advanced into the area, and was situated exactly halfway between Abergavenny and Brecon Gaer in order to control the territory north and south of the River Usk and to control the river itself, which was considered an important highway into the interior.

The fort was discovered north-east of Pen-y-darren fortress, but was separated from it by the chain of mountains surrounding them in the present county of Powys.

Earthworks have been observed here since the 19th century, initially by the Revd H.T. Bayne in around 1800, and then later mapped by a local surveyor in 1803. The renowned antiquarian Theophilis Jones recorded it as a Roman site in his first edition of his *History of Breconshire* in 1809.

The site was examined in 1804 and was confirmed as standing on a detached knoll of sandstone on the west side of the Rhiangoll, a northern tributary of the River Usk. At the time of the visit, outlines of the fort's eastern and south-eastern defences were clearly visible, although they were slightly hidden in places by the existing boundary walls and farm hedges. As the knoll rose 15–20ft above the surrounding ground, the fort had the distinct advantage of overlooking the vicinity, and was therefore able to offer the garrison a warning of any attack from the rebellious natives. This was a common stratagem employed by the designers of Roman forts.

In the north-eastern corner a bank of stones and layers of soil had been placed on the natural ground surface to form the fort's outer defences, and it was here that the excavators chose to section. It was found that the main defences comprised a single ditch to protect the rampart, with the Romans making full use of the natural slope. There was a pit in the eastern section of the defences which suggested that at one time timber uprights had formed a palisade. In another rebuilding phase, the Roman builders had erected a stone wall on top of the earlier bank and raised the height of the rampart by the addition of a layer of red soil and stones. These defences had later been demolished and the red soil dispersed outside the line of the wall to form a berm that provided an extra area of defence.

Within the fort, the excavators found coarse pottery and beakers that had been indented with thumb prints to make a pattern before the clay was fired. Black burnished pots also emerged, as well as the rim of a two-handled jar in a sandy-red colour. A *mortarium*, which was thought to have been made in Kent, was dated to between the late first and the early second century. It had been stamped with the potter's mark, although only the initials I.R.O were legible. Fragments of a Samian cup also emerged, dated to around AD 150–160. This indicated that the fort was still functioning in the mid to late second century.

On the whole, finds were scarce, possibly due to the disturbance of the land from continuous cultivation. Consequently, no trace of any internal structure could be found, apart from a kerb behind the rampart which was thought to have been part of the *Via Sagularis*. Had it not been for the discovery of pottery, no one would have known that the Romans had built a fortress here.

The earliest dated coin to have been discovered was a *denarius* of the Emperor Nero (AD 54–68), with the inscription '*Imp Nero Avgvstvs*' and '*Ivppiter Liberator*' on the reverse, thus confirming that Pen-y-Gaer was among the first fortresses to have been built in Wales.

There were signs that the fort had been abandoned around the time of Hadrian, when the garrison joined others at the beginning of the second century to build his northern defences.

BRECON (Y GAER) (CICUTIUM)

The proud remnants of the Roman fort known as Y Gaer, which simply means 'the fort', and also as Brecon Gaer is situated on farmland in the picturesque village of Aberyscir, where the River Yscir forms its western and the River Usk its southern boundary. It is also situated three miles from the modern town of Brecon and about 10 miles from Pen-y-darren. The fort now lies beneath modern farmland, with sheep and cattle grazing over what had once been a powerful symbol of Roman dominance in the area.

The fort was known as Cicutium by the Romans and was garrisoned by a regiment of 500 Spanish cavalry, the Ala Hispanorum Vettonum. A cavalry unit was divided into *turmae* of 30 horsemen, under the command of a decurion. And as the Romans were considered not to be good horsemen, they recruited their cavalry units from conquered provinces, in this case from Spain. The horses were usually very small stallions and the Vettones rode them without the aid of stirrups. We know this because engravings that have been found in which the horsemen are seen with their legs hanging free. This would have presented no problems to such expert riders, and as the Vettones controlled their horses with their legs they were still able to strike down an escaping enemy, which was their role after a battle.

Y Gaer is considered to be a superb example of an auxiliary fort, and as bricks bearing the stamp of the Second Augustan Legion appeared here it was thought that the fort was built by them, under whose command the Vettones served.

At the height of its importance, the fort protected the hinterland and was on the direct route southwards to the other forts of Coelbren, Neath and Loughor. In its position in a secluded valley, with the ridges of the Brecon Beacons rising some 3,000ft nearby, the fort was protected from the harsh winter winds. Also, since it was based in mountainous terrain, mounted patrols made policing the area more effective. In such a location, Y Gaer became the pivotal centre for military movement into central Wales. It appeared as an awesome structure on the landscape and covered seven acres, which is considered large for such a small garrison.

Y Gaer is among the largest of the Roman auxiliary forts in Wales and is considered to be the most famous. Even in the 11th century its ruins were mentioned in charters as a *vasta civitas*, and in about 1090 Bernard of Newmarch is said to have used the fort's stonework to build his castle in Brecon town. As the fort decreased in size and was practically erased from sight by stone robbers, it still produced various miscellaneous objects on the surface. In 1684 legionary tiles were found marked LEG II AVG, and in 1763 people began finding Roman coins. A gold coin with a winged figure of Victory was discovered in 1854, along with other coins of the Emperors Augustus, Vespasian and Valerian. A piece of a bronze plate, which had probably come from the armour of a trooper, also emerged. Then, at the end of the 19th century, the significant discovery of a Latin inscription on a tombstone was made, declaring that the young man so remembered had served in the cavalry there. The tablet, made of sandstone, had been split into two pieces, but the surviving left-hand portion bore all his details. In fact, the inscription was considered to be among the best of late first-century workmanship and was a major archaeological find as it gave vital clues as to the name of Y Gaer's garrison. It read:

DIS·[M]
CAND
NI·FILI
HSP·VETT
CLEM·DOM
AN·XX·STIP·III·H

The Candidus Tombstone. (Brecon Museum)

Translated: 'In memory of Candidus...son of...trooper in the Vettonian Spanish Cavalry, set up by his heirs...Clemens and Domitius. He lived 20 years and served three'.

The last line details his age and length of service, with the final letter 'H' being the abbreviation for Hispanorum, the Latin name for Spain. The tombstone had been mistaken for a Roman milestone and was found on the side of the road leading to Battle Fawr farmhouse in the neighbouring village. Despite a thorough search, the right-hand portion could not be found. Nevertheless, the surviving portion remains a graphic and poignant memorial to a young soldier who died all those centuries ago in a land that was not his home. This historic tablet is now in the Brecon Museum.

In the 16th century another historic tombstone was found which had also been used as a Roman milestone. Made of sandstone, it stood 6.5ft above the ground and bore the figures of a man and a woman. As portions of the figures had worn away, they were both mistaken for females, and the stone became known as Maen y Morwynion (the Maidens' Stone). Below the figures was a panel 27in long and about 20in wide containing an inscription, but weathering had destroyed all but the last line, which was preserved, no doubt, by the growth of turf around its base. It read 'CONIVNX EIVS H.S.E.' and was regarded as characteristic of the ones found on first-century tombstones. This stone is also at the Brecon Museum.

Excavations of the fort were carried out during the summer of 1922 by R.E. Mortimer Wheeler. Among those who assisted him were his wife, Tessa, and Mr V.E. Nash Williams, who had later succeeded him as director of the National Museum of Wales.

Upon arrival at the site, the outline of the fort was clearly visible beneath the parched grass, making identification of its defences easier. It was found that originally the fort had been constructed with clay ramparts and timber buildings in around AD 75, during the time of governor Julius Frontinus's campaigns against the rebellious Silures. The ramparts were found to have been supported by two defensive ditches, with the outer one 5ft high and 18ft wide, resting on cobble footings, and the inner one 15–16ft wide and 6ft deep. Here, Roman objects began to appear in the form of first-century Samian ware and other pottery.

There had been stone turrets at each corner, built into the rampart wall. As the corners were rounded, they left no 'blind' spots for the archers. These walls, as much as 12ft high, provided a formidable defence, as did the west gate located at the top of a sloping hill. Its entrance would have looked exaggerated from a low viewpoint, creating the illusion that it would be difficult to assault. Each gateway had a huge wooden door which was locked at night and protected by a gatehouse on either side. The gatehouses protecting the west gate were larger than the others and projected out from the wall. This gate, which led directly to the most important building in the fort – the *Principia* – would also have been considered more important than the others and had probably been used by visiting dignitaries and for ceremonial occasions. None of its stone decorations have survived, but fragments of plaster with blue, red and yellow patterns were found lying inside the interior of one of its gatehouses, indicating what a splendid entrance it must have been.

This photograph shows the surviving north wall.

It soon became apparent that ploughing had taken place over the interior of the fort, but excavations revealed that the original timber buildings had been destroyed by fire around AD 120, 50 years after its founding. The rebuilding of the fort was, however, interrupted when the troops were withdrawn from Wales and sent to the north of England in AD 122. Following this, in around AD 140, an ambitious program was undertaken to reconstruct the fort in stone, and during this time the original rampart was reinforced by a stone wall, a part of which, incredibly, is still standing as much as 12ft high. In places the rampart was found to have been raised as well as strengthened with stone. Remnants of the stone battlements were also found.

About 30ft from the fort's wall was the *intervallum*, which had a slight camber and had served the double purpose of providing access to the ramparts while also placing the barrack blocks out of the range of enemy missiles. On each side of the west gate the rampart had been cut to construct the flanking guardrooms. Here, a grey-fumed cooking pot, dated AD 130–160, with a wavy line decoration on the neck was found in a dump, as was a black-fumed beaker with an elaborate rim, dated AD 140–200, probably imported during the early Antonine period. Scattered on the surface of the west gate were coins of the third and fourth centuries, indicating that the fort was in occupation during those periods. There were two of Carausius (287–293), one of Constans (342–348) and one of Valentinian I (364–378). The Praetorian gate was also uncovered. It had been protected by flanking guard towers, and its archway was considered an unusual feature for military establishments of that period.

Each corner of the fort had been occupied by an internal turret, with the south-west one having a commanding position on the brow of the steep slope above the junction of the Rivers Yscir and Usk. Bearing this in mind, the builders had taken special precautions to stop the turret from slipping downhill. This measure had also been taken on all the other surviving corners of the fort's wall. The south-east turret in particular was found to have been among one of the finest surviving stretches of the wall.

Excavations of the east gate showed that it had retained much of the stonework above its foundations and had been built at the same time as the rampart wall. There was no evidence of the original timber structure, but the door-sill and door jambs of the northern stone guardrooms were all found in a remarkable state of preservation, standing to a maximum height of 7ft. There was little evidence, though, of the guardroom having been used, probably due to the marshy ground outside which had discouraged anyone from using it. Two spearheads dating to the early second century were interesting discoveries on the floor of one room. The southern guardroom, however, had been largely destroyed in ancient times, but fragments found on the road surfaces running through the gateway showed that it had been decorated with ornamental panels.

The main street, the *Via Principalis,* was found to be 30ft wide and displayed deep grooves along its surface, which had been made by the wagons bringing in supplies through the west gate. Lining the street was the *Principia*, which had been built on sloping ground. Its plan was considered unusual in Britain as, when rebuilt in stone, it had an open courtyard, flanked on three sides by long halls. These would normally have been verandahs, but from the solidity of the foundations it was clear that they had been enclosed as long halls. One of these, known as a fore-hall, straddled the *Via Principalis* and was 147ft long and 40ft broad; it extended across the entire width of the building. These fore-halls have been known as *Exercier Halle*, or exercise halls, associated with mounted troops. At Y Gaer, this great hall, built during the second century, strengthens the supposition that troopers exercised their horses here during the winter months. On the northern side of the *Principia,* the other long hall was thought to have been where the horses were stabled. Because of its elevated position, much of its stonework had been robbed in the past, but the remaining fragments of its walling provided a clear picture of its internal layout.

The regimental shrine and treasury (the *Sacellum*) occupied a position between two rooms and was located in front of the fore-hall. It had been built with extra care and attention from yellow wall plaster. A roof tile bearing the stamp of the Second Augustan Legion was also found. On the whole, the workmanship of the entire building had been far superior to the others, as was usual for one of such importance. It is considered that it had been a building 'of some distinction'.

In the centre of the *Principia* was the cellar or floor-safe, which was 7ft long, 5ft wide and 3ft deep. Access was through a trapdoor in the floor. It was found to be full

This photograph shows the remains of the north-east guard tower attached to the north wall.

of rubble, among which was a second brass of Trajan and a *denarius* of Vitellius, probably dropped by those who had installed it. It is known that such structures within the *Sacellum* did not appear until the second half of the second century, so at Y Gaer the little cellar is an interesting example of the military floor-safes still in the initial stages of development. It was noted that in places the floors of the *Principia*, with the exception of the *Sacellum*, had been destroyed by modern ploughing.

The space on the eastern side of the headquarters was occupied by a so-called cross-hall, which usually divided its verandah from the furthermost range of rooms. In an auxiliary fort this range commonly consisted of five rooms, but with only three at Y Gaer it was considered exceptional in a headquarters building of this enormity and was also considered unusual in Britain. It was possible that these rooms, and those on the opposite side, were sub-divided by timber screens which have not survived. This building was estimated to have been no less than two-storeys high.

To the far left of the *Principia*, against the northern defences, was the granary, but there was also a difference to its usual design in that it did not have a raised floor but one which had been laid with rough slabs. Evidence shows that these had later been taken away. It was thought that the granary could have been converted into a barrack block during the fourth century. There was, however, space for another granary, but with one being capable of serving a garrison of 500 men, another one had obviously not been considered necessary. Therefore, this left a large unoccupied space which was then taken up with a stone-lined well. This was found to be full of water to within 4ft of the top. Inside, two fourth-century coins were found, but the pottery was a great deal earlier, perhaps AD 90–130, including fragments of Samian ware showing an early festoon design. Further down the well, the filling consisted largely of building stones, hazel nuts and the bones of an ox. For the most part, the well had been filled with debris dating from the intensive late first to early second century occupation of the fort.

The commandant's house was a large rectangular building, also built on sloping ground next to the *Principia*. Fourteen post holes and two layers of flooring were all that remained of its first-century predecessor. Indications were that the house had undergone two timber reconstructions, both of which had ended in fire, validated by the discovery of a charred post. When rebuilt in stone, the house was of a normal plan but was again of exceptional size and consisted of four ranges of rooms grouped around a courtyard. This probably opened through a verandah. A drain carried off the rainwater from the courtyard in the direction of the rampart. In the drain, two Samian bowls of the Trajan–Hadrian period were recovered intact.

A second brass coin of Domitian (AD 86) dated this work to the late first century. Another interesting find was the rim of small glass bowl, coloured dark blue, with a pattern of yellow and green drops.

At a later period, an annexe had been built on at a right angle to the house and alongside the *Via Principalis*. This may have been built to install extra kitchens, as entertaining was usually carried out on a grand scale to impress visiting dignitaries. An iron key was found lying on the late first-century floor, with some bone dice marked with the figures six, four, three, two and two. The duplication of one of the numerals was considered unusual. Close by were three gaming counters. In all, about 30 gaming counters were found in various places around the fort, which were a good indication of how the garrison commander and his men spent their leisure hours. The counters had been made of white, black, dark blue and yellow paste. Finally, the building showed signs that it had been destroyed during the occupation of the fort, and that even its footings had been stripped by stone robbers.

In the northern half of the fort, the legionary bathhouse was found to have been built on an unusual axis and in an unusual location in comparison to the other fortresses. Excavation revealed that it had the usual suite of cold and heated rooms and a semi-circular cold plunge bath, although none of the original floors or *pilae* that had supported them were present. They had been removed and replaced by a rough filling of broken building materials. It was also found that the flues had been lined with bricks, all of which bore the plain oblong logo of the Second Augustan Legion. The bricks were mostly 8in or 11.5in square, similar to those commonly used for the *pilae*. Water from the semi-circular bath had been emptied through a square outlet into a drain which travelled along the whole width of the building. Such was the thoroughness of Roman plumbing, that midway along the drain a manhole had been fitted so that the channel could be cleaned out.

The use of legionary tiles and the excellence of the masonry suggested that the baths were fully functional before the evacuation of the fort in the Antonine period. However, the discovery of a third-century *olla* in the outlet from the semi-circular plunge bath showed that it was no longer flushed by water at that period, and that the bath had long ceased to be used, probably because a plunge into cold water during the winter was considered far too rigorous. Fragments of a bronze parade helmet, comprising pieces that covered the ear, tip of the nose and part of the upper lip, were found in a pit close by. Although the bronze was in a decomposed state, it was salvageable. Helmets of this type were quite elaborate and were worn at tournaments and ceremonial parades. Examples have only been found on two other sites in Britain – one in Lancashire and the other at Newstead, both of which dated prior to AD 100.

Although the barracks had been laid out in their usual pairs at Y Gaer, the inner units of each pair had been built back-to-back and designed to house 80 men. Each block comprised eight units, and were 180ft long and 30ft broad. As nothing of the internal divisions had survived, they might have consisted of timber screens. Evidence showed that none of the barrack blocks had gone through the stone-building programme but had remained wooden throughout their use. The discovery of a charred plank suggested that they had burned down at some point.

From the quantities of early second-century pottery found there, occupation had taken place from about AD 75–120. Nothing dating from later than the Trajan period in the second century could be found. Thereafter, all evidence of occupation diminished to almost vanishing point in the Antonine period. This conveyed the impression that the pot shards were the result of a total clearance by the troops, and that the disposal of rubbish between the backs of two adjacent barrack blocks had taken place during the evacuation of the entire garrison around AD 140, when the regiment was transferred north. Among the discarded pottery were some finely decorated pieces featuring a lion between two leaves. This pattern was similar to one found on an *ovolo* at Pompeii, and it was stamped IIVST. Another panel showed Diana and a small hind, while another had the figure of Victory holding a small bowl. These fragments, however small, fully displayed the potter's expertise in producing what was not only everyday domestic ware, but also delightful works of art that have survived the centuries for us to admire. Two highly decorative intaglios, one in carnelian and the other in onyx, which had been lost from rings, were found showing minute engravings of mythological figures.

The latest coin to have been found at the fort was the one dated AD 367–375, during the reign of Gratian, showing that Y Gaer continued to dominate the area until the end of the fourth century. It is also interesting to note that the presence of legionary bricks and tiles in the reconstructed areas show that the Second Augustan had also been actively engaged in maintaining their fortresses.

After the fort's defences had fallen into ruin it was re-occupied, probably by the local inhabitants. During their occupation, the new inhabitants roughly patched up the fallen rampart by the south gateway and reinforced the defences with a dry-built stone wall, increasing its thickness by 5ft. It was observed that the workmanship contrasted greatly with the original, making it obvious that it had been rebuilt by persons less skilled than the legionaries.

A small community also established itself outside the northern defences, their timbered dwellings flanking the RR 621 Roman road which came up from Cardiff by way of Caerphilly and Gelligaer. Workshops of blacksmiths and tanners were also present alongside this road leading into the fort. The RR 621 then continued on a northerly course towards Castell Collen. A second road, the RR 62, entered the fort from the east and cut through the *vicus*. Alongside this was the fort's cemetery on one side and a large *Mansio* on the other, the latter suggesting that this area was well visited by those who required to stay a night or two.

The few remaining ruins at Y Gaer are scheduled as ancient monuments, and as they are on private land operating as a working farm permission to view them must be obtained from the owner. The surviving north wall, now situated inside the paddock, is the first and most noticeable feature on approaching the farm from the roadway leading up from the village.

Aerial photography identified a practice camp outside the defences, with another one under the present farmyard.

The Romans also installed two enormous marching camps on the summit of Trecastle Mountain within Brecon Beacons National Park, and within easy reach of Brecon Gaer. These camps were designed for troops on the move, both as halting places for those on manoeuvres and for those being marched from one fort to another. They were even built for stays as short as a single night and were also as well defended as the fortresses. Marching camps extended across the whole of Wales and were considered an important feature in the campaigns to conquer the land the Romans called Britannia Secunda.

The two camps on Trecastle Mountain, known as Y Pigwyn (meaning 'Beacon'), were unique in that one had been built inside the other, with the larger outer one having a circumference of one mile, being 1,454ft long and 1,254ft wide, giving a circuit of 5,416ft and measuring 37 acres. The inner camp measured 1,254ft long and 996ft wide with a circuit of 4,500ft, totalling 25 acres.

Two entrances were found on each side of the enclosures, but not opposite each other. The width of each ditch and rampart was about 14ft, and they were well preserved in places. In fact, the camps are the best preserved marching camps in Wales. The inner camp was considered to be large enough to have accommodated an entire legion and its auxiliary cohorts.

As no structural remains were found, it was supposed that the troops had been accommodated in tents during the summer, known as *papillos* as the flaps were likened to butterflies. As each tent held only eight men, several hundred would have been required.

The Romans had obviously chosen this lonely mountain top as it gave them uninterrupted views across the region, and it was suitably situated on the borders of both Silurian and Demetae territory so they could supervise the movements of both tribes. It was also a position from which the Romans could launch their invasion into Demetae territory, and this is probably what they did.

A Roman road stretched along the southern walls of the camps to connect with the fortresses of Brecon Gaer and Llandovery, with the former being only four miles across the border in Demetae country.

There were also several cairns representing ancient burials on the summit, one of which was that of a native chief, and two conical-shaped cremation urns were also found.

An interesting discovery was a tombstone with a Latin inscription reading:

IMPERATORI NOSTRO MARCO CASSIANO / POSUMO PIO FELICICI AVG.

From this tombstone, the name Marco Cassiano emerged. It is possible he was a Roman soldier who had died in one of the fierce battles that were said to have raged in the vicinity.

Tightening their grip on the area, the Romans installed three more practice camps to the east, with another smaller marching camp to the west of Trecastle Mountain.

CLYRO

The fortress at Clyro was discovered on farmland overlooking the river at Hay-on-Wye, to the north-east of Brecon Gaer, and had its south-eastern sides sloping downwards to the river. It was about half a mile from Clyro itself.

The fortress had been built with the usual rounded corners and at an angle, with one of its corners facing directly northwards. It was thought to have been of a considerable size, being quarter of a mile long and half that wide. Some of its ramparts have survived and were well defined on the north-eastern slope. Being on a rise, the ramparts would have had excellent views across the terrain with the Brecon Beacons just 20 miles away. One of its corners has also survived, but the one in the south was lying immediately beneath the existing Boatside Farm, where the farmer reported seeing a metalled roadway leading away from the north-east gate.

Aerial photography from 1960 revealed two ditches almost 90ft apart, but on the ground a ditch was found 12ft wide that had been cut into the rock. The excavation failed to uncover any internal structures, although some circular ovens were found alongside the *intervallum*. Domestic finds included some bright red Samian ware and a wine flagon from the mid-first century, indicating that the fortress had only a short occupation compared with other fortresses in the area. It was thought that the fort had been abandoned around AD 60, during the early years of the Flavian campaigns.

During its occupation there had been a plentiful supply of fresh water. One source was a spring outside its eastern walls and the other was a spring called Monks' Well, situated a short distance from its south-western corner.

The fortress was considered to have been of some strategic importance, as it provided Clyro with an essential link between the forts in the Usk Valley and those in the Leintwardine area on the eastern borders.

A marching camp, around 26 acres in extent, was also discovered not far from the fortress, thus making a formidable union during those early years of the Roman incursion.

CAERAU

The little fortress at Caerau was discovered during an aerial survey in April 1960 on farmland situated south of Beulah in the county of Breconshire, now Powys. Although the land had been ploughed continuously, its ramparts were still visible, being 18ft wide and 3ft high in places. The whole circuit measured 340ft x 325ft, giving an area of just two acres. With the south-eastern side sloping steeply down to the River Cammarch, the fort had commanding views in all directions except in the north-east. The fort only required a small garrison, and this could have been a detachment of about 500 infantry or a cavalry unit.

Examination of the remains revealed that the ramparts had been made of clay, set on a cobble footing and then faced with turfs. The defences consisted of double ditches surrounding the enclosure. No internal structures were found, but Samian ware and some coarse pottery were found dated to AD 75–90, which give an indication as to when the defences were constructed. Around the beginning of the second century the defences were modified with a higher rampart, but only one ditch was retained.

Interestingly, outside the north-east gate there was evidence that a *vicus* had become established there when test pits dug in 1970 revealed the floors of several buildings. Bricks and tiles were also found, and these helped to identify the location of the bathhouse there.

In the absence of any internal structures, it is possible that the garrison dismantled them before abandoning the fort when they were transferred north to help build Hadrian's Wall.

To the north, and situated between the fortress and Beulah town, an enormous marching camp was found extending across six fields and measuring just over 36 acres. It appeared as low banks in the pasture, but no internal structures were found. To the north of the fortress there were also signs that a *vicus* had been present when floors of buildings were uncovered during the digging of trial pits in 1970.

To the south of the fortress, aerial photography then located what appeared to be two more practice camps lying alongside the RR 623 Roman road going northwards, although there were no signs of any defences. These military installations certainly enforced the Roman grip even more on such a small area inside Silurian territory.

CASTELL COLLEN

astell Collen was originally designated as a practice camp, but its characteristics were more akin to a fortress, and after 25 excavations revealed some remarkable details of its interior it deserves to be included among the great Roman fortresses of Wales.

It was situated in mid-Wales, in the parish of Llanfihangel on the banks of the River Ithon, a tributary of the Wye, and a mile north of Llandrindod Wells. It was almost square and covered five and a half acres.

It was considered a key military station, along with the auxiliary fortresses of Brecon Gaer and Caersws, and formed an important link of communication into mid-Wales. It also had a full defensive force made up of a detachment of the Second Augustan Legion.

The Romans called it Magos, but it was called Caer Fagu by the Silures. The site acquired the name Castell Collen in modern times for easier reference, as there was a nearby farm of that name when it was discovered.

Castell Collen was also as well defended as an auxiliary fortress, with a timbered palisade which was later replaced with a stone wall and battlement. It also had the range of principal buildings usually found in permanent forts, including the headquarters, the commandant's house, the granary and the bathhouse.

The commandant's residence revealed that its design and size had been worthy of his high rank. It was 60ft long and 30ft wide, with the usual suite of rooms situated around a courtyard. There was also a hypocaust which had amply heated his rooms and private bathing suite.

Excavation of the granary revealed a series of ventilation holes that had kept the grain dry. The bathhouse measured 110ft in length and was much larger than expected. It was also found to be in a good state of preservation. There was a spacious entrance hall which measured 44ft across and an open courtyard surrounded by a cloister, making it an elaborate structure for a station that was not designated as a permanent fortress. Here at Castell Collen, the bathhouse afforded the soldier every luxury, which must have compensated for his rigorous training. Excavation of the drains revealed a rich harvest of jewellery that had been lost by the bathers, including an ear pendant made of black stone set in a gold mount. The bathhouse was among the few buildings which could be fully excavated, and a quantity of pottery recovered from the building was instrumental in dating its construction to around AD 100–110. Next to the bathhouse was the latrine. It was a good size, 20ft square, and was entered from outside the baths through a wide passageway. It had also been flushed by water from the baths. A drain, extending over 60ft east of the camp, eventually discharged the waste into the river.

The river provided a natural defence, as did the elevated spur of land on which the camp had been built. This elevation provided unbroken views across the surrounding countryside. Another significant feature was that the ground sloped precipitously down to the river. To prevent the rampart from slipping on this side, the Roman

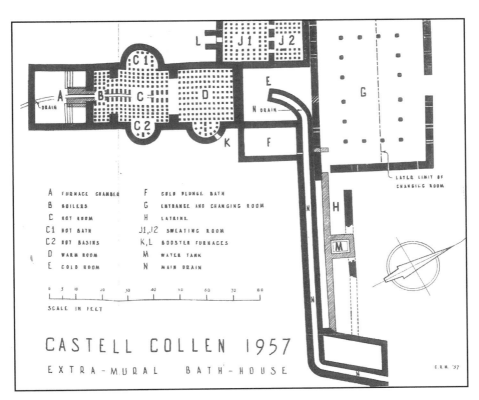

A FURNACE CHAMBER
B BOILERS
C HOT ROOM
C1 HOT BATH
C2 HOT BASINS
D WARM ROOM
E COLD ROOM
F COLD PLUNGE BATH
G ENTRANCE AND CHANGING ROOM
H LATRINE
J1,J2 SWEATING ROOM
K,L BOOSTER FURNACES
M WATER TANK
N MAIN DRAIN

SCALE IN FEET

CASTELL COLLEN 1957
EXTRA-MURAL BATH-HOUSE

builders had planted a row of timber stakes and then added blocks of stone in front of the wall, which also helped to impede any attack. The southern approaches to the camp had been over a bridge.

The defensive ditch had been cut to a 'W' shape and was 21ft across and about 5ft deep, but when it had become silted up the Romans built another one 20ft wider. Usually, sharply pointed stakes were included to inflict serious injuries on any attacker by tearing the feet of both man and horse, and it was in the ditches where most casualties and deaths had occurred during battles.

A coin of Faustina (died AD 141) was found among the debris in the *Sacellum* of the headquarters, along with pottery and bricks from the hypocaust. Another significant find was a highly decorative fragment of a Latin inscription recording the building activities of the Second Augustan Legion, who defended the camp. The fragment also contained a carving of the legion's insignia – the body of a goat with the tail of a fish, representing Capricorn – the birth sign of its founder, the Emperor Augustus. Also discovered was a hoard of 80 silver and bronze coins, most of which were dated to the third century; gold and bronze ornaments, one of which was in the shape of a hen, and two spear heads, with one attached to a flat blade 6in long. Pieces of window glass also emerged in great numbers throughout the site.

In the north-west corner of the camp was the parade ground. Even this was protected by a defensive ditch and there were traces of an entrance near its centre.

Some evidence of a road running westwards was discovered, which may have been used by the Romans to reach the lead mines in the area.

Around AD 150 the camp was reduced in size from five and a half acres to three, during which time most of the western defences were demolished. With a smaller perimeter, the rampart was widened by 5ft then strengthened to a height of 7ft in a neat herring-bone pattern that had escaped the plundering.

Occupation of the camp was thought to have continued until the close of the third century, but the area remained populated because a civilian settlement had been established outside its gates.

Castell Collen was one of the few Roman sites where a full excavation could be carried out.

COELBREN

The Romans established an auxiliary fort at Coelbren in around AD 74–78, on the crest of a hill 730ft above sea level, south of Brecon Gaer and halfway between the modern-day towns of Ystradgynlais in the Swansea Valley and Glyn Neath in the Neath Valley. It was originally built from earth and timber, then it was remodelled in stone shortly after AD 140.

The fort was first excavated by Colonel W.L. Morgan, R.E., in 1904–07, who found that the outline of the fort was almost square, with sides 100 yards long and with the usual rounded corners. The site had been ploughed level and had a fall of 30–40ft in every direction from the ramparts to meet the general level of the surrounding ground. At excavation it had the appearance of a broad platform which was covered with patches of heather. The fort was located next to an extensive marsh called Gors Llwyn and was at the junction of three large streams: the Camlais, the Nantybryn and the Nant-y-Fedwen. The bog itself is known as being notoriously difficult to cross in any season, and even more so in the winter. In this respect, the marsh provided the fort with a reasonable defence on this side.

On examination, only the rampart on the south and west side had survived in the form of a low bank measuring about 30–45ft across. Its outer scarp was visible on the north and eastern side and was standing to a height of 4ft. The bank continued eastwards along the line of the rampart for over 300ft, but as the area had been disturbed by ploughing the eastern boundary had disappeared. There were also two ditches about 6ft below the ramparts, with a combined width of approximately 32ft.

An aerial view of the fortress site at Coelbren. (By kind permission of the Glamorgan & Gwent Archaeological Society.)

In Roman times the fort would have had four entrances, one at each point of the compass, but the position of the north entrance was not so well defined, as the gap in the rampart looked as though an access had been made for a modern footpath to cross the site, rather than it being a Roman gateway. The eastern entrance was obscured by a modern bank, probably created by the piling up of earth after ploughing, and the entrance on the western side of the fort was represented by a causeway across the ditches. The remaining entrance in the south had been completely destroyed.

Interestingly, the section of the north bank east of the modern road showed that it was 30ft wide and had been made wholly from turf on a foundation of tree branches. The rampart itself had been solidly built to take wooden galleries and watch towers. On closer examination, it was found that the rampart had been constructed with alternative layers of clay, turfs and brushwood, mainly birch. Its outer section was founded on a bed of oak logs, some 16ft long and all laid at right angles to the line of the rampart. In places the logs were in two lengths with a gap in between, although the overall length was again about 16ft. It was assumed that the log base was laid as a reinforcement to enable the rampart to stand more firmly on the natural soil without slipping. Where the area was not so solid, the Roman builders had laid a double layer of logs. In contrast, the eastern rampart, and a part of the western rampart, were founded on stones rather than logs. At the corners, the foundations were more elaborate and consisted of two layers of boards which had been sawn up to 2ft wide and were still showing marks made by the axe. In places, piles of oak nearly 2ft square formed buttresses which acted as supports to take the extra weight of platforms holding heavy artillery and other defensive machines. These were connected by wooden galleries and bridges with strong towers situated at the corners and at the entrances.

Forming part of the fort's defences was a wide berm which had been fortified with wooden spikes. Remarkably, these were still in place, having been preserved from rotting by the levelling of the rampart. This clearly illustrated the measures taken by the Romans to defend their walls because of the insecurity felt in the area.

Outside the fort, the causeways of the Roman road leading to the south and east were clearly visible, being 18ft wide and standing about a foot high. That on the east had a line of greener grass down its centre, suggesting that a culvert might have existed there. An aerial photograph showed that the Roman road from the east led directly into the fort.

A poppy head beaker, which is now displayed at the Swansea Museum. (By kind permission of the Swansea Museum.)

Excavations of the interior revealed fragments of timbered buildings, and in several places there were signs that brick floors had been laid on wooden foundations, but over the intervening centuries the floors had crumbled into red-brick dust. Horizontal strips of timber that had been squared off appeared to have belonged to a barrack block with a floor of roughly cobbled stones. Extensive layers of ash and burnt material gave away the presence of hearths where the troops had cooked their meals. This area was probably along the rampart roadway where cooking operations were usually carried out. There were also extensive layers of brick ash thought to have represented the remains of previous buildings, giving rise to the supposition that there had been two separate periods of occupation at Coelbren, with the first having been burnt down to make way for newer buildings in the second phase of occupation, as sometimes was the case in Roman forts.

As a result of constant ploughing over the entire site, very little of the fort has survived. However, various objects of interest were found which gave some impression of its Roman occupants. These included fragments of Samian pottery of Flavian date and fragments of *amphorae, mortaria, ollae,* a flagon and a flanged bowl. An interesting discovery was a dark grey coloured 'poppy head' beaker, so-called because of its distinctive shape. It had an unusual decoration of a raised beaded design and is now on display in the Swansea Museum. Coloured wall plaster was also found.

All the fragments were mostly from the late first century extending into the third century. Included were many discs made of sandstone, 2.5in across, which had probably been used as pot covers, and as several decorative pieces were spread around the area it was probable that they had been part of a common form of decoration around the fort. Terracotta beads of various sizes and greenish-blue 'melon' beads also came to light, as did a small leaden ballister ball which was probably a stray that had been fired by the artillery. A large quantity of glass also emerged, scattered over a wide area with some appearing above a layer of blue clay. The colour of the glass varied from blue to light green and represented bottles and vases of various shapes. There were also numerous specimens of window glass. Iron nails were also in plentiful supply, which had obviously survived beyond the timbers into which they had once been hammered. A quern, used to grind corn, also emerged, as did fragments of several *amphorae*, which were dated to the third century and varied from 0.5in to 1in thick. There were also many potsherds of black coloured ware. This ware was made by the Durotrigian potters who occupied the territory we now call Dorset. It was easy to manufacture and was sold to the Roman army in large quantities because of its durability and practicality. The tradition of making black, burnished kitchen ware was, however, ostensibly an Iron Age one, but because of the Roman contracts to make them they were found on most military sites in the second century.

Large quantities of coal were also found, but as they were far too numerous to have been accidentally brought to the site it was thought that the coal must have been brought for smelting purposes in the garrison's workshops, where various deposits of slag were found alongside some glazed materials.

A layer of gravel, 1.5ft thick, turned out to be the surface of a road that went through the fort and was thought to have been the *Via Principalis*, from which smaller roads radiated.

From the evidence gleaned, we can suppose that the fort was abandoned at some point between AD 190–220 and was repaired and re-occupied towards the end of the third century. The destruction of the fort was thought to have been intentionally carried out after the troops had moved out, leaving it to be ravaged further by the local populace who had come into the area to farm the land. Stone was scarce, and it is already known that farmers robbed the fortress's walls to build their own. Piles of stones had been placed intermittently along the road leading to Neath. The purpose for these was not clear, but it is probable that they were left there as a guide to travellers unfamiliar with the locality.

Running from the east and south entrances was the *Sarn Helen*. This was an important Roman road, named after a Celtic princess, and ran the entire length of Wales, linking Roman forts and settlements from Neath in the south to Caernarfon in the north. Here at Coelbren it was a major route of communication between the fort and the one at Neath, and being in hostile territory it provided swift access for reinforcements in times of trouble. As Coelbren was so far inside enemy land, it was considered to occupy an important strategical position in this part of Wales. It is possible that the *Sarn Helen* was constructed at the same time as other major roads in the vicinity during the first century.

When the site was converted to agricultural land, the systematic ploughing of the area destroyed many Roman remains, and the final destruction occurred in the 19th century when immigrant labourers, who had been drawn by the prospect of employment at the nearby Banwen Ironworks, further robbed its buildings to build their cottages. The Roman road was also systematically robbed.

There was another significant Roman presence to the north-east of Coelbren in the form of a massive marching camp at Ystradfellte, measuring 45 acres. This was sited on the Roman RR 622 road that ran northwards out of the camp. A long stretch of this road can still be seen to the north of Coelbren, which passes through several forestry plantations with the River Nedd cutting across its path.

The camp's presence was originally identified by a slight elevation on the surface, and its southern rampart could be traced along a narrow gap between the trees. Nowadays, a pathway crosses the interior diagonally from east–south where its entrance gates had probably stood. The site is now a scheduled ancient monument.

A notable find along the RR 622 close to the camp was an inscribed tombstone recording the death of the Roman Dervacus, who had probably served at the camp. The lettering on the stone was badly cut but noted he was the 'son of Justus'. This historic stone is known as Maen Madog. A large square pit, thought to have been his grave, was found close by, but it was not considered unusual, considering the lapse of time, that the stone had become dislodged from its original mounting. Nevertheless, it had recorded the burial place of a lost soldier.

NEATH (NIDUM)

Still in Silurian territory, the Romans established another auxiliary fortress here on the banks of the River Nedd within the town of Neath, Glamorgan, and called it Nidum after the river. The Welsh name for the town is Castell Nedd, and this is how it is known to all Welsh speakers.

Nidum was first mentioned in the *Antonine Itinerary* as being on *Iter XII*, route 12, which placed it halfway between Bovium (Cowbridge) and Leucarum (Loughor). But while no Roman establishment has been found at Cowbridge, Roman coins have surfaced there in the past.

Excavations in progress. (By kind permission of the County Museum, Neath.)

The placing of Nidum in such a location made the antiquarians aware that a Roman fortress was lying either in or around the present town of Neath, but like so many other fortresses the precise location remained a mystery, as it too was lying under centuries of redevelopment and was therefore difficult to find. From time to time Roman artefacts appeared in the area, giving an indication that a Roman site was somewhere close by, and so the search went on.

In 1835 a large hoard of 500 Roman coins, ranging over several reigns, was found at Gwindy, and in 1892 a milestone from the reign of Diocletian (284–305) was found on the line of the Roman road about a mile south of Neath, which is now preserved in the National Museum of Wales. In 1919 another hoard of 150–200 coins was found buried in an old quarry during the building of the Anglo Persian Oil Company on the outskirts of the town. It was thought that this hoard was probably loot from a robbery during the third century. The quarry was only a short distance from the line of the Roman road – the *Via Julia Martima*.

Then, nearer to modern times, a postman, while digging in his garden on the outskirts of Neath, came across a piece of sandstone identified as a Roman soldier's tool for sharpening his sword and other weaponry. It was surmised that this had become lost when the soldier, after being given a plot of land upon his retirement, and keeping the tool for sharpening his farming implements, had subsequently mislaid it, as normally, he would have been obliged to hand over the tool with the rest of his kit. A similar sandstone tool was found in the Bone Cave of the Dan yr Ogof caves in the upper Swansea Valley, where a group of people had found shelter in the Roman era.

It was not until trenches had been dug in Neath for a new housing estate in 1949 that workmen struck brickwork that was identified as Roman foundations. And when fragments of Roman pottery also emerged, it soon became apparent that the long lost fortress of Nidum was lying beneath their feet. The National Museum of Wales was immediately informed, and its director of archaeology, the late Dr V.E. Nash Williams, who was also an expert archaeologist, arrived to examine the finds and direct future excavations. The pottery enabled the dating of the fort's founding to be placed at around AD 74–78.

It was discovered that the fort was lying on low ground to the west of the town on the banks of the River Nedd, just 340ft from the water's edge. It was also lying beneath the grammar school playing fields and straddled the main road.

The fort's location on the banks of a wide navigable river was typical of the Roman's military strategy. Being at the head of the tidal Nedd, it enabled their ships to sail directly in from the sea to deposit supplies and men right at the fort's front door. Its location also overlooked the river valley and controlled the crossing of the great east to west Roman trunk road from Caerleon to west Wales. There was also another major road in the vicinity, the *Sarn Helen*, which stretched northwards to Caernarfon where another great fortress called Segontium was established. Thus, Nidum would have been considered one of their most important fortresses in guarding the crucial routes into their newly conquered territory, and in expanding their new province.

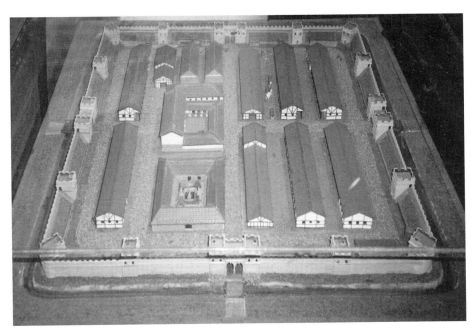

A model of the fort at Nidum.

Nidum had been built to the usual military plan and was almost square shaped. It measured 540 x 500ft and occupied nearly six acres, which made it one of the largest auxiliary fortresses in Wales. Such a fortress would have garrisoned 1,000 men, thought to have been a detachment of the Second Augustan Legion from Caerleon.

During excavations, alongside the road running parallel with the modern North Abbey Road, a pebbled wall which had survived to 6ft high was found along with fragments of Samian ware. Part of the stone rampart was also uncovered, along with its stone guardhouse with walls over 3ft thick. Excavations revealed that the defences had originally been made of clay and earth, but the rampart had later been riveted with stone. Attached to the rampart were internal towers 17 x 11ft thick with walls also 3ft thick, whose stonework had been extensively robbed in the past.

In 1950 massive blocks of stone revealed the whereabouts of the south-east and south-west gateways. Both had dual archways over a 22ft-wide roadway, guarded by flanking stone towers, measuring nearly 9ft square internally, and massive wooden doors. Two iron spikes found in the ditch outside a gateway suggested that a wooden bridge had been built there to give access into the fort. The foundations of both gateways are now protected behind iron railings so that passers-by can view them. They are the only existing structures of the fortress that can be seen.

It is known that the 12th-century Neath Abbey, now an imposing ruin overlooking the approaches to Neath town, was built from the stonework appropriated by the monks from the fortress. However, after a lapse of some 1,800 years, this stonework was recovered from the Abbey and taken back to the excavations where they were incorporated into the rebuilding of the south-west gatehouse.

While the internal buildings had initially been built with timber, these had been burnt down after a short abandonment of the fort and were rebuilt in stone, along with the gateways and rampart wall, during the early years of Hadrian's reign in around AD 100.

A coin of Faustina Senior was found on the floor of one of the barrack blocks, which suggested that occupation had continued until at least AD 140, possibly by a cavalry unit.

There was an assortment of domestic kitchen ware recovered from the site. These included beakers, pie dishes, flanged bowls and rib-necked flagons, mostly of the late first to early second century. Among them were *amphorae* for storing wine and olive oil, with an early carrot-shaped one dating from the first century. Remarkably, a complete *amphora* several feet in length was taken out of the ground whole, despite the fact that a mechanical digger had been removing soil from that very spot a short time before. Robust *mortaria* with interiors made up of sharp fragments to facilitate the mashing up of food were also found, as well as *ollae* for stewed dishes. Numerous flooring and heating tiles made up the list of items recovered, with coins ranging from Augustus to Trajan, 23 BC–AD 111. The heating tiles were box shaped and had a variety of shaped holes, mainly diamond, to allow the heat to pass through.

A discovery which amused the finders was a single brick with slide marks left behind by a meat bone that had been thrown upon it by its maker, and curiously it also had two sets of paw marks, one small and the other much larger and deeper. From this scenario, it appeared that the brick maker had tossed his bone away to land on the wet clay, and that the small impressions were those of a puppy which had tried to get at the bone, but only succeeded in pushing it away with its nose. The other much deeper paw mark was made by a larger dog which had also tried to get a free meal, having no doubt frightened the little puppy away. Luckily, this brick, although badly scarred, had not been rejected and was used for building, remaining intact despite years of destruction to tell us what had occurred all those centuries ago when a brick maker tossed away the remnant of his lunch.

Other interesting artefacts found at the fortress are now on display at the Neath Museum. They include a complete flagon made of coarse ware, which was the most common pottery

An exhibit of a quernstone used for grinding corn into flour. (Neath Museum)

for everyday use. Samian, on the other hand, being far superior with a high smooth glaze and often decorated, was used by the officers and visiting dignitaries. There is a second-century 'scale' beaker, so-called because of its distinctive scale-like decoration. Made of fine pottery, this piece has red and blue colours in its design, and although it was been recovered whole, it had been slightly squashed after centuries in the ground. Iron objects included the handle of a hand mirror, a scabbard for a dagger, several artillery ballista balls, an arrow head and numerous iron studs from the soles of soldiers' sandals. These were added to stop the soldiers from slipping on muddy or wet surfaces, and it was estimated that through constant use the soles only lasted 10 days. A quernstone found there was about 14 inches across. This was a popular domestic utensil for grinding corn into flour.

It is possible that the abandonment of the fortress occurred when seven cohorts of the Second Augustan Legion were transferred north with the rest of the army, in AD 122.

There had also been a large civilian settlement outside the fortress walls, but owing to modern development on the site this could not be excavated. However, the finding of a milestone bearing the Emperor Diocletian's name (AD 284–305) in the vicinity confirmed that the *vicus* had continued to flourish until the fourth century.

On the whole, the excavations were successful in producing conclusive evidence of a very busy military establishment in what is now the centre of Neath, which has become an integral part of the town's historic past.

Just north of Neath, and overlooking the present town of Tonna, the marching camp of Blaen Cwm Bach was discovered on a lonely mountain top in 1958, and like Y Pigwyn it had a circuit of over a mile long. Despite being close to a farm and a forestry expansion, much of its circuit was traced and found to be rectangular in shape with rounded corners. The camp measured 2,880ft east to west and was 1,670ft wide, giving a total area of 61 acres, thus making it the largest of the military installations in Roman Wales.

The remnants of the camp's ramparts had been riveted with stone and lined with clay on the inside during a later stage of its occupation, and those on the north-west corner were sloping below the scarp, which had probably been designed to allow the troops to obtain fresh water from the streams located there.

The discovery of stone walls within the encampment suggest that its role had not been entirely temporary and that it had probably contributed to the military strength in the area.

The enormous size of these marching camps meant that they had taken up the natives' valuable agricultural land which must have left them all the more poor, and had, from the Romans' point of view, ensured their complete subjugation to Roman enslavement.

LOUGHOR (LEUCARUM)

The Roman fort of Leucarum at Loughor, Carmarthenshire, was erected on the banks of the estuary of the River Llychwr, eight miles from the present town of Swansea. The name of the fort derives from the Celtic word 'Leuco' meaning 'shining and bright', said to describe the waters of the estuary. This waterway now acts as the dividing line between the present counties of Glamorgan and Carmarthen. Leucarum was mentioned in the *Antonine Itinerary* as being half way between Moridunum (Carmarthen) and Nidum (Neath) and as being on the *Iter XII* (Route 12).

The estuary provided a safe anchorage for Roman shipping, and the broad river gave swift access into the interior. Being on a major road, it also ensured a direct line of communication into the tribal lands of the Demetae, who were the next tribe the Romans set out to conquer. This road was to lead them into mid-Wales and onwards to the north. Since early times there has been a ford here which can be crossed every four hours at low tide, and this must also have been a great advantage to the advancing Romans. Also, Leucarum was within convenient marching distance of the neighbouring fortresses of Moridunum and Nidum.

The first Roman remains to have been discovered at Loughor were those of the bathhouse during the construction of the Great Western Railway in 1851, which was situated outside the south-west corner of the fort. Unfortunately, due to construction works, this area could not be excavated. The same construction work also limited the number of Roman artefacts that could be found there.

The view of the estuary and sand banks.

However, a significant find was a 4ft high altar standing on a pedestal 3ft wide. Discovered in the rectory garden, it had been used as one of the steps leading to the house. Made of fine-grained white sandstone, it had the appearance of marble when found. At the top of the altar was a shallow depression to take burnt offerings. Interestingly, down its right-hand side someone had carved an Ogham inscription made up of strokes. This is the earliest form of writing from the ancient British and Irish alphabet, consisting of 26 letters and written as strokes on either side of a continuous line with the number of strokes representing a letter. In deciphering the inscription, the letters 'L' and 'E' were made out, suggesting that the writer had endeavoured to write 'Leucarum' to show travellers the way by using the altar as a signpost. Only a few Ogham inscriptions have been found in Wales, but this one gave an important clue as to the location of the Roman fortress. Now looking somewhat weathered after centuries of neglect, the altar is on show at the Swansea Museum, with the deep scarring of the inscription clearly visible down its right side.

In 1954 evidence from aerial photography officially confirmed the presence of the fortress and that its south-east corner was lying beneath Loughor's ruined mediaeval castle.

In the October, during road widening, one of the Roman walls was revealed behind a row of recently demolished cottages at the southern end of Castle Street with fragments of Flavian first-century pottery. These chance finds indicated that at its earliest, the fort was occupied around AD 75. This particular excavation was carried out by Mr J.M. Lewis from the National Museum of Wales, who had come across the Roman remains while examining the castle foundations.

An aerial view of the fort's site in the south-west corner of village, which shows the excavations of the granaries. The church represents the central location of the fort. (By kind permission of the Glamorgan & Gwent Archaeological Trust.)

An exhibit which shows fragments of a dagger sheath inlaid with silver. (By kind permission of the National
Museum of Wales, Cardiff.)

Trenches cut into the steep sides of the castle motte soon located a corner tower belonging to the fort, making it apparent that the foundations of the castle had encroached upon the Roman ones.

Further excavations brought to light the ramparts on the north, east and south sides, enabling the excavators to estimate that the internal width of the fort was around 375ft, but owing to railway lines intersecting at that crucial point the west rampart could not be found. It was probable that it had been destroyed by all of the construction work. They did, though, discover that the defence ditches had been later reinforced with stone and that a cobbled base had formed a sound foundation for the rampart, although this too was later replaced by a stone structure. Turrets had occupied each corner of the fortress wall, but only one was found, that of the south-east corner. It measured 9ft square internally, with walls over 3ft thick. The rampart wall had been rebuilt with sandstone and was at least 30ft wide to provide a good line of defence. Even here it was obstructed by the overlaying mediaeval wall of the castle. Along the *intervallum* were the foundations of five timber buildings which were thought to have been stores. It was not possible to locate the gateways. From the general plan, it was thought that the north gate could have been sited where the modern bridge now crosses the estuary, and that the south gate, which gave access to the bathhouse and the fleet's anchorage, was located somewhere in the region of Castle Street. It is more than likely that a gate would have faced the estuary to enable supplies to be offloaded into the fort. Sentries, too, on duty in its flanking towers, would have kept a sharp lookout for any invaders coming in from the sea.

Excavations were conducted on waste ground to the east of Ferry Road, in an effort to locate the northern defences and the north-east corner of the fort, but a telephone pole and a garden wall prevented this. What was found were some fragments of first-century pottery which were instrumental in dating the fort. Metal objects included spoons, a pair of tongs, which, despite their great age and some rusting, were still working, and several small bronze bells with their individual clappers. Amazingly, the smallest bell still had its clapper firmly attached to it. There was a loop at the top of each bell, suggesting that they may have hung from a ceremonial standard. In contrast, a heavy anvil also surfaced – a type that was carried around by the soldiers and used for sharpening daggers and swords on manoeuvres. Each of these particular anvils had a long spike which was struck into the ground to steady it during use. On the same site, several domestic items also emerged. They included jars, bowls and several *mortaria*.

One historic find was the delicate fragments of a first-century dagger sheath, covered in silver. When placed together, rivet holes showed where it had been attached to its wooden base and that it once had a delicately carved pattern. This beautiful specimen was about 3.5in long and displayed excellent workmanship.

Dagger sheaths and sword scabbards were made of wood covered with leather and were often embellished with bronze and other metals that also helped to reinforce them. The scabbards were attached to the soldier's body by four rings hanging on narrow shoulder straps, and daggers (*pugios*) were worn around the soldier's waist on a buckled leather belt on his left side. The soldier carried his sword (*gladius*) on his right side, so that it could be drawn underarm while still holding his shield with his left hand. Daggers had a short iron blade that was double edged and would be used if the sword was lost in battle. It was also used effectively in close combat to kill an enemy. The swords had long handles surmounted by a rounded pommel, made of either bone or wood. Ivory was also used and favoured by high ranking officers. Completing the soldier's armoury was a long narrow apron made of leather strips reinforced with metal studs, so as to protect the lower half of his body. His upper body and head were also well protected with metal pieces covering his chest and shoulders, his helmet having a wide collar to protect his neck and pieces to cover his cheeks. The javelin (*pilum*) was another effective weapon carried by the Roman soldier into battle. Its long iron shank was designed to bend on impact so that it could not be thrown back by the enemy, yet it was powerful enough to penetrate an enemy's shield. All the equipment was stored in a room adjoining the soldiers' sleeping quarters and was their sole responsibility. The cost of replacing lost items was taken out of their pay packets. Hob nails that had come from the soldiers' footwear also appeared in large quantities.

Excavations continued at the northern tip of the fort where a trench was cut through a stone structure to reveal the site of a kiln. This was no more than a pit dug into the sand with its sides shored up with large cobbles. This crudely made kiln had also been lined with branches to form a kind of cradle in which blocks of limestone had been set. Examination of the charcoal revealed that oak had been the fuel. Even after 18 centuries, it was possible to see that the heat generated by the kiln had left the cobbles severely scorched and had turned the sand red. As there were no limestone quarries in the immediate area, it was more than likely that the Romans had obtained it from West Gower, where it would have been easily shipped to the site. A number of deep pits were also discovered from which the Romans had extracted gravel for building work. Later, when they had become unproductive, the pits had become convenient dumping places for unwanted refuse.

The site of a cemetery was also discovered where cremation burials had taken place during the late-first and early-second century. This gave credence to the theory that an

*A bronze statuette of a mouse which was
found in the commandant's house.*
(By kind permission of the National Museum of Wales,
Cardiff.)

early church had once occupied the site. Here, three cremation burials were found close to each other. One was in a stone-lined coffin, inside which was a small pot filled with a fibrous material. This was identified as a pomander that had been left as a 'grave gift'. The other two burials contained domestic pottery items and a bowl made of pale grey ware, decorated with a lattice design that had probably been made with a comb.

It was discovered that the *Principia* was lying immediately beneath the existing structure of St Michael's Church, and could not be excavated. This marked the church as being placed centrally over the fort. The commandant's *Praetorium*, which should have been alongside the headquarters, was uncovered in the north-west corner. This was considered quite an unusual location for such a prestigious building, but as the commandant had a choice about where he wanted his house sited he chose a more level piece of land. Not only that, but being in that corner he also had better views of the estuary from his windows.

The *Praetorium* had been mainly constructed in stone, and the surviving walls indicated that it had contained 22 rooms. A large area of metalling indicated that there had been more than the one obligatory courtyard. This double courtyard was considered unique in auxiliary fortresses. Foundations of a covered walkway were also uncovered, and traces of coloured plaster with floral and abstract patterns in orange, yellow, brown, black and green were visible on three sides of its walls, which were considered to be of a very high standard, giving the commandant all the luxurious surroundings of a Roman villa. The remnants of charred planking and broken tiles suggested that the building had been floored with timber and covered with a ceramic roof. Interestingly, inside the house an area of burnt debris was found, among which were large quantities of charred wood and collapsed planking. These were thought to have been cupboards and shelves, and the order in which they had fallen suggested that they had done so in quick succession. Iron hooks and brackets which had fixed the shelves to the wall were also among the charred remains, seemingly just where they had landed. This scenario suggested that the building had accidentally caught fire and that evacuation had been swift. A significant discovery among the rubble was a free-standing bronze statuette of a mouse with a round-shaped morsel between its paws. The ornament was about 2in high, 2.5in across and had probably been the commandant's personal property, perhaps a mascot. A similar statuette was found in a Roman grave in York, but the one at Loughor was regarded as a major find. In fact, this particular mouse had actually escaped two major fires. One occurring in his own century at the fortress, and the other centuries later when the warehouse in which he was being stored with other relics in Swansea was burnt down. The statuette, bronze bells and the silver sheath are now at the National Museum of Wales.

Other buildings successfully excavated were the three granaries found to the east of the *Principia*. All had been constructed with timber and were rectangular in shape. It was found that they had been built on bases of evenly spaced circular posts set in parallel trenches across the width of each building. They measured 99ft long and 63ft wide and were lying north to south. The floors had been raised about 3ft above the ground to keep the buildings well ventilated. To compensate for the overall sloping of the ground, the builders had cut the base posts at different heights to keep the buildings on an even keel. There was also evidence that the granaries had eventually been demolished to make way for two new structures, but what they were could not be defined. When photographed from the air, all three granaries were clearly visible in the south-east corner of the village. Substantial quantities of loose amounts of grain were also found on this site and gave an indication of the soldiers' diet. These included barley, lentils and hazelnut shells, as well as wheat for baking bread. Quantities of barley grains were also found along the *Via Praetoria*, where they had presumably spilled during transportation.

In Roman times barley was mainly used as animal fodder and for brewing beer. As a good amount of horse-keeping equipment was also found on the site, it was more than likely that the garrison contained a cavalry unit – a *cohors quingenaria equitata*, which would have included 140 mounted troops.

Another archaeological excavation was carried out as late as 1970, recovering numerous fragments of Samian ware of various sizes and in various stages of preservation. These revealed elaborate borders and picturesque designs with mythological characters and hunting scenes with dogs, boars and horses, all typical of the era. Exotic animals such as lions also featured. A red clay container, thought to have been a pomander, and a complete tripod pitcher were recovered intact. There was also plain and glazed pottery that had come from the fort's kitchens. The glazed ware was dominated by the presence of jugs, and it was possible to reconstruct some of these objects back to their original state. These examples of first and second century domestic ware are now on show at the Swansea Museum.

Another exciting find was a hoard of 60 coins ranging from AD 250–263 in a layer of silt above the ruins of the south-east corner turret. From these, it was thought that the fortress may have continued in operation until the fourth century as part of the coastal defence system and abandoned early in that century.

Leucarum was one of the largest auxiliary fortresses in south-west Wales, and it seems likely that during its lifetime it was occupied by a variety of units, including a cavalry unit that required space for six barrack blocks.

Owing to the fact that the village had been built on top of the fortress, a full excavation had not been possible, and once the archaeologists were satisfied that they had explored every aspect of the fortress, they covered up all the excavations so as to return the village back to its normal state. Consequently, there is nothing left of Leucarum fortress to be seen. Sadly, its foundations have become buried and are out of sight again. Only its treasured relics remind us of its once powerful presence.

Roman dominance of the area was further increased with the installation of three more practice camps at Mynydd Carn Coch, just two and a half miles to the east. Two of these had been built close together, with the largest one measuring only 97 x 99ft. The third camp lay one mile to the east of Stratford Common and was regarded as the largest in Wales.

CARMARTHEN (MORIDUNUM)

The Roman fort of Moridunum (modern Carmarthen) stood at the junction of three valleys on the northern slopes of the Towy Valley and commanded a strategic position on a comparatively level ridge of land at the tidal limit of the river, only seven miles from the sea. The site was also protected by hills to the north and it had a clear view of the land to the south. The location also had the advantage of rising ground to the north and marshy ground to the north-west. It was probably these natural features that influenced the Romans into choosing the site for their fort. Moridunum also had the advantage of being at the junction of three major roads, one being the *Sarn Helen*, which led northwards to Segontium in Caernarfon.

The fort also attracted a substantial influx of people from the surrounding area who established their homes outside its defences. In time, this community grew into a sizeable town between the late first and fourth century. The Romans called it Moridunum after the Celtic words 'mori', meaning sea, and 'dunum', meaning fort. However, it was not until the latter half of the 20th century that the existence of the fort and town became known following redevelopment work in modern Carmarthen.

In spite of the lateness of its discovery, Moridunum was first mentioned by the Egyptian geographer Ptolemy in the first century, who even stated its precise location and correctly described it as the principal town of the Demetae. In the 12th century there were visible signs of its existence when Geraldus Cambrensis (Gerald of Wales) noted on his travels: 'This ancient city is situated on the banks of the noble Tywy, surrounded by woods and pastures, and roughly enclosed with walls of brick, parts of which are still standing.' Mention of these walls also appeared in the 14th-century *Cartulary of the Priory*. Even into the 16th century, Elizabethan antiquarian William Camden mentioned Moridunum in his *Britannia*, published in 1586.

However, the 19th century produced several tangible items of its existence. In 1804 two Roman altar-stones were found, including the famous 'Nato' stone on which was a Latin inscription 'bono(o r) ei p(ublica) nato', which is believed to have referred to a fourth-century Roman Emperor. Further evidence came to light in 1871 when a tessellated floor, along with portions of an ancient wall, were discovered while digging a well at 136 Priory Street. Then what was presumed to be part of a Roman bathhouse was unearthed in 1897, when a cellar for a house called 'Bryn Roma' was being constructed along the Esplanade.

Finds also continued into the 20th century. In 1905 stone foundations came to light just off Priory Street, during the building of St John's Church. Again, two altars were found. The one from the garden of the rectory is now kept in the porch of St Peter's Church, and the other is in the Carmarthen Museum at Abergwili. These finds brought renewed interest to the theory of a Roman settlement existing at Carmarthen.

In 1954 a superb silver gilt trumpet brooch came to light in a workman's trench in St Peter's Street. Another interesting discovery was a large amount of Samian ware, of both Flavian and later dates, when part of St Peter's churchyard was removed for road widening.

In 1961, during a small excavation at Dyffren House, a stone drain with a smaller adjoining one was discovered immediately to the west of the bathhouse site, and this renewed interest in the location, as did several interesting finds which included more fragments of Samian ware, dating to the first century, and two Roman coins: one of Gallienus, dated AD 261–268, and the other a Claudius II, dated AD 268–70. Several examples of fourth-century *mortaria* were also recovered there.

However, it was the discovery of a pebbled roadway beneath demolished properties at Spilman Street in 1968 that really motivated serious excavations to take place under the guidance of Professor G.D. Barri Jones of Manchester University, when money for excavations had become available.

During his excavations in 1968 and 1969, the professor was able to establish that the particular earthwork he had uncovered was military in character, and confirmed that he had made the eagerly awaited discovery of the auxiliary fortress, also referred to as Moridunum. The estimated area of the fort was put at 4–5 acres. He was also able to establish that the entire defences had been built in two separate phases, with the first dating to the latter part of the first century. These defences had been made of clay and turf, 14ft wide and about 7ft high, fronted by two V-shaped ditches. The second phase was constructed after a lapse of time when the inner ditch had become silted up and had been rendered useless. A much wider rampart was then made across the in-filled ditches, which was reinforced by a stone wall 7ft thick, thus making the total width of the rampart about 48ft. The ditches produced a quantity of first-century Flavian pottery, which reinforced the theory that the fort was established around AD 75. This date was further confirmed by the substantial quantity of first-century coins found lying within palisaded enclosures with a coin bearing the inscription of the Emperor Vespasian (AD 69–79), found to the rear of Church Street, and first-century Samian ware. It was also established that the Roman fort was lying just beyond the mediaeval castle in the Spilman/King Street area of the modern town.

The Dyfed Archaeological Trust, formed in 1975, took over the excavations, and for the first time there was a full-time, regionally based archaeological service to respond to the planned development in the town that threatened the Roman remains.

In 1985 trial trenches were cut in the Carmarthen district council's car park in Spilman Street, and under the surface of the entrance were the remains of another clay bank that had been overlaid with turfs. This was identified as being the rampart of the *intervallum* road that ran around the whole of the interior. Examination of the bank showed that five timber buildings had once stood there. The barrack blocks were also located, but their remaining timbers revealed that they had been rebuilt on several occasions. However, the discovery of further defences within the main site indicated that a much smaller fort had been built inside its perimeters, probably to accommodate a much smaller garrison when the bulk of the troops had been transferred north. Large deposits of burnt clay and charcoal, found directly above the original floors of the timber buildings, suggested that they had been deliberately set on fire before the fort was abandoned, thought to have been in around AD 150. Unfortunately, excavations in this area only revealed a small portion of the fort. There were no signs of its southern rampart and it was also not possible to locate any of the principal buildings. Fragments of pottery and coins were the only signs of occupation, suggesting that it had been for a short duration only.

In 1968, south of the *Via Decumanus*, behind the north-west rampart, the explorers made an interesting discovery when the foundations of four large buildings, identified as being of third-century origin and residential in character, were found butting up against the road. This discovery led to the location of the civilian town of Moridunum. One of the buildings was 59ft overall and had been divided into two rooms 26ft wide with a colonnaded portico 6ft wide. Another substantial building measuring at least 61 x 69ft was another interesting discovery. From their appearances, these buildings had been levelled at some stage to make way for an even larger structure, 80 x 110ft. Evidence also showed that the rooms had been floored with *tesserae* of terracotta and preseli stone which was regarded to be a luxury. One room had been heated by a hypocaust and had its furnace set into the wall. The construction of this building was dated by the coins of Magnentius and his brother Decentius (AD 351–353) that were unearthed in the foundations. Another interesting find was a chatelaine – a set of short chains for holding keys. A large stone structure with a courtyard from the second century was also discovered during excavations of properties No. 1–5 The Parade in 1986. The function of such a large building was thought to have been an inn, an essential feature for a growing rural community.

The town prospered well under the Romans, probably through trading initially, and as the inhabitants embraced the Roman way of life the Romans bestowed upon the town the title of Moridunum Demetae, thereby making it the tribal and administrative centre of the Demetae people. Judging from the number of enamelled seal boxes found, many of the citizens had learned to read and write. Many of these seal boxes have colourful designs and are well preserved. The reason they have survived so long is the technique of using glass in the enamelling.

Excavations in 1969 established that the Roman town was lying under the modern streets of Richmond Terrace in the north, Old Oak Lane in the east and Little Water Street in the west, and that it stretched over 32 acres.

In those unsettled times the town would have needed some kind of protection, and a defensive plan, similar to the fort, was carried out with the initial phase of the town's construction in the first century. This consisted of a clay bank fronted by two V-shaped ditches and a rampart strengthened

A display of enamelled seal boxes and a coin of Vespasian.
(By kind permission of the Carmarthenshire County Museum.)

A display of bronze escutcheon, enamelled brooches and fibulae. (By kind permission of the Carmarthenshire County Museum.)

with a timber palisade. Closer scrutiny of the ancient town's foundations then gave a clearer picture as to what life had been like there from the second to the fourth century.

Sometime before AD 150, a planned street system had been laid out on the eastern side of the settlement, with further development then taking place when numerous rectangular timber buildings were added. Evidence revealed that this particular area had been a busy industrial quarter with houses fronting a gravelled street, with some buildings incorporating both living quarters and workshops. One such building, which was believed to have belonged to a corn merchant, had hearths set into the walls and had cobbled stone floors on either side of a central corridor. In the yard outside was a granary 15 x 13ft in extent. This had a raised floor supported by massive timber posts to keep out rodents. Some charred grains of wheat were also evident around the burnt-out holes that had supported the timber uprights, suggesting that the wheat had been accidentally burned while being roasted for malting purposes. There was also a commercial bakery nearby where a number of clay ovens were found for baking bread, as well as stone querns, which indicated that some corn grinding had been carried out by hand. Several 'Aladdin' shaped terracotta lamps were recovered whole from the area. These had been filled with oil to provide light in the homes. In other buildings, hearths and quantities of iron slag suggested that iron smelting had taken place. The abundance of nails and iron roof fittings indicated that they had been used on the timbered houses that had once covered the Priory Street site, which also had thatched roofs. Scraps of leather found among the rubbish in another building suggested that a saddler, or a cobbler, had also traded in the street.

A display of terracotta lamps in the museum at Abergwili.

Excavations in the garden of No. 104 Priory Street uncovered the foundations of a second-century temple. As its walls had been extensively robbed, very little of the building remained, but those which had been left enabled the archaeologists to identify that the inner square – *cella* or sanctuary – had been built within a larger square. The outside enclosure measured approximately 70ft square, while the inner one measured 44ft square. It was thought that the temple had been timber built, founded on sill beams with panelling in-filled with wattle and daub and then lime washed. The temple had also been built on a massive foundation pit which was 4ft deep. Such a foundation would have been substantial enough to have supported a three or four-storey building. The temple was considered small for its type, and evidence showed that it had been built before the other timber buildings around it.

The remains of some of the buildings in the area revealed that they had become derelict or had fallen into disuse by the late second century. Others had been deliberately dismantled and the site cleared. This was followed by a period of abandonment when the site appeared to have been used for garden cultivation. From the amount of rubbish and loose stones lying around, the vacant properties had obviously been turned into refuse dumps. On the whole, industry had prospered well in the town for as long as 250 years. Evidence also emerged that even after the area had been abandoned, streets continued to be laid, and that occupation was resumed in the third century with many trading activities still going on. Coins, pottery and evidence of further street maintenance suggested that life in the town extended well into the fourth century.

The rusted shield boss with spearheads attached, which was removed from the excavated refuse dumps.

From the various refuse dumps, two iron shield bosses appeared among the discarded items, one of which had two spearheads attached to it, although all of these items had corroded due to acidity in the soil. However, the finds were in a good enough condition to establish that one spearhead was wider than the other and had a more leaf-shaped blade. An L-shaped lift-key was also found. This three-toothed key was the commonest type found on Roman sites, and was operated by a simple tumbler operation.

The most significant discovery at Moridunum Demetae must surely be that of the amphitheatre, discovered in 1936 by the acting borough engineer, who noticed a semi-circular depression in the hillside below the Park Hall housing estate at the western

The amphitheatre at Moridunum.

end of Priory Street, lying just outside Moridunum's boundaries. It was only because of his efforts to stop modern development in the area from proceeding that excavations were able to be carried out and the amphitheatre saved from further destruction. It had already suffered partial destruction because of the main road leading out of Carmarthen cutting through it which demolished one of its seating banks. Excavations to establish the line of the arena were carried out in 1968 by Manchester University as part of their excavation programme.

They found that the amphitheatre was probably constructed in the second century by cutting into the natural hillside to form a seating bank around the arena to accommodate about 4,500–5,000 spectators. The amphitheatre would also have attracted people from the surrounding areas, as well as the legionaries in the earlier days. Its function was thought to have been more theatrical than religious or gladiatorial.

Today, the amphitheatre is open to the public, and can be found along Priory Road, a short distance from Carmarthen town centre. Access to the site is by way of a short track leading in from the roadside pavement and, as one will see, the entire area is now completely covered with grass. The retaining wall around the arena has survived to a height of about 4–5ft, as have a short flight of steps which led spectators to their seats. The seating banks have eroded through time, and the one nearest the road has been partially destroyed by the construction of Priory Road. Only a part of it has survived in the shape of a small mound which now forms a barrier between the amphitheatre and the roadside. The arena, too, has suffered from modern intrusion by an invasion of overgrown trees and shrubs infiltrating from the back gardens of the cottages lining the road. This growth has also obscured the far end of the arena from view.

It is not known how many entrances the amphitheatre had, but excavations uncovered several road surfaces which suggested it had a long period of use. Only one entrance is now visible.

Recently, while excavating near the amphitheatre, a large grey earthenware pot containing the cremated bones of a woman was found. Curiously, among the bone fragments were quantities of grape pips, which posed the question: how did they get there? The cremation had obviously marked the site where the people of Moridunum had been buried.

With the discovery of Moridunum Demetae, the town now has the distinction of being one of only two walled Roman towns in Wales, the other being Venta Silurum (Caerwent).

The burial urn found near to the amphitheatre.

LLANDEILO

The existence of Roman remains at Llandeilo, situated almost halfway between Carmarthen and Llandovery, had long been suspected. There are antiquarian records which state that a possible Roman structure was lying beneath Llandyfeisant Church, and that a number of Roman coins, including a late first-century hoard with an ass of Tiberius (AD 10) and a third-century hoard, were found here before 1920.

In 1980 an aerial survey identified clear stretches of the Roman road running from Carmarthen, with one stretch underlying the present A40 going west from Carmarthen to Llandovery. The location of a Roman fortress at Llandeilo on this road, within a day's march of either stronghold, appeared to have been an obvious choice for the advancing Romans. But in spite of Roman pottery appearing on the surface, as well as the coins and a milestone bearing an inscription to the Emperor Tacitus (AD 275–276) found in 1967, the exact whereabouts of the fort remained as elusive as ever. It therefore fell to a geophysical survey, carried out in April 2003 by Cambria Archaeology, to prove beyond reasonable doubt that the Romans built an auxiliary fortress here.

The survey, which showed radar-like images of features below the ground, provided some surprising results when it was seen that there was not only one fort

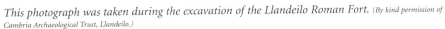

This photograph was taken during the excavation of the Llandeilo Roman Fort. (By kind permission of Cambria Archaeological Trust, Llandeilo.)

beneath the surface but two, one superimposed upon the other, with clear details of their individual defences. The survey had indeed exposed the largest auxiliary fortresses to have been built in Roman Wales. It transpired that they had been built close to an Iron Age settlement, and had been built in close succession to each other. Also, the location was just where the archaeologists had suspected, in the area of Dinefwr Park where many of the Roman finds had appeared. In addition to showing the fortresses, the survey showed images of a civilian settlement outside the defences with traces of habitation along the roads leading out of the forts. A structure located outside the defences in the north-east corner was thought to have been the bathhouse. There were also clear indications that the Roman road linking the fort at Llandovery ran out of their front entrances.

The internal layout of the earlier fortress could not be determined with certainty because of the overlying features of the later superimposed one, and so another geophysical survey was carried out in 2004 and 2005 on behalf of the National Trust who had purchased the park with plans for constructing a golf course.

Fort No. 1 (the largest):
The internal dimensions of this earlier fortress were measured as 768 x 480ft, giving a total area of just over 10 acres. It had three defensive ditches on its south-eastern side and two on its south-western. The images of its northern defences were obscured by the interior of the second fort. However, its gateways were identified on both the south-eastern and south-western sides, and a four-post structure, 20ft square, was visible on the line of the rampart which suggested the location of a huge watch-tower.

A large thermal response was detected on the inner line of the south-east defences which was interpreted as the possible location of a kiln or a large hearth where fires had burned, probably for metal working. It was also known that the soldiers had cooked their food there.

In the area of the *Principia*, the excavators came across a burial ground and retrieved an earthenware cremation urn which had filled with soil. From its discovery, it appeared that the people from the *vicus* had moved into the fortress once it had become abandoned and had found that this central area was a more suitable place to bury their dead.

Excavation of the defensive system was carried out when it was found that the inner ditch had been back-filled with the rampart when the fort was decommissioned to make way for a second fort. In the ditch filling, there were fragments of pottery, brick and tiles. Other finds were shards of Samian ware from South Gaul and coarse pottery of the late first to early second century.

From the pottery recovered, it was possible to estimate that this fortress had been operational up to the middle of the second century and, judging by its size, it had probably been garrisoned by a large infantry unit supported by cavalry. The foundations of their barracks were found to have gone down into the bedrock.

The most noticeable feature of this fortress would have been its front entrance with supporting watch towers. Evidence for this were the four sets of post holes measuring almost 3ft square, suggesting a massive double entrance which would have highlighted the importance of the fort to the area.

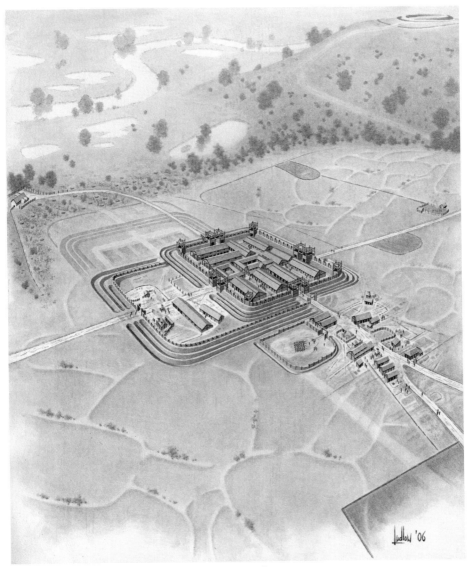

A reconstruction of Llandeilo Roman Fort by Neil Ludlow. (By kind permission of Cambria Archaeological Trust, Llandeilo.)

Fort No. 2 (the smallest):

This additional fortress, which had been built inside the defences of the other, measured 448 x 352ft and was approximately four acres in extent. Three of its four entrances were identified, and most of its four sides were clearly visible. The south-east line of its defences was represented by at least four ditches, and there was a wider berm between the second and third ditches which had apparently been crossed by a bridge.

The Malvernian Pot, photographed before and after excavation. *(By kind permission of Cambria Archaeological Trust, Llandeilo.)*

Among its internal features were large post holes which suggested that timber uprights had supported a colonnade fronting onto the *Principia*. All the internal buildings had been made of wood, and there was no evidence to suggest that any structure had been rebuilt in stone.

A large crushed *amphora* was recovered from a pit and a whole straight-sided pot from Malvern was recovered from another. The pot was recovered whole, but unfortunately it broke while removing the soil from its interior. This remarkable brown-coloured pot – now pieced together – was about a quarter of an inch thick, which had probably assisted in its survival, and measured about 12in high with a diameter of about 7in across. It is now proudly on display at the offices of Cambria Archaeology at Llandeilo, where I had the privilege of seeing it and holding it in my hands.

The fort saw a reduction in activity during the early part of the second century as the Roman troops had left south-west Wales in large numbers by the mid-120s.

According to its size, this fortress also held a large garrison, and it was abandoned around AD 140, after which the civilians of the settlement took up residence by making it an extension to their community.

The most exciting find, however, must have been the discovery of a treasure trove – a hoard containing 2,366 Roman coins from the second half of the third century. This remarkable discovery was made by a workman undertaking drainage work on farmland. All he did was kick a large stone out of the way, when the coins, which had obviously lain behind it, just spilled onto the ground as if from an invisible slot machine. No container was found, so it was presumed that the coins had been kept in a cloth bag which had rotted over time.

The discovery was communicated to the National Museum of Wales in Cardiff, and was also reported to H.M. Coroner for Carmarthenshire, as is required by Law, after which the coins were delivered to the National Museum for safe keeping.

The coins were analysed by Mr Ed Besley at the National Museum, who reported that they were all of Roman Imperial billion (highly-debased silver), with the majority comprising copper alloys and 1–10 per cent added silver. The coins ranged from over a 300-year period, with the vast majority (718) coming from the reign of Tetricus I (AD 271–73).

Other coins found in significant numbers were: 463 coins from the reign of Victorinus (AD 269–71); 299 coins from the reign of Gallienus (AD 260–68); 288 from the reign of Claudius II (AD 268–70); and 283 from the reign of Tetricus II (AD 273–74).

Other coins reaching double figures came from the reigns of Divus Claudius (AD 270) (64 coins) and Carausius (AD 286–93) (65 coins). The latest coin to be dated was that from the reign of Carausius (AD 286–93), struck at the London mint around AD 291.

Around 66 hoards attributable to the reign of Carausius have been found, 19 of which are in Wales. Another enormous hoard of 2,583 coins was discovered at Pennard on the Gower in 1966, and a hoard totalling 693 coins was found at Erw-hen, Carmarthenshire, in 1965. Also in Carmarthenshire, another Carausian hoard was found near Laugharne Castle, making south and south-west Wales a favourite dumping ground for Roman savings or spoils from ancient robberies.

LLANDOVERY (ALABUM)

The remains of a Roman fort, known as Alabum, were located in the tiny village of Llanfair-ar-y-bryn, on the outskirts of Llandovery town, in the present county of Carmarthenshire. The church of Llanfair-ar-y-bryn (St Mary's Church), whose spire dominates the landscape, marks the precise location of the long-lost fort and stands immediately over the *Principia* in the centre. The site of Alabum also crowns a piece of land that falls sharply on all sides which appears to have been the main requirements favoured by the Romans in siting their fortresses. The site was also close to a main river – another favoured requirement.

Over time, the fort had been completely obliterated from the landscape, but an 18th-century vicar of Llandovery was reported to have collected many Roman relics that he had dug up from his garden and which gave rise to the assumption that some kind of Roman building was lying beneath the surface. The relics included a broken altar, fragments of pottery and some coins of Constantine.

When antiquarians Edward Lhuyd and Colt Hoare visited the site, in 1700 and 1800 respectively, Lhuyd reported that there were 'manifest signs of a place possessed by the Romans', referring to the defences, which could then be seen on all three sides.

In 1873 another antiquarian recorded having seen a rectangular outline with rounded corners, which he measured as 391 x 582ft, to give a total area of nearly five acres. He also saw a division running down its centre. This was probably the *Via Principalis*. Over time, as the expansion of the village covered the fort, much of its walls were being robbed for building purposes until only its foundations were left.

In 1961 and 1962 archaeological investigations were carried out by the late Professor Mike Jarrett, who revealed that the fortress had been destroyed by fire, probably to make way for the next building phase. In March 1983 further investigations were carried out by the then Dyfed Archaeological Trust, now Cambria Archaeology, who confirmed that the fort had undergone four major phases of construction, with the earliest having been made of earth and timber, and that the defences had been reinforced with wood. Its internal buildings had also been wooden.

To provide a clearer picture of the fortress, a geophysical survey was carried out in September 2004 by the Dyfed Archaeological Trust as part of the Cadw-funded study across Wales to determine the whereabouts of Roman fortresses and roads. Previous surveys have produced good results. It appears that Roman sites are well suited to this particular kind of surveying technique.

Overall, the survey produced a surprising result when images revealed the presence of two separate fortresses, with masses of overlapping images where buildings of the second fort had been built over those of the first. There was also a 'substantial annexe' to the north-east of the fort, consisting of three parallel defensive ditches and associated features such as kilns or ovens which suggested several periods of activity. The *Via Principalis* was also well defined by a drain running down both its sides. A break in the rampart marked the position of the *porta principalis sinistra*

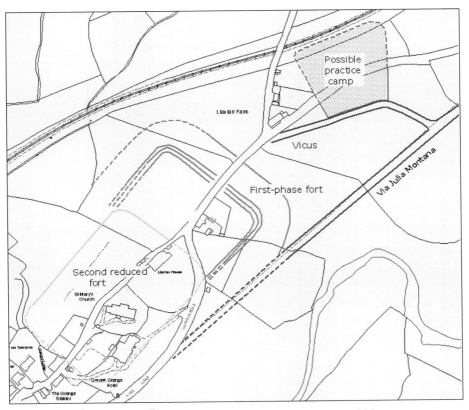

A plan of Llandovery Roman Fort. (By kind permission of Cambria Archaeological Trust, Llandeilo.)

– its western gateway. One building, measuring 48 x 180ft, even produced a high magnetic response, which suggested it had been destroyed by fire.

Another interesting feature of the survey was the clear evidence that there had been a *vicus* along the roads leading out of the forts, as well as a Roman burial ground. Also leading away was a road identified as being the *Via Julia Montana* which ran off in a north-easterly direction. This road ensured the quick transit of troops from one fortress to another.

In 2005 an additional geophysical survey was carried out on the archaeological assessment of the area before the proposed road improvements took place and destroyed this historical site. It revealed that a fourth outer ditch had been constructed and that the original fort was larger than first thought. It also confirmed that the fort had undergone several transformations during its lifetime, including a reduction in size to accommodate a smaller auxiliary fortress in its southern half, leaving the rest of the original fort to be retained as an annexe, perhaps to be used for stores, workshops or for corralling horses. There were also clear indications that there was another road leading off the *Via Julia Montana* which ran into the *porta praetoria*, the front entrance to both fortresses.

Archaeologists working in trench six with Llanfair-ar-y-byrn church in the background. (By kind permission of Cambria Archaeological Trust, Llandeilo.)

In June–July 2006 Cambria Archaeology, under the direction of Dr Nikki Cook, undertook a trial archaeological evaluation of the site to assess the character and extent of the surviving archaeological features shown in the 2005 survey. In all, seven trenches were cut across the triple defences and the *vicus* lying just outside them, and as a result a wealth of Roman pottery emerged including black-burnished ware and other pieces of British manufacture from the Severn Valley, the Malvern area, Caerleon, Dorset and Barnstaple in Devon, all of varying dates ranging from the first to the second century. There was also a quantity of *amphora* jars for storing olive oil and wine, and an abundance of greyware and some Samian. One almost complete Severn Valley *amphora* was recovered, along with a handle of one bearing the letters T A A S A C, which was the stamp of the potter Asiatici.

However, the most exciting find was the roadway that had led off the *Via Julia Montana*, seen in the previous survey. It had a well-maintained metalled surface made of compacted pebbles that had been brought up from the river bed. Being found just below the top soil, it was fortunate that the road had escaped damage from ploughing. The main A483 road, which has been constructed right through the middle of both fortresses to dissect them into two halves, follows the same north-easterly route as the Roman road and runs almost parallel to it. A stretch of the Roman road is now lying beneath the A483.

A number of features such as post holes for timber uprights suggested that buildings belonging to the *vicus* had once fronted the road. Two possible wheel ruts were also noticed which established it as a well-used road carrying wheeled traffic right into the fort.

On the north side of the road there was a distinct camber which sloped downwards towards a possible roadside ditch. On the south side, signs were that many of the buildings had extended into the road, and that some of its surface had been robbed, probably by the civilians who had used the stones to create solid surfaces for building. The clay walls of one structure were also uncovered, including a small area of compacted stones which might have been one of its floors. Such dwellings were simply made, but as time progressed and Roman techniques were adopted, tiles soon replaced earthen floors and became a popular commodity for roofing. In fact, several roofing tiles were found here. These orange-coloured tiles were sturdily made, rather rough in texture, and because of their thickness they were quite heavy. From the amount of *amphorae* found, it was clear that the housewives had cooked with olive oil, and that the people as a whole had followed the Roman culture in drinking wine.

As more Celts adopted the Roman way of life, they may also have participated in its religious ceremonies, as a pedestal base of a tazza was found. This was a shallow cup for burning incense. Such discoveries enable us to look back into the lives of these people who had survived one of our most turbulent periods in history, and whose everyday lives have now become part of our great heritage.

From the various discoveries, the conclusions were that the fortress had undergone several transformations during its lifetime and that it had been built around the year AD 70. It had also been temporarily abandoned and then re-commissioned when the second fortress continued with the task of enforcing Roman dominance of the area while still maintaining its position at the top of the highest point on the landscape. It was finally abandoned around AD 160.

Another nearby feature of interest was a V-shaped ditch outside the north-eastern defences, which appeared to be part of an enclosure. This was thought to have been a small practice camp used by the garrison.

A large marching camp was, however, found at Beulah, outside Llandovery, between the A483 road and the Roman road. On examination, it looked as though all traces of the camp had been ploughed away as, apart from the west and north sides appearing as low banks beneath the pasture, there was nothing else to see. It would seem that the location of another marching camp here meant that the Roman army had attached some importance to the area as a whole.

PUMPSAINT

The auxiliary fortress of Pumpsaint (Five Saints), was found in the present village of that name, about eight miles north-west of Llandovery. Since the village is close to the famous Dolaucothi gold mines, which were exploited by the Romans during their occupation, the fort was more than likely erected to guard them and the roads along which the gold travelled that lead directly to the Roman mints where it was converted into much needed currency.

The finding of Roman items close to the village, including a hoard of gold in which was a second-century pendant in the shape of a wheel and a length of gold chain, gave rise to the suspicion that a Roman settlement was close by. The wheel was a symbol of the Celtic thunder god Taranis, and the chain, made of heavy links and which was not part of the pendant, was similar to those attached to Roman lamps. Interestingly, an *intaglio*, cemented on to a pebble in readiness for engraving, was also found, as was a painter's stone pallet with various colours still visible. A vessel identified as a pan for washing gold was another valuable find.

The name Pumpsaint derives from an old local legend of the five saints: Gwyn, Gwynio, Celynin, Gwynaro and Ceitho, the sons of Cynyr of Cynwl Garo, who had supposedly left impressions of their heads on a large stone they had sheltered against in a violent storm that had been raised by a sorcerer luring them to his caves.

This tall, free-standing block of sandstone bearing deep impressions around it, now standing in a wooded glade in the grounds of the Dolaucothi mines, is known as the Pumpsaint Stone, and was probably used in the crushing process of the gold when it had laid beneath vertical hammers. The five brothers became the subject of a poem in the 16th century and even the neighbouring chapel of Llanpumpsaint is dedicated to them.

Further evidence of a Roman presence came when the clay floors of timber buildings were found following erosion of the River Cothi's banks on the south side of the village, along with some Samian ware of the first century. These were considered exciting finds, and a rescue operation of the area by the Carmarthenshire Antiquarian Association began immediately, set up by a local action committee to settle the question of whether there had been a Roman presence in the village once and for all.

This action coincided with the planning of a road improvement scheme through the village which involved the removal of the car park of the Dolaucothi Arms Hotel and the hotel's vegetable garden, comprising three quarters of an acre. Trial trenches

A gold pendant, as displayed in the Carmarthenshire County Museum, Abergwili.
(By kind permission of the Carmarthenshire County Museum.)

The Pumpsaint stone.

at once revealed the existence of Roman remains to a considerable depth, and this encouraged further exploration of the site over a period of two months during the summer of 1972.

The first major discovery was a granary with massive stone-built walls, which confirmed that a Roman fortress had once occupied the site. There was a road running along the western side of the granary that had been resurfaced no less than 11 times, and beneath the foundations of the building were the timber remains of its predecessor. Even the stone granary was found to have been deliberately demolished to make way for new defences sometime during the second occupational period when a reduction of its south-eastern corner had taken place.

The western defences and the barrack block were found beneath the rear garden of the hotel. A post hole for a timber upright in one barrack indicated that it had a timbered portico for protection against the weather. There was also a range of buildings standing on either side of a road running north to south through the centre of the fortress. Nearby was a gravelled surface with a drain leading to a stone-lined latrine, thought to have been part of the barrack block. Some Flavian-dated pottery was instrumental in establishing that the fortress had been occupied from the mid to the latter part of the first century, indicating that the Roman invaders were soon erecting a chain of auxiliary fortresses in the area to establish their rule over the territory and put down any insurgence by the Demetae.

When the northern defences were located, it was possible to establish the precise outline of the fort and its size which was in the region of 375 x 450ft, giving a total area of four acres. This put Pumpsaint in the second rank of Roman auxiliary fortresses in Wales and is comparable in size to Coelbren.

Excavations continued in the pasture on the eastern side of the village, referred to as Town Field. Here, the defences differed from the ones in the west. There were no traces of any stone revetment or secondary ditches and the rampart had been completely removed. It was then thought that the Romans had built a smaller fortress inside the first one, and had decided not to strengthen the defences along this side, as with the river running at the bottom of a steep bank there would have been little need for an outer ditch. Examination of the ditches revealed that the garrison had filled them in with material from the dismantled rampart. This included layers of charcoal and daub from buildings destroyed by fire. It also appeared that during the reduction, the Romans had also demolished their barracks to make way for a series of three structures thought to have been workshops. This action probably occurred when there was no longer a need to accommodate the same number of troops.

Although relatively little pottery was found, indications were that occupation of the fortress did not extend longer than the middle of the second century. It is to be remembered that the fortress of Moridunum (Carmarthen) had also been vacated around AD 150, a time when most forts in Wales were abandoned in favour of their occupants travelling north, as part of Hadrian's campaign to strengthen his defences in the north of England.

THE GOLD MINES OF DOLAUCOTHI

The Dolaucothi gold mines are situated in open countryside in the picturesque Cothi Valley, just a mile from the village of Pumpsaint, and were fully exploited by the Romans. They are the only known Roman gold mines in Britain.

Gold was first extracted at Dolaucothi during the sixth century BC and led to Tacitus describing Britain as being 'rich in gold, silver and other ores', which probably temped the Romans to invade. With their arrival in the area, the mines would have instantly fallen under their control, with all the mineral rights going directly to the Emperor. Roman mining operations probably started the instant the troops had established their fortress across the river in AD 75.

The discovery of a bathhouse at the bottom of the Cothi Valley during the 19th century suggested that an organised settlement had been established there in Roman times, no doubt inhabited by the workers who had been drafted in and the convicts condemned to serve their time in the mines. Numerous querns for crushing the ore had also been found lying broken around the area for many years, and it seems incredible that during the years preceding these discoveries no one was aware that the mines existed in the locality. The Romans obviously had made no record of them, and those who followed were ignorant of their existence. Consequently, the woodland kept its secret for hundreds of years, until 1844 when a geologist by the name of Warington Smythe did a survey of the land for the current owners and surprised everyone by declaring that he had discovered caverns full of gold quartz. Even Henry Tudor, later Henry VII, who presented land to those families who had helped him at the Battle of Bosworth in 1485 during his struggle to gain the throne, was unaware of the immensity of his gift when he rewarded the Dolaucothi family for their loyalty.

Eventually the mines became part of the Dolaucothi Estate, which had been in the hands of the same Johnes family since the 16th century. The estate covered 2,500 acres, and included several farms and the village of Pumpsaint. In the 1940s the estate was handed over to the National Trust.

The mining complex itself is surrounded by lush woodlands with the mines divided into three groups: a small group being situated to the north of the centrally placed cluster and another small group in the south.

While most mines go underground, the ones at Dolaucothi go inwards into Cwm Henog and are situated in the middle of a woodland at the top of the mountain's rocky slopes. In Spring it is covered with bluebells.

At the bottom is the area that was once the opencast quarry where the Romans started their mining operations, and which was 40ft deeper than at present. This large open space is now occupied by several buildings housing the reception, a shop and a tea room. There are also the corrugated buildings in which the Victorian miners stored their equipment, as are several of the tall-sided trolleys that once transported the ore around the site.

Cwm Henog with the water wheel to the bottom right of the photograph.

After the Romans had exhausted the quarry, they dug two separate mines extending 160ft into the mountain, now known as Upper Roman Adit and Lower Roman Adit, and they are open to the public. Helmets and wellington boots are provided to those visitors who require them.

From a tool found in one of the mines, it appeared that the Roman miners had used a long-handled implement called a gad. The iron head had a sharp point at one end and a flat piece on the other. This was struck with a hammer so as to cut the rock with greater precision.

As the ceilings throughout the two mines rise to about 7ft high, visitors are able to walk upright and are also able to follow the angle of the gold seams, or even see the tool marks left by the Roman miners. Noticeable, too, are the square-shaped entrances which are typical of the way the Romans hacked their way into the rock. These square-shaped entrances can also be seen in the Roman mines on the Continent.

In the Upper Roman Adit, the Romans cut another long gallery, but this had closed for safety purposes as there had been a roof fall along its route. Here, visitors come into contact with the sloping shaft sunk by the Victorians to reach the Roman workings, and which was probably one of the methods they used to get to the gold-bearing quartz. The Victorians also laid tracks through the woodland to carry the ore down to the processing centres, but they had not excavated all of the ore. Large clumps of it are still visible at the far end of the Upper Roman Adit.

During their time here, the Romans also used the most advanced methods of technology known to them, for besides manually removing the quartz with their primitive gad, they also dislodged it by plying powerful jets of water on to the rock surface. For this purpose, and for washing the ore afterwards, they built enormous reservoirs with sluices to contain the volume of water and aqueducts to carry it across the difficult terrain. The Cothi Aqueduct alone was seven miles long and channelled two million gallons of water per day from a place close to the Cothi's source. The route taken by this amazing aqueduct can be seen going along the base of the neighbouring mountain and it is a testimony to the brilliance of Roman engineering. In one instance, the water had been carried through a narrow rocky gorge and had ended in a reservoir called Melin-y-Milwyr (the Soldiers' Mill), where, no doubt, Roman soldiers had been employed in washing the ore. Today, the Soldiers' Mill is nothing more than a deep depression in the woodland, with most of the water having seeped away. It too is a lasting reminder of the Roman period.

The individual reservoirs at Dolaucothi are certainly among its most ingenious features. One in particular had been cut into the lower slopes of Cwm Henog and was bounded by impressive banks of up to 24ft wide and 45ft in length. A break in its banks may have allowed the water to flow out to where the ore was washed.

The leat supplying this water, called Cwm Henog Leat, was considered to be of Roman date. It also carried water to other reservoirs around the opencast. At its western end, the leat disappeared into the 19th-century workings. This consisted of an impressive rock-cut channel, between 3–4ft deep and 3ft wide, which had also carried water across the north-west slopes of neighbouring Alt Cwm Henog for a distance of over 100ft. It was seen that parts of the channel had been reinforced with roughly built dry-stone walling and had obviously been the work of the Roman workers. Another impressive reservoir on the lower slopes of Cwm Henog, measuring 32 x 96ft, had two channels appearing from the west end of the bank with each one measuring about 9ft wide. However, the eastern end of the reservoir now lies hidden beneath a dense growth of rhododendrons.

Another method for extracting the ore was by building a fire against the rock face and then placing the heated rock into a tank of cold water. This rapid cooling process would cause the rock to crack and expose the quartz which could then be easily removed by hand. A large water tank was found sunk into the floor of a 64ft cavern and was considered to have been where the heated rock had been cooled by the workers. The presence of partly burnt timbers nearby reinforced this supposition.

Once the ore had been extracted, it was ground into smaller pieces by water-powered machinery consisting of suspended hammers which pounded it against a large rock beneath. (It is possible that the deep depressions around the Pumpsaint Stone may have been caused by this process.) After this operation, the broken pieces could be crushed into even smaller pieces, either by hand-operated querns, as suggested by the specimens found around the site, or by water-powered millstones for greater efficiency.

After crushing, the ore was washed along a series of channels, called water tables, in order to separate the gold from the remaining rock waste. It was then collected at the bottom in rough material, preferably a sheep's fleece as the oil in the wool helped

The entrance to the Upper Roman Adit at the Dolaucothi gold mines near Pumpsaint.

to trap the fine grains. When the fleece was full, it was then burned, leaving the gold behind. This method was highly favoured by the Romans, who went on to remove an estimated half a million tonnes of rock, from which they would have extracted just three-quarters of a tonne of gold. It was found that one tonne of ore produced only a small quantity of gold, equivalent to the size of a cube of sugar.

After smelting the gold into ingots, the Romans then transported it under military convoy to various mints, the main being the Imperial Mint at Lyon in France. Here, it was made into coins to provide much needed currency for paying the soldiers' wages and for buying luxury goods such as jewellery, fine cloth, fine Samian ware from the factories of Gaul and olive oil from the Mediterranean. The Roman army relied greatly on the imports of olive oil for cooking and for providing fuel for heating.

A priority for the Roman miners was ventilation. This was achieved by digging another tunnel to the outside. In those days, lighting was by way of lamps fuelled by animal fat or olive oil, which gave off large amounts of black greasy smoke. In Victorian times, the miners depended on candles in the darkness which the miners had to buy themselves, but as the children working alongside them could not afford to buy such luxuries they were compelled to share their elders' meagre light.

Apart from the Roman mines, visitors can also be taken to the mines worked during the 19th and 20th centuries. Pickaxes were then used, and the marks of these can also be clearly seen along their walls.

In modern times, full-scale mining operations did not start until 1870, but in 1910 alone 360 tonnes of gold quartz was extracted. There was also further mining between 1934 and 1939 when a deep shaft was sunk down the middle of the large opencast to connect with the gold-bearing seams. In 1936 a further 381 tonnes were mined from the old workings, but the standard techniques of separating the gold from the waste did not work effectively, so other methods were used. These also failed and, in the end, as no one from Britain could treat the ore from Dolaucothi, it was sent to Hamburg in Germany for processing; although this operation also came to an end with the outbreak of World War Two. After that, the mines were not considered practicable and were consequently closed down.

In April 2000 the Cambrian Archaeological Trust invited a team of French archaeological experts to carry out a geological survey of the mines, during which an interesting find was a section of a Roman drainage wheel. Drainage was an important factor to prevent flooding and these wheels, which had a diameter of 13–14ft and were about 12ft high, were set in pairs along a sloping gallery and operated manually to expel excess water by rotating their outside paddles. A replica of one of these wheels was made for the television programme *Time Team*, and it is on display in the former opencast mining area next to the children's section where they can 'pan for gold' along a water-filled trough, similar to the one used in Roman times.

Gold-bearing pyretic shale has also been found on the site. This is seen as having distinctive weathered yellow-white incrustations, which in effect are tiny grains of gold trapped in the dark grey to black coloured shale.

Although there is still a small quantity of gold left in the mountain, and all mining operations have ceased, the site has become one of great national importance and, under the auspices of the National Trust, the Dolaucothi gold mines have become a popular tourist destination, with thousands coming here to learn how the gold was mined and the various techniques used.

The underground part of Dolaucothi has been leased from the Crown by the University of Wales, Cardiff, and then sub-let to the National Trust during the summer months when guided tours take place. The university also uses Dolaucothi as a teaching facility and has set up a comprehensive exhibition in the reception area showing the history of gold throughout the ages.

As the mines are also of such great archaeological and scientific importance, they are protected by the Schedule of Ancient Monuments. And, as the surrounding fields are likely to contain buried archaeology, even agricultural use is forbidden. The preservation of this historic site is therefore one of the many functions the National Trust has in Wales.

LLANIO (BREMIA)

Llanio is considered to have been of some importance in the area, as it commanded a strategic position at the junction of two major roads, three miles from Tregaron and seven from Lampeter, on the left bank of the River Teifi, Carmarthenshire. It was also within marching distance of the auxiliary fortress at Pumpsaint. It was designated as a practice camp where Roman troopers came to improve their battle skills, but it had all the characteristics of a well fortified base where lead was smelted on a large scale.

The fort also commanded the *Sarn Helen* to Dolgellau and, more importantly, protected the road to the valuable gold mines at nearby Dolaucothi and the lead mines situated further north. In this respect, the approaches to Llanio were well guarded.

Llanio was also built to the usual military design, being rectangular in shape with rounded corners. It measured 525ft long, 381ft wide and was five acres in extent.

The fort was discovered in 1887 when paving stones were unearthed during ploughing operations. The farmer also found a section of a Roman road lying just 15in below the surface, and as an oval mound looked suspiciously like a structure beneath the surface the Cambrian Archaeological Trust carried out an exploration that year.

Traces of at least three buildings were found outside the southern defences, and, following the discovery of a wall 3ft thick, the bathhouse was eventually uncovered. Brickwork which had formed part of the heating system was found within 2ft of the surface. This hypocaust had been made up of short pillars 7in high and running in parallel rows, nine deep. Some of the flue tiles were found in an excellent state of preservation, and large slabs of stone on which the pillars had rested showed signs of being exposed to great heat. Adjoining the hypocaust was a room measuring 18 x 20ft with a floor covered in large red-brick tiles, many of which had been incised with a pattern of circles. One of the circles had a line crossed through its centre to make a cross. It was thought that these tiles for this bathing room had not been produced locally but had been brought in by ponies over the Black Mountain, some distance away. Many of the flues made from tiling were box shaped with holes cut into their sides to allow the heat through, and many of these were in an excellent state of preservation. There was also an abundance of soot to mark the site of the furnace. Another furnace was found which aroused a great deal of interest in that it marked where the Romans had smelted the lead they had mined in the area. It was rectangular in shape and several feet deep. From among the debris they extracted a large piece of lead which, when melted, weighed 16lb. As the remnants of the furnace contained a high level of arsenic, the excavators had to wear protective clothing. The compressed layers of burnt deposits revealed that this particular furnace had been smelting lead for a considerable time.

The walls of Llanio had been extensively robbed in the past, and, while most of the structure was said to have 'vanished from the surface' long before 1700, parts of its defences could still be seen on all three sides.

However, it was the discovery of five inscription stones, one of which referred to the second cohort of the Asturians, that established the remains as military as well as establishing that the cohort had been based at Llanio. The Asturians were natives of north-eastern Spain and had been stationed in Germany before arriving in Wales. Records show that they were also garrisoned on Hadian's Wall during the third century. This particular stone was found embedded upside down in the walls of a neighbouring stable and was subsequently rescued.

Another stone inscribed in Latin was nearly a foot high and only 6in wide. This gave the name of Martialis Ennius Primus, with the symbol preceding his name denoting that he was a centurion. The stone had probably been part of his tombstone. Another tombstone gave the name ARTI, which was translated as Artus or Artius, and the third stone, about 13in long, gave the centurion's name as Verioni. It was more than likely that all three tombstones had been removed from the camp's cemetery, which lay a short distance away.

One other interesting object that surfaced while digging for peat in the area during the 19th century was a small carving of a woman's head which had been perfectly preserved, despite it being made from wood. It was regarded as an excellent piece of early craftsmanship, with the carver taking great care to create an intricate pattern to represent braided hair that extended to the nape of the neck. There was a socket hole to indicate that it had broken off a statuette. In the same field, it was said that a sepulchral mound had been found full of cremated bones, but these had been taken away and used as compost.

Closer to the river bank, a mass of stone foundations were found littering the area, and excavations revealed that these had come from at least one large building which contained several rooms and was identified as being residential. This suggested the presence of a *vicus*.

TRAWSCOED

Going northwards from Llanio, another first-century fortress was built here in the territory of the **Cornovii** in around AD 70. It occupied gently sloping ground close to the north bank of the River Ystwyth, about eight miles from its mouth. It was a site chosen by the military for commanding the valleys of the Rheinol and Ystwyth and for being on the strategic military road leading to Canovium (Caerhun, Conway) in the far north.

The fort measured 550 x 460ft and was discovered on 6 April 1959, when earthworks were found north of the modern B4575 road cutting across it. To the south, the western defences were located, but the rampart had been disturbed to form a large mound 36 x 122ft wide. The area of the fort was estimated to be in the region of five acres, which was large enough to garrison a regiment of 1,000 men or 500 cavalry.

Scattered ash and clay over the inner edge of the rampart located the site of the ovens, and the position of the south gate suggested that the fort had been facing towards the river. It was identified as the *porta principalis sinistra*, and the gate on the west as the *porta praetoria*.

In April 1962 further excavations were carried out to determine the character of the fortress, but continuous cultivation of the land with constant ploughing had interfered with the occupation levels. However, the foundations of a timber building were traced to a length of 48ft, running parallel with the ramparts. The building was 22ft wide and sub-divided with partition walls 12ft apart to make three separate compartments. In the corner of one room lay the carbonised remains of wooden planks which had probably been the flooring. It was assumed that this building had formed part of a barrack block which had been burnt down.

A section was cut through the eastern defences, south of the estimated position of the *Via Decumana*, and revealed that the rampart had been increased to 19ft wide and was standing over 2ft high. Here, the Roman builders had used puddled yellowish-white clay with occasional layers of rock particles to give it extra strength. This street had been constructed with closely set cobbles, and they looked as good as the day they had been laid.

Because of the interference to the site over the years, domestic items were scarce and hard to find, but a few pieces of Samian ware, cooking pots and buff-coloured *mortaria* were safely recovered. Previously, some storage jars had been ploughed up in the field lying to the south of the modern road. These articles showed that they had come from the Flavian mid-first century to the Trajanic second-century occupation of the fort. Sections cut through the defences showed that there had been at least two separate periods of occupation, borne out by the fact that the rampart had been doubled in size. There was no specific evidence to suggest that the fort had been abandoned.

Aerial photography revealed the site of a *vicus* to the north of the fort, complete with outlines of its streets. Excavations showed that the inhabitants had lived in timber buildings fronting the extension of the *Via Decumana*, close to the fort's gateway. This particular gateway was found to have been in an excellent state of preservation. A single building, measuring approximately 24ft wide, and at least 21ft long, had a clay oven and a sunken floor, but there was evidence that this building had been burnt down during the Flavian period to make way for a more level building area along the roadway. More timber buildings flanked the extension of the *Via Principalis* for some distance, and several other buildings contained working crucibles, with one having an oven. From this, it appeared that the settlement had been extremely industrious during the late first century, and that it went on to function into the second. The evidence also suggested that the people had burnt down their existing homes so they could make way for new ones.

Rubbish pits are good indications of what people throw away, and one such pit yielded shards of different pottery from the mid-first-century Flavian period to the second-century Trajanic. Occupation of the *vicus* was apparently very short, lasting just 50 years, from AD 70–120.

There was no evidence to support later activity there, and the inhabitants probably abandoned their little community when the fortress ceased to function.

PENNAL

P ennal was one of the smaller auxiliary fortresses, situated at the tidal limit of the Teifi Estuary, just north of Trawscoed and on the line of the road crossing Cadir Idris.

The identification of Pennal as a Roman military site was made by the antiquarian Edward Lhwyd when he discovered structural remains and flue tiles beside the river, supposed to have come from the hypocaust of the bathhouse.

In Lhwyd's day the site was known as Cefn Gaer, but Roman remains were first discovered here in 1693, when Samian pottery surfaced in the field opposite the farmhouse occupying the site. The fragments contained a curled leaf design, said to have gone out of fashion by the mid-Flavian period in around AD 85. These then suggested that the first occupation of the fortress had occurred during the mid-first century, at about the same time as Caersws and Forden Gaer.

In 1793 some more Roman artefacts were recorded, which included a little gold chain only 3in long and a string of silver beads. Also recorded was a 'brasse pann'.

During the excavations in 1865, a single outline of a quadrangle enclosure with rounded corners was identified, measuring 830ft long on the south-east side and 630ft on the south-west. There was also evidence that there had been a *vicus* attached to the fortress.

Further excavations were carried out in 1933, and among the discoveries was a coin of Julius Caesar (54–44 BC), an earlier coin of Tiberius (AD 14–37) and a coin of Domitian (AD 81–96).

As the site was monopolised by farm buildings lying on its western corner, excavation there was not possible, but the outlines of the fortress, supported by the presence of a *vicus*, indicated that it had undoubtedly fulfilled an important role in this remote part of Roman Wales.

CAERSWS

The Romans established two individual auxiliary fortresses here at Caersws in central Wales, close to the River Severn, and situated to the north-west of Trawscoed. They were among the largest to be built.

The first fortress, known as Caersws I, lay on a spur of land overlooking the Severn and was the larger of the two. It was considered to have been the first to occupy the site and was regarded as having been pre-Flavian, perhaps associated with the earlier campaigns to control central and northern Wales. No earthworks were found, and it was not excavated.

Caersws II

By contrast, the second fort stood on level ground close to the north bank of the River Carno, just above the flood plain, and was first established during the reign of Vespasian in the AD 70s. It was designed for an auxiliary unit of the largest size, perhaps a *cohors miliaria* of 1,000 men. It was built to the usual military plan with rounded corners and enclosed an area of 7.7 acres.

Caersws itself was regarded to be at the strategic centre of Ordivican territory, with several valleys meeting here. It was also the furthermost limit to which an invader from the east could penetrate, with the mountains providing a natural stopping point. Three major roads radiated out of Caersws; one going north, the second going west and the third going eastwards to connect with the fortress at Forden Gaer, leading eventually to the legionary fortress of Wroxeter on the eastern borders. With these military bases established in the area, the dominance over the **Ordovices** was complete and ultimately led to their final defeat.

The earthworks of Caersws II had been the object of antiquarian interest for at least 200 years, having first been noticed by Pennant in the late 18th century. Then in 1804 Roman pottery was noticed by the banks of the Severn.

In the late 19th century part of the fort's walls could be seen above the ground, and lines, visible under the dry grass during the summer, were thought to have been streets inside the fortress. On investigation, this large site was found to have been ploughed extensively over time, during which more fragments of Roman pottery emerged scattered over a large area.

The bathhouse was traced outside the fort in 1854, and, like at most of the Welsh forts, it was the first of the large buildings to be discovered and was, as usual, located close to the river. It had a drain and an aqueduct leading to the river. On excavation, there was a good depth to the sandstone walls which had accounted for the good state of the bathing rooms, two of which had hypocausts made from mixed and re-used materials of red and yellow tiles and slabs of slate. Some of the tiles were hexagonal but a few random ones bore the stamp C.I.C.F. and were embellished with a pattern of ivy leaves. One had a fuller legend which read C.I.C.F.S.P.P. This inscription proved to be greatly significant as it suggested that the garrison of the fort had been the first cohort of the Celtiberians who had been in occupation during the third century. There were also many coins that had been lost by bathers, and these ranged from the reigns of Antoninus Pius (AD 138–161), with two of Victorius and Tetricus (AD 268–273), thereby indicating that the bath building was still in use during the late third century.

In 1909 the Liverpool Archaeology Committee undertook excavations here, and sections cut across the fort's streets revealed that in rebuilding the fort the Roman engineers had raised them as much as 6ft as a protection against the winter floods. It also became apparent that the earlier streets had been built much flatter, while the latest ones had been given a camber. The Roman engineers had also protected the two defensive ditches lying in front of the rampart, and had used gravel to protect the ditch systems in the north.

There appeared to be three construction periods at the fort, with earlier timber buildings having been demolished to make way for new ones, and the rampart had been heightened with clay and the ditches strengthened with a stone wall. Reconstruction work had also taken place at the barracks in the northern section. These had been dismantled and never replaced, while those in the southern half of the fort continued to be occupied until the third century, as indicated by the pottery.

The headquarters, measuring 70 x 90ft, was found to have a 6ft deep cellar/strong room in the *Sacellum*, which was much deeper than at any of the other forts. This also showed signs of reconstruction at a later date. Stone bases that had supported a colonnade in front of the building were also uncovered, as were quantities of roofing tiles bearing the stamp of the 20th Legion.

The commandant's house contained two rooms which had been heated with a hypocaust, also made from re-used material of red and yellow tiles and slabs of slate. Most of the tiles were plain, but a few random ones were marked with the garrison's initials and were also decorated with ivy leaves. There was a good depth to the sandstone walls which accounted for the rooms being in a good state of preservation. When the *Praetorium* was finally demolished, the area was sealed with a covering of stones into which late third or early fourth-century pottery shards had been trodden.

Alongside the headquarters was the buttressed granary. This consisted of a single stone building, 95ft long, and 33ft wide, with the remains of its walls standing two courses high, although none of its internal cross walls had survived after being robbed in the past. The floors had been covered with flagstones, and there were signs that fires had been lit on them. This suggested that the granary had perhaps become living quarters for the local inhabitants after the garrison had left. Quantities of charred grain were found, among which were spelt wheat and bread wheat. Rye was also present but in small quantities, which contrasted with the granary found at Caerleon where a substantial amount was recorded.

Elsewhere in the fort, fragments of decorative Samian ware were found, and the vessels were described as being of 'fine quality' and had been imported from the factories of Gaul. The dating of this pottery indicated an intensive occupation during the last quarter of the first century and the first decade of the second. Owing to the chemical makeup of the soil, some of the Samian had not preserved very well. Metal objects included spear heads, bronze key heads, a silver bell with its clapper still intact and several Dolphin brooches.

Outside the fort, rubbish pits which had been filled up by the garrison during the second century were full of broken pieces of pottery, oyster shells and other oddments. An interesting discovery was a trumpet-shaped fibula with an enamelled decoration consisting of a zigzag pattern down each side that was assigned to the first century.

The excavations at Caersws revealed that it was unlike any other fortress in Wales and had been occupied continuously throughout the second century, far longer than any other in Wales. Like Brecon, the garrison was largely reduced in AD 120, although they remained in occupation until AD 200, when the fort was repaired. Soon afterwards the garrison was withdrawn. After the year AD 280, all traces of military occupation came to an end.

An annexe built on to the fort was first discovered from the air in 1972, and excavation revealed that it had come into being early in the second century when the outermost ditch on the north-eastern side of the fortress had been put out of action and replaced by a stone wall. A small tile kiln was found within its western side and showed that it had been used to manufacture floor and roofing tiles for the fortress. These also included the small hexagonal tiles found in the bathhouse, making it clear that the tiles there had been custom-made.

It became evident from the discovery of several timber buildings outside the fort's south-eastern walls that it had attracted a larger-than-usual civilian settlement starting from the late first century. Rubbish pits, wells, clay hearths and floors of various dwellings, and burials (some cremations) were found south of the ramparts. One grave revealed the outline of a wooden coffin with nails attached, and another contained a pair of hob-nailed boots, indicating that the man had been buried with his boots on.

The dwellings were thought to have been wattle huts lying along the main road leading from the fort to the banks of the river. It was here that most of the Samian ware was found. There were also other varieties of rare glass and an immense quantity of discarded pottery. Behind the buildings were some pits that had been dug by the inhabitants for extracting clay for building purposes. Interestingly, scraps of metal found among the rubbish on the floors strongly suggested that the lead ore, which abounded at Plynlimon, had been smelted there. An estimated 100lb of lead was recovered in one spot alone. A significant find was a bronze fibula in the form of a cock with enamelled wings. An oak trough in a perfect state of preservation was found in one of the three cleared-out wells. Another yielded a barrow load of leather clippings, which had evidently come from a saddler's shop. Coins were also plentiful, dating to the early part of the second century.

One building was found to contain a narrow range of rooms fronted by a verandah and separated by a cobbled yard. Several of the rooms had stone or clay floors and contained at least five ovens. Five small weights were also found, and it was thought that this building had been a bakery in a row of retail shops which had fronted the road. Other remains suggested that the community had a tavern and iron, bronze and leather workshops. The finds of pottery suggested that occupation did not last longer than the middle of the second century.

One of the most significant finds was that of a Roman villa with two identical bathing suites. Several rooms were successfully excavated, one of which was paved with blue and white stones. A fragment of a polished cut-glass drinking vessel, which was very expensive in Roman times, was an indication that this had been the home of a wealthy family. Pieces of window glass also emerged, as did fragments of urns and jugs of various designs.

The foundations of a semi-circular building were also found against the main southern wall, and this may have served as a small winter apartment where the sun shone all day. Beyond, in the area between the building and the river, a human skull was found embedded in the clay which had a set of perfectly preserved teeth from someone middle-aged. Nearby was a curious burial where two skeletons had been buried 'toe to toe'. No coffins were found. Close to the burials were fragments of *amphorae* and *mortaria*. An urn full of cremated bones also surfaced. The conclusion was that the villa had been occupied to the fourth century.

Also outside the ramparts were the earthworks of ancient homesteads which had been occupied long before the Romanised citizens had occupied the land.

CARNO

The Romans also erected a small fortress here, eight miles north-west of Caersws and south-west of Carno village in the county of Montgomeryshire. Initially, traces of the ramparts were faint, but the excavations of 1964–65 showed that they had been built with turfs and were 12ft wide. There was also an inner bank measuring 15ft across which, for a small fortress, were substantial defences. The entire circuit measured 404 x 325ft, giving a total area of 2.5 acres.

The fortress became known as Caer Noddfa (Fort of Refuge), which derived from the time when the Knights Hospitaller of St John cut back the rampart in the north corner to build their hospice in the 13th century, thus reversing the role of the fortress by providing hospitality and succour to those in need.

The road from Caersws passed along its south-west side, and it is possible that there was a good communication between the two fortresses. As there were no signs of any internal buildings or pottery it was not possible to date the remains.

FORDEN GAER

For a number of years, earthworks at Forden, lying about a mile from Montgomery town and only a few hundred yards from the banks of the River Severn, had long attracted the attention of antiquarians who believed that they belonged to a Roman fort.

In 1929 the Powysland Club, under the presidency of the late Earl of Powys, decided to explore the site with the assistance of a working party from Aberystwyth University College. The fort lay on the Roman road leading to the auxiliary fortress of Wroxeter in the east, and was also connected to Caersws in the west.

Excavations soon confirmed the existence of a very wide rampart which formed part of the fort's defences, and that the internal measurement of the fort was 5.5 acres. There was, however, extensive plough damage to the site.

The area covering the interior of the fort was markedly higher than the surrounding ground, and the rampart rose in parts as much as 13ft above the existing surface of the deep depression with another encircling it, thus making a very effective defence system. It was thought that the doubling of the clay bank served a dual purpose: not only did they keep out intruders, but they helped to stem the flow of the frequently flooding Severn.

The outer bank consisted of gravel and a thin covering of clay. The inner ditch was 14ft wide but only 5ft deep. A post hole in the clay 15ft under the corner foundation probably marked the line of a stockade built during the earliest occupation of the fort. Its sides had been backed with cobbles. There was further evidence that the rampart had been refaced during the third and fourth century. The north and south entrances were clearly marked, but those on the east and west were not so apparent. Evidence pointed to a late first-century occupation, probably around AD 80–100, the latter date marking the reconstruction of the fort. From that date to the early third century the fort appeared to have been fully occupied, and the second phase of its history continued well into the second half of the fourth century.

Two sections, 4ft wide, had been cut through the rampart, and it was discovered that the Romans had fortified it with 10ft long planking. Many other fragments of pottery were found between the layers of the rampart, including a Samian cup with an internal groove, said to have come from the first century. This was helpful in dating the work to that period. Much of the Samian was highly decorated, and one had an animal with a long bushy tail, probably a squirrel. A black cooking pot with a lattice pattern also emerged, as did fragments of a large *amphora*. Further down was a burnt layer in which several fragments of Samian ware were found, with some coarse fragments of a grey vase. When pieced together, the diagonal lines of a lattice pattern emerged. A large urn and a jug handle with triple reeding were also found and were dated to the early second century.

A cross-section revealed there were three layers in the north to south road with traces of wood in the clay which might have been supports for timber uprights. In this mixture, some more Samian fragments surfaced of mid-Flavian date. The burnt layer showed that an earlier timber building had stood on the site before it had burnt down. A rebuilding programme then followed when the rampart was strengthened by the addition of the wooden planking, at a time when most of the other forts in Wales were being rebuilt in stone.

Attached to the rampart were the foundations of a rectangular building, about 110ft long, with a division of five rooms in the rear. The interior was covered with a gravel paving which suggested a courtyard. Towards the centre was a thinly set pavement of small cobbles. This was dated by the range of early Samian and mid-Flavian pottery found there. A carinated bowl of brown ware and a screw-necked jug were also found. Several pits in the area contained a variety of objects, including several pie dishes, cooking pots of early second century date, an early type *mortarium*, stamped by the potter, and many pieces of an *amphora*. Even coins from the reigns of Hadrian to Antoninus Pius had found their way there, obviously dropped by their unsuspecting owners when depositing their refuse. Someone had also thrown away a fibula, because its pin and catch plate had broken, and another discarded fibula, 2.5in long, had a trumpet-shaped bow with a zigzag pattern down its sides and had originally been filled with enamel. This specimen was dated to the early second century and was similar to the one found at Segontium. A curious find was a circular disc, which was 1.75in in diameter with a human face and curled hair carved in relief on one side. This was probably part of a belt buckle. A horse sandal was also found among the rubbish. These sandals were often put on injured hooves to prevent the spread of infection.

Excavation of a heavily metalled road running east to west, made of river gravel and 10in thick, produced a *denarius* of Trajan, dated AD 98–99, and also a cylindrical bowl with external ridging that was characteristic of first-century examples. A narrower road, with a substantial gutter made of rough quarried stone, produced another Samian dish from the second century. The bed of the third road was largely composed of fragments of roofing tiles and showed a deterioration in workmanship. Strangely, someone, probably one of the workmen, had scratched the number XIII in the soft clay. One wonders what he meant by writing this particular number and if it had any significance.

A building, with its rooms facing the defences, was also discovered with fragments of roofing tiles, showing that it had been well covered. A hypocaust tile also meant that modern heating techniques of the day had also been applied, while some of the rooms had been paved. No identification to the building was given, but to have had such luxury it had probably been the residence of a high-ranking officer, perhaps the commandant.

In the lowest stratum of the *Via Praetoria* an early *denarius* of Trajan was found, and the study of ceramic material indicated a renewal of activity during AD 110–120.

A number of other interesting finds were made during the excavations: a leaf-shaped arrowhead and a core scraper appeared on the top soil, along with a child's bangle. Another fibula, dated AD 80–120, was among the metal objects which included a pewter pan handle and a harness buckle. Some of the pottery had been stamped with the potter's name – PRISCVS. This potter was known to have worked at Lezoux, France, in the second century. His stamp has been found at many Roman sites which were occupied during the Hadrianic–Antonine period. Some pottery possessed a rosette stamp. These appeared between the years AD 190–260 and the third century, and constituted 30 per cent of all the stamps found. A coin of Julius Caesar was also discovered in the rubble. This displayed an elephant trampling on a serpent and was dated 50–49 BC. The coin was plated, and it was probably a contemporary imitation and not part of the official issue. Glass fragments of a greenish tint were also found in an excellent condition and denoted fine craftsmanship. These had come from square-sided bottles and a high-sided vase. One fragment had come from a vase of an intense blue colour. Below the metalling of the east to west road (the *Via Principalis*) was the base of a cylindrical bowl showing external ridging on the foot stand. This was a classic first-century example.

It was concluded that the fort had been occupied for a short duration only, and discoveries from the Antonine–Severan period appear to represent the time when the fort was fully active. A study of the ceramic discoveries indicated a renewal of activity during AD 110–120. The site then remained in occupation until early in the third century when a general rebuilding and levelling up had taken place. The last period of occupation was a long one, with another complete rebuilding programme as a result of fire. The coins show that the site was still in occupation in the fourth century. After AD 380, the fort appears to have fallen into decay.

However, three independent sites suspected of being Roman were examined in response to the erosion of the river bank to the south of the fort, which had exposed evidence of habitation.

On Site No.1 two periods of occupation were detected, but plough damage was extensive, with plough marks extending right down to the natural soil, and the main Roman road had been removed down to its core. It was discovered that the continuous erosion of the river bank was affecting this area. The first occupation was probably in the first century. This was represented by a length of road flanked by drainage gullies leading from the south gate of the fort. Phase II of the occupation took place in the second century. A timber structure was found extending northwards towards the fort.

On Site No.2 substantial postholes were found which were thought to have supported an aisled hall, perhaps built after the troops had left. There were many fragments of Romano-British pottery to suggest that people had made homes there.

Site No.3 was a large square enclosure, about 320ft across, located in a neighbouring field some distance to the west of site No.2 and close to the River Camlad. Here, too, Romano-British pottery was found, but, although plough damage had virtually destroyed the interior, this site could also have been part of the little settlement.

JAY LANE

Having invaded Wales along its eastern borders in AD 47, the Roman army soon established a small auxiliary fortress in Jay Lane as early as AD 55–57, and it was the first of three fortresses they built in the vicinity of Leintwardine (now Shropshire).

The remains of the fortress were identified by the curving mounds lying beneath the grass, and although post holes in the clay indicated where timber structures had stood it was not possible to find anything of the fort itself. Its interior had been completely ploughed away, as had the rampart, but the defence ditches had survived and were characteristically V-shaped. They measured 7ft wide and only 3ft deep. The filling in the ditches suggested that the rampart had been rivetted with turf which had later been thrown down into the ditches. For unknown reasons the outer ditch was never completed.

The position of the main gates and gatehouses were identified by their large post holes in the clay and shale, with some showing where the large square timbers had stood. In places, the post stumps had either rotted in situ or had been rocked or dug out after dismantling. Of the fort's corner towers, only the one in the south was located. Measurements indicated that it had been 15 x 18ft overall. There had also been wooden towers spaced at intervals along the top of the ramparts. Three of these were found.

Measurements of the interior indicated that the area on either side of the *Via Documana* in the northern half of the fort was 122ft, which would have provided space for six barrack blocks, but this, and the space in the southern half, was considered to be below the limits required for a part-mounted military regiment requiring stables and stores for their horses. Consequently, it was considered that Jay Lane had held a smaller unit, an *ala quingeneria* consisting of 500 cavalry.

All the finds came from the ditch filling outside the north-west gate and included samples of coarse pottery and the glossy red Samian ware. One find of particular note was an attractively shaped bowl with external grooves extending down to the foot ring, identified as having been of Gaulish manufacture. Two other bowls had come from the Flavian period and were also of south Gaulish make. One had been made during the Neronian period. A flint scraper which had survived from the Iron Age also emerged. Unfortunately, coins found in the ditches were badly corroded, and this had made identification impossible.

The fortress had only a short life span. It was dismantled around AD 78. Twelve years later, the military built another fortress at Buckton just a mile away.

BUCKTON

This auxiliary fortress at Buckton was established around AD 90 and was the second fortress to have been built in the vicinity of Leintwardine, just over a mile from the site of the Jay Lane fortress. It was considered to be in a better position, as the site had clearer visibility over level ground.

Here, again, the interior of the fort had been eradicated over the years, leaving only the remains of its defences to speak of its existence. It was considered that there had been a turf bank 12.5ft high and that a stone wall had been added some time later.

When there was a general reduction of garrisons in the west, Buckton was dismantled in the year AD 140 and its stonework removed to ground level. It is probable that this stone was then used for building the bathhouse at Bravonium (Leintwardine), as the stone used there was not found east of the River Clun. It was thought that, like Jay Lane, the fortress had been garrisoned by a detachment of cavalry.

In its time, Buckton had been part of a formidable force, ensuring Roman domination over the entire area in collaboration with its sister fortress at Bravonium.

LEINTWARDINE (BRAVONIUM)

Having taken control of the area, the Romans soon established a civilian settlement here around AD 50 and called it Bravonium. It was mentioned in the *Antonine Itinerary*, placing it on *Iter XII*, and again quoting the correct mileages between the town and other important Roman sites, namely 75 Roman miles to Chester and 74 Roman miles from Caerleon.

The town went on to flourish quite successfully until the second century when the military decided it was a desirable place to set up an auxiliary fortress, the main attraction being that the town lay at the junction of two rivers, the Clun and the Teme, and that it commanded the Teme Valley route into central Wales. Another deciding factor could have been that the site was astride the major road Watling Street West, and that it was also midway between two other major towns of Magnis (Kenchester) in the south and Viroconium (Wroxeter) in the north. It was thought that the military needed the site as a base for the transit of troops when the garrisons in other parts of Wales were being withdrawn. In such a strategic situation, its value as a military site was enormous.

Excavations began in 1964 and revealed that the fortress had been constructed around AD 160 and defended by three V-shaped ditches, 17ft wide. As the fortress had been built on a high plateau, the approaches to it were quite steep, which had been an advantage from a defensive point of view. It was found that the ramparts enclosed an enormous site measuring 860ft from north to south and 560ft from east to west, totalling a massive 13 acres, making it larger than Llandeilo and the largest auxiliary fortress to have been built in Roman Wales.

Excavation of the interior was not possible since the modern town of Leintwardine had been built over its structures, but it had been possible to identify the *Via Sagularis* behind the ramparts. The fortress's baths were also located lying to the south beside the banks of the Teme. The only other buildings uncovered were those which had belonged to the Romano-British town, including the foundations of what had been a large mansion supplying travellers with a night's lodging.

It was thought that there was no military presence here beyond AD 196 when the fortress was abandoned. Bravonium was more noted for being a British/Romano town of some prominence which went on to flourish until the fourth century.

Bravonium was also known as 'The Town of the Quern', its Roman name having derived from the Celtic word 'breuan' meaning quern.

A significant find from the settlement was an inscription on a block of purplish sandstone dedicated to the god Jupiter. The stone, which had been the central part of an altar, measuring nearly 1ft high, 1ft deep, and 14in wide, had a carved inscription reading:

IOM...DIVOR O AV...SALVT EV...ORVM
In full: I[ovi] O[ptimo] M[axiom] [et numinus] DIVOR[um] O[mnibus]
AV[gusti] SALVT[i] E[i] V[er et].

This was translated as 'To Jupiter Best and Greatest [and] the divine [spirits] of all the Emperors. For his well being [and] theirs, this offering is made.'

The town was eventually destroyed by fire in the fourth century and was possibly not inhabited again for another 100 years.

About a mile south of Leintwardine was the hill fort known as Brandon Camp, which was re-used by the Romans as a storage depot. Here, aerial photography of the interior identified the presence of several granaries which were later confirmed by the excavation of the site.

WROXETER (VIROCONIUM)

The Romans made full use of their arrival in Cornovian territory along the eastern borders of Wales by establishing another small auxiliary fortress here on the banks of the River Severn, just to the north of their other fortresses in the Leintwardine area.

The intention of the fort was to guard an important river crossing which would have been a great asset in ferrying goods and supplies along its stretches. The Romans called it Viroconium after the territory in which it was built, and the fort was recorded twice in the *Antonine Itinerary* which placed it on *Iter II*.

The fortress had the advantage of being on elevated ground, which gave the sentries a greater opportunity for supervising all movements on the river, as well as commanding the Severn Valley which offered easy access into central Wales. Elevation of the site also meant that there was a steep slope down to the river outside its western defences, and that the ground was even higher along its northern side. The fort had also been defended by two large V-shaped ditches on its northern side, both of which were about 14ft wide and 8ft deep, but on its southern side the ditches had been made slightly smaller at 10ft wide and 6ft deep. All of them had become silted up, but were found to contain some excellent pieces of Samian ware and other pottery which had been thrown in there. Among the Flavian and pre-Flavian dated Samian bowls was a South Gaulish cup and a flat-rimmed *mortarium*.

The fortress measured 515ft east to west and 470ft north to south, which enclosed an area of 5 acres, and while the ditches were clearly visible there was no sign of the rampart or any of the internal buildings, but a stone-walled pit was found, as was a gutter lined with wood which was found running along the defences. It was, therefore, thought that the entire fort had been built of timber and had probably been the first military station in the area.

In 1783 a discovery was made, by chance, of an inscribed tombstone showing a mounted horseman striking down an escaping enemy. Its Latin inscription was crucial in identifying the garrison. It read:

TIB CLAVD TIRINTIVS EQ COH…THRACVM ANNORVM LVII STIPENDIOR XX…H S E

Translated: 'Tiberius Claudius Tirintius, trooper of the Thracian Cohort Equitata, aged 57 years with 20 years' service, he lies here'.

The Thracian Cohort was a part-mounted unit who had come from the region of modern Bulgaria, and the relief clearly indicated the role these troopers performed after a battle: they struck down the enemy escaping from the battlefield. This historic stone now resides in the museum of Rowley's House at Shrewsbury.

Another significant discovery was a bronze diploma or military discharge certificate. These diplomas, written on bronze, were awarded to auxiliary soldiers on completion of 25 years' service, and granted Roman citizenship to both them and their heirs. It also legalised any marriages they may have made. It was also possible for the individual soldier to obtain a copy with the addition of his name and unit. One such diploma, granted to Mansuetus, an ex-infantryman of the Second Cohort of Dalmations, was found at Wroxeter and dated from AD 130. In all, three bronze diplomas were found inside Carnovian territory, which suggested that the recipients had preferred to live out their retirement in the area.

After the fortress was abandoned during the second half of the first century, a legionary fortress was built to the north at Chester to house the 14th Legion (Legio XIV Gemina) in a campaign to oust the Cornovii from their strongholds in the area and particularly those in their citadel on the Wrekin which lay to the north-west. But the legion was later replaced by the 20th Legion (Legio XX Valeria Victrix), who had moved up from Devon. However, on the creation of a new legionary headquarters at Chester in around AD 77, Viroconium was demolished after abandonment and the site cleared to make way for a civilian settlement. As a result, the 20th Legion was transferred north to their new headquarters at Chester.

A relic from this period was the tombstone of a soldier of the 20th Legion, whose death was dated to around AD 61. He was named as 'Gaius Mannius Secundus, son of Gaius of the Pollian voting tribe, 52 years old, with 31 years of military service.' Gaius came from northern Italy, and like all soldiers in the legions he was a Roman citizen.

Soldiers of the 14th Legion were also buried here. One named Titus Flaminius was 45 years old when he died and had served with the 14th for 22 years. He was also from northern Italy. His role was recorded as an *Aquilifer*, who carried the legion's eagle standard – a tall staff surmounted by an eagle – and wore a headdress made from a wolf's head. The role of an *Aquilifer* was considered to be a great honour. Another, Marcus Petronius, was said to have been a *Signifer*, also a standard bearer.

After the departure of the Roman military, Viroconium became a market town with the survivors from the Cornovii strongholds making new lives for themselves there in an era of peace and reconciliation. The town probably started as a timber-built settlement which grew into a prestigious centre of great prosperity in the second century, enabling its citizens who had embraced the Roman way of life to enjoy all its benefits. By the fourth century, Viroconium had become the fourth-largest town in Roman Britain.

Excavations were carried out in 1913, which suggested that occupation of the town had begun around AD 80. By the middle of the second century the town had grown to cover 200 acres, and it became the provincial capital of *Britannia Secunda* and the administrative and tribal capital of the Cornovii. For this new role, Viroconium became Viroconium Cornoviorum. This title was regarded as unique, not only within the province of Roman Britain but across the Roman Empire itself. An interpretation of the town's name, 'The Town of Virico of the Cornovii', referred to Virico, the chieftain who had suffered the same fate as his warriors when the Romans invaded and burnt down their stronghold on the Wrekin.

The pioneer settlers of Viroconium had also built defences to safeguard their new town. At the beginning of the 18th century, excavators revealed that the walls formed a rough oval shape around the town and were 6ft thick, built with large cobbles obtained from a nearby quarry, and they had been laid on a bed of clay without mortar. As an extra defence, the settlers copied the military and had a berm 11ft wide. They also created deep ditches with a 45 degree slope.

A ceremonial inscription was found in the ruins of the forum and provided valuable information about the town's identity. It read:

IMP CAES DIVI TRAIANI PARTHICI FIL DIVI NERVAE NEPOTI TRAIANO HADRIANO AVG PONTIFICI MAXIMO TRIB POT RIM COS III PP CIVITAS CORNOVIORVM.

This translates as 'To Imperial Caesar Trajanus Hadrianus Augustus, the son of the divine Trajanus Parthicus, the grandson of the divine Nerva, chief priest holding tribunician power for the 14th time, Consul three times, father of the country, the city [or council] of the Cornovii [erected this].'

This impressive stone plaque dedicated to Hadrian was found among the ruins of the forum where it had probably been given pride of place over its entrance.

The most outstanding Roman building to have survived is the great wall of the basilica, which was built on to the baths and used as a great exercise hall. It was an enormous building, 245ft long and 67ft wide, and formed an impressive entrance to the whole bathing complex. The wall of this magnificent structure, called the Old Work since the 16th century, is 72ft long, made of red sandstone blocks and stands 20ft above the ground, making it the tallest Roman structure to be still standing in Britain.

Beyond the great structure with its enormous squared opening are the surviving foundations of the *frigidarium* and the other public bathing rooms, with the rows of *pilae* for their underfloor heating systems still in place. In its time, the basilica had been divided by colonnades or arches, with a central nave 30ft wide and two aisles, each estimated to have been 14ft wide and as much as 60ft high to support its enormous roof. Its interior would have resembled that of a modern cathedral, similar to Caerleon and Chester.

The basilica revealed a few secrets of its past glory. Inside, its walls had been plastered with coloured stucco and its floors covered with decorative mosaics. The floor of the central nave had a herring-bone pattern of red brick, while the north aisle (and possibly the south) had a mosaic floor with a plain geometric design in panels of about 8.5 x 18ft coloured a greenish-black, with a little red on creamy white. Another, measuring 15ft square, had a geometric design in red, green, grey and purple colours enclosed inside a grey-green border. This had apparently been destroyed soon after discovery, but a drawing of the mosaic was made to record it for posterity. In the debris were several padlocks, a chain link, a trident candlestick and, curiously, a steel axe-head. Fragments of sculptured stone revealed that the building had been well adorned with many stunning architectural features.

The baths replaced the earlier Flavian complex which was abandoned before it was completed in the first century. Adjoining the baths was a large public lavatory and a market place with a central courtyard. All these buildings were successfully excavated and are now open to the public. Looking to the north-east, one can appreciate the vastness of the baths' interior and wonder at the impressive wall left standing. For the benefit of the modern-day visitor, all the different bathing rooms have been gravelled over in different colours to make identification easy.

The *frigidarium* was entered through double doors from the basilica and is marked with black gravel. Leading off this room, on either side, was the *tepidarium*, the warm steamy room, and to the sides of these were the dry heat rooms (*laconica*) where bathers were allowed to sweat. Beyond the *tepidarium* was the hot steamy room (*caldarium*). Their floors were built lower than the *frigidarium's* in order to allow the warm air to circulate from the furnace at the far end. For reasons of economy, in the third century these two rooms were closed down, turning the old *laconica* into a new *tepidarium* and creating a new *caldarium* with a furnace.

Interestingly, a letter from a woman who had rooms above the baths complained about the continual noises coming from them. She complained about the shouting of those who suddenly burst into song and the cries of 'the drink sellers, the sausage sellers, the pie-man and the restaurant touts' who, with their own distinctive melodies, were making her life intolerable. The letter was a great historical find and provided a vivid account of the daily occurrences at the baths. One can almost see the men splashing about in the water, with their voices reverberating around the large rooms as they called out to one another. Remnants of animal bones and oyster shells were an indication that bathers had snacked in between their swims.

In the south-west corner of the baths block stood the *macellum* or market hall, with a courtyard surrounded by a porticoed walkway. This had later been altered into sets of square rooms to accommodate shops selling high-quality goods and food.

The forum originally occupied an entire block. This also had an enormous courtyard surrounded on three sides with porticoes that had doubled as a market place. At the farthest end was a massive hall where public meetings and the assizes had taken place, similar to the one at Venta Silurum (Caerwent). At present, the surviving column bases, which had supported the colonnaded frontage, provide an excellent boundary along the edge of the site (now grassed over). Towards the end of the second century the forum suffered a catastrophic fire which destroyed the front of the building and caused the inscribed dedication to fall from its place of honour. Stacks of Samian bowls and *mortaria* were also found, which might have been the entire stock of one of the shops there.

Just south of the forum and facing Watling Street were the remains of a large building measuring 98ft overall. The remains of sculptured stonework and statuettes identified it as a temple. The discovery of two altars indicated that it was dedicated to Jupiter and had been built in the second century. Its façade had been supported by six columns nearly 2ft in diameter and had been about 15ft high. The temple also had a cobbled courtyard surrounded by a wall 2ft thick. In the eastern half of the courtyard

This photograph shows the entrance from the bascilia into the bathing complex.

was a line of stone foundations which appear to have supported a series of wooden pillars and a wooden roof covering a walkway. The bones of an ox, which had probably been the object of a sacrifice, were found in the south-east corner. The temple was said to have been similar to the Temples of Isis and Apollo at Pompeii. It went out of use during the fourth century when the town went into decline.

It was suspected that there was another temple lying to the north of the forum, with another one to the south-east of the baths complex. The foundations of this latter building measured approximately 100 x 50ft, and since it occupied a prime site in the centre of the town it must have been an extremely important building. Coins of Philip I, Trajan II, Decius and Gallienus helped to date it to the third century.

The excavations also revealed that Viroconium Cornoviorum had a well laid-out street system dividing it into rectangular blocks for residential homes, some of which had contained as many as 20 rooms with private baths and flushing toilets. To accommodate such a demand on the water supply, which also served the great baths, the waters of the Severn's tributary were diverted along a V-shaped aqueduct to enter the town through its eastern defences.

Remnants of slag which had come from bronze smelting were also found, including some good-quality bronze objects such as fibulae and brooches showing that some members of the population were skilled in bronze working. One of the brooches was in the form of a cockerel. There was also a set of toilet implements hanging on a single ring, and a bronze head of a woman was thought to have been made from a wax model. A hearth for extracting silver from lead was also found. Apart from metal working, the people had become involved with glass working and leather tanning.

It is known that the Celts, who had made up the population of this town, were experts at metal working long before the Romans invaded and had created many objects of great beauty in both silver and bronze.

The underfloor tiles of the hypocaust that heated the caldarium and tepidarium.

Excavations beneath the basilica and the baths in 1969 uncovered the gravel floors of the former military barracks in which were three lead-weighted darts or javelin heads.

Curious finds were also discovered in the cemeteries lying to the east and north of the town. In 1810 several earthen urns and a glass vessel 14in in diameter with two handles were found, which contained small bones and silver coins. The burials also revealed several lamps, silver buckles and a small bronze mirror. Another bronze object, thought to have been a lancet with a short steel blade, was found in a wooden box lined with leather. A bodkin was also found in its own little box and had its copper lock still intact.

There were abundant traces of burning throughout the site, leaving no doubt that the city had suffered at the hand of Saxon invaders towards the middle of the fifth century. As a consequence of this, a gruesome discovery of human remains was made inside one of the hypocausts, suggesting that the people had hidden in there to escape the massacre but had either become trapped by the fires raging above or had suffocated from the intense smoke. The skeletal remains included three women, an old man and a child, three of whom had died in a crouching position, while two were lying down. Curiously, near the old man's body was a pile of coins. A number of nails and decomposed wood adhering to the coins implied that they had been contained in a wooden box and that the man had taken his savings into hiding with him. There were 132 coins in total and they ranged from the reign of Tetricus, Constantine II and Valens, with the latest coin giving an indication of when the city was plundered and destroyed by the invaders.

In time, a new town emerged from the ruins of Viroconium to become modern-day Wroxeter.

WHITCHURCH
(MEDIOLANUM)

Moving northwards from Wroxeter, Ostorius Scapula tightened his grip on Ordovican territory on the eastern borders by establishing another auxiliary fortress at a place we now know as Whitchurch in Shropshire. Like Wroxeter, Scapula sited the fortress on their major military route of Watling Street, which directly connected it to the legionary fortress at Chester. The Romans called their new fort Mediolanum from the Celtic word 'medio' meaning 'in the middle of', which aptly describes its position midway between Wroxeter and Chester. The *Antonine Itinerary* placed it there, quoting Mediolanum as being 23 miles from Wroxeter, and listed it on their main route *Iter II*. In modern terms, the distance is just over 20 miles. Ptolemy, who had an uncanny knowledge of the area, also placed it correctly in the middle of the Cheshire Plain.

Aerial photography showed that the modern A49 road was lying immediately over the Roman road leading to the fortress, and a long stretch of it was found just north of Dodington. And while the main road deviated to the left, the Roman road ran in a straight line to connect with High Street, under which its cobbled surface was found. The High Street was thought to have been the location of the *Via Principalis*.

As the present town was built immediately on top of the fortress site, excavations were difficult, and only its western and northern defences could be uncovered. Some foundation trenches were found which were thought to have belonged to some of the fort's internal buildings. However, none of these were uncovered, just post holes where their timber uprights had been.

The fortress was initially identified by its western defences lying alongside Newtown Road during the excavations of 1965–66, and it was dated to the time of the Flavian Emperors, around AD 75. During the excavations a V-shaped ditch was fully exposed and found to be 10ft deep and 10ft wide, narrowing into a flat bottom just 10in across. This deadly device had been specifically designed to prevent those who had fallen in from escaping. The demolished clay rampart had been 12ft thick and lay in a solid mass at the bottom of the ditch – just where the soldiers had intended when they dismantled the defences and put the fortress out of action around AD 100. The date of the rampart's demolition was verified by the fragments of Flavian and Trajanic pottery found in the ditch. However, the fragments of the black burnished and red/buff pottery made in the Severn Valley were instrumental in dating the building of the fortress to around AD 75. Evidence suggested that occupation had been for a short period only. The decorative Samian ware and various domestic pottery used at the fort was also helpful in establishing the length of occupation.

As no other defences could be found, it was only possible to guess the line they had taken. To determine the actual circuit of the fortress, the archaeologists took the western defences as a starting point and, following the contours of the land, they went northwards into Yardington and across the top of the High Street into Bargates. As the top of the High

Street fell sharply to the south, it was supposed that the fortress's perimeter had also followed that route and that the fortress had been on the hill – a place favoured by the Romans for commanding high ground. The complete circuit measured seven acres, making Mediolanum one of the largest of the auxiliary fortresses in Roman Wales.

However, the excavations of 1956–66 in the Yardington area revealed the demolished remains of timber buildings with clay floors and patches of charcoal where furnaces for metal working had stood. The signs were that these dwellings had occupied the site long before the fortress had been built, and that the Romans had deliberately burnt them down to make way for the fortress and then dumped their charred remains into the fort's defences. This little settlement had coincided with the earlier occupation of Wroxeter in the mid-first century.

After the abandonment of the fortress, the site then became the focus for a thriving new settlement when migrants, who had probably been ousted from their mountain strongholds by the Romans, arrived to build new lives for themselves. It was at Yardington that the early timber buildings of the settlement were found. The settlers also built their homes southwards along Watling Street, and there was evidence that they had become self sufficient and industrious throughout the second century, with traces of several furnaces suggesting that the area had become an industrial complex where metal working had taken place. There were also kilns for lead smelting which produced quantities of lead clippings. Bronze, too, had been worked at the site.

As they still lived in dangerous times, the settlers thought it prudent to defend their homes and constructed a clay rampart 27ft wide with an outer ditch around their town. The defences followed the line of the hill occupied by the fortress, and using the techniques of their past masters they made use of the natural clay for building the rampart. A stone wall was later built in front of it around AD 170, and a portion of the town's second-century rampart was found in the Yardington–Bargates area which had survived to a few feet high.

By the middle of the second century, many of the timber buildings had assumed an industrial character, indicated by quantities of charcoal and furnace rakings found on rough mortared floors. A post hole suggested that one of the workshops had been covered with an open-sided shed. This industrial activity was carried out on the immediate fringe of High Street, but by the end of the century, when expansion put a premium on available land, this industry was forced away from the centre. It may have moved to the Yardington area where evidence of continued metalworking was found. This industry was seen to continue well into the third century when the settlement of Mediolanum had reached its peak to emerge as a well established town in its own right.

The residents of this early settlement had found that the area to the east of Dodington had provided them with a suitable burial place, and here again it was demonstrated that families had placed the cremated remains of their loved ones in a variety of containers, the most popular being flagons and storage jars, and that many of them had been decorated with simple designs. One such flagon was found with its neck and handles removed for use as a cinerary urn. These first-century to early second-century specimens are now on display at the Whitchurch Museum.

As Mediolanum grew in stature, its citizens began to have a greater expectation for their town and pulled down their timber buildings to replace them with more robust stone-built ones. The clay and cobbled foundations of one such structure were found lying almost up against the old western defences. This building was described as a 'courtyard type' and possessed an internal portico with its colonnade probably enclosing the central courtyard. The columns were supported by a wide base, 2ft high, and the design also included a walkway paved with pebbles set in clay. Only the cobbled foundations of this splendid house had survived, along with one course of its walling. Both its external and internal walls, which were nearly 3ft thick, had been strong enough to support an upper storey with a roof. The foundations then revealed the entire layout of the house, which included eight rooms. The largest, thought to have been the living room, measured 18ft across, but the portico's columns added another 8ft to its width, making the overall measurements, including the portico, 50 x 50ft. The external measurements amounted to 87 x 87ft. A grand room indeed! Outside the house was a section of a U-shaped drain containing pieces of roofing slate thought to have been brought from Flintshire. Remarkably, nails secured to the timbers were still in place. A few square feet of the original earth-beaten floor had also survived, but the building had been partly demolished by stone robbing. Comparative buildings were found at Caerwent.

There was also evidence that light industry had taken place over the site of this building when a U-shaped mortared furnace floor, up to 7in thick, was discovered, and judging from grooves in the mortar a windbreak had been installed. Inside the furnace bowl was a mixture of charcoal and clinker, which had come from the collapsed dome during the last firing and contained pieces of lead that had been cut from larger sheets. At the other end of the site, a trough kiln over 11ft long was found which had been cut into the footings of the south wall of room four and was entirely filled with charcoal. This particular kiln had been used for evaporating brine obtained from the neighbouring springs, which had made Whitchurch a salt-producing centre in the mediaeval period. The method of producing the salt was to keep the brine simmering in shallow vessels over a charcoal fire to produce crystallisation, during which the salt would be scooped off. A circular pit, over 4ft in diameter, was found nearby, and this was probably where the brine had been stored. Another interesting discovery was a small shaft furnace, which had been cut through the clay and cobbled foundations of room two and contained quantities of iron slag.

It was also apparent that another stone structure had been built over the previous building, which had possessed a hard-packed earth and gravel surface into which a coin of Tacitus (AD 275–76) had been trodden, thus giving the approximate date of construction to the mid-third century. A length of walling had also survived, and like its predecessor the building had a long life span. Prior to re-cutting the drain for this building, broken crockery and other rubbish had been used to level up the ground, and in the rubble was another black-burnished pie dish. This put the occupation well into the fourth century. The rubbish also contained waste from another furnace with some finely decorated Samian ware that had been discarded by the occupiers.

Adjoining building two was a length of walling at least 58ft long which had belonged to another stone structure, with an internal wall enclosing a room that had been re-floored and raised by 6in. Fragments of wall plaster showed that its decoration had been a little more up-beat than its neighbour, having had its walls coloured red, green and white, although its floors had been destroyed so no comparisons were possible. Several fragments of glass were recovered, ranging from the thicker green and blue glass of the early second century date to the thinner white window glass thought to have belonged to the forth century, suggesting that this house had also survived a long occupation. An interesting discovery in the cobbling of what appeared to have been the approach to the house, was a series of holes created by the insertion of roughly cut timbers of not more than 4in square and trimmed to a triangular shape. This particular structure could not have carried much weight, so it was thought that it might have been a hitching rail for tethering horses.

A bizarre discovery beneath a floor in one of the rooms was an underfloor grave containing the skeletal remains of a young adult male, about 20–30 years of age, which had a circular hole in the skull just above the right ear. The hole indicated that he had undergone surgery known as 'trepanation', when a circular piece of bone is removed from the head. Curiously, the removed disc had been replaced before burial, and was found lying inside the skull. This burial suggested that something sinister had occurred in that room. Firstly, it was against Roman law to bury adult corpses within a settlement, and if the young man had died on the operating table then the surgical team, in perhaps trying to hide a botched-up job, had committed another crime by concealing his death and hiding his body under the floor. Obviously, the crime was never discovered, so the culprits, having escaped detection, had taken their deadly secret to the grave.

Examination of the skeleton revealed that the young man had been about 5ft tall with a good physique, but his right wisdom tooth had badly decayed which would have caused him excruciating pain, and this was probably the reason why he had sought medical help. Examination of the hole showed that it had been cut with a circular saw, the same kind of tool used in today's trepanations, with the instrument also having a projecting spike. This kind of operation has been carried out for centuries for injuries and pain to the head, but during the Middle Ages trepanation was carried out rather barbarically on people with mental illnesses, assuming that cutting a hole in their heads would allow the demons sending them mad to escape. However, the operation conducted on this young man is the first evidence of it having been carried out in Roman Britain. Beside the skeleton, one of the culprits had dropped the lid of a castor box, and this dated the burial to the fourth century. Castor is a substance used in medicine and had perhaps been administered to the young man for some reason during that fateful operation.

The excavations of 1965–66 also unearthed quantities of animal bones which suggested that cattle had been slaughtered in large numbers for meat. There already existed idyllic pasture for grazing, and with the production of salt for curing, the meat could be transported for marketing. Its exportation must have been a contributing factor in presenting Mediolanum as a market town when agriculture had taken the place of light industry. And as the production of salt continued long after the 13th century, Mediolanum emerged into the thriving market town we know today.

CAER GAI

Caer Gai was one of the fortifications established during the campaigns of Ostorius Scapula, the second Roman governor of Britain, for the occupation of North Wales in the latter part of the first century, and was situated at the southern end of Lake Bala. While it was designated as a practice camp, it was considered to have been of considerable importance in this part of Ordovican territory as it was the connecting link between the fortresses of Tomen-y-Mur and Mediolanum (Whitchurch). Caer Gai was also on the military road that led directly to the legionary fortress of Deva (Chester), parts of which were found leading out of the camp's north-east gate.

The camp was mentioned by Robert Vaughan of Hengwrt, a Merionith antiquarian who lived from 1592–1666, as 'the camp of Caius, built by Caius, a Roman', who was probably the commanding officer. On the other hand, it was said that the ancient inhabitants of the area had called the camp after Cai Hir ap Cynyr, King Arthur's brother-in-law who was the Sir Kay of the Arthurian stories, and who was reputed to have lived there. William Camden also made reference to the camp in his 17th-century publication *Britannia*, and according to the *Annales Cambrae* of 1656 the camp was still retaining its prime position of strength and importance after becoming a centre of government long after the troops had left.

The camp had been built on a craggy rock, 100ft above the River Dee, which skirted it to the south-west, and comprised a square enclosure about 140 yards each way, to give a total area of four acres. From the ramparts the ground fell sharply away in almost every direction and created an excellent defence, while on its eastern side Mother Nature had provided a credible obstacle in the form of a deep torrent with a ravine running along half of that side.

A small excavation revealed that the ramparts had been constructed with large blocks of sandstone and had been built with meticulous care without mortar, and such a degree of workmanship was considered far too grand for such a small base. However, a surviving section of the wall clearly showed the skill of the Roman stonemasons.

The gateways to the north and south gave access to the camp, and a well-trodden path was found crossing its interior that had been made by miners going to the nearby Ystwyth lead mines. Post holes for timber uprights remained deeply embedded in the clay and indicated that the ramparts had been surmounted by a wooden palisade. In the south-east corner, holes indicated the location of a wooden tower and a squared sentry post or guardhouse.

During the excavations of 1885 the remains of the bathhouse were found on a slope outside the defences from where its waters would had been conveniently discharged into the river. There, the remnants of a wooden shrine were found which had probably been erected by the soldiers to the goddess Minerva, the protector of warriors, to whom they made their daily offerings for their well-being. A similar shrine, in sandstone, had been erected by the legionary soldiers outside the fortress at Chester.

The interior was never excavated, but in 1949 small finds were made to the north-east of the site which included a quantity of Flavian pottery and some grey urns containing cremation burials which marked the site of the military cemetery. Other finds included the base of a flask, *mortaria* and roofing tiles.

Nearby was a trench only 2ft deep, which was filled with black soil and charcoal and contained several highly decorated fragments of Samian ware. A significant find was a broken block of sandstone, which at one time had been part of an altar. The block was only 10in high, 23in thick and 30in long, but fortunately the block bore a Latin inscription that was deemed relevant to the camp, and contained an important piece of evidence. It read:

IULIUS GAVERONIS F FE MIL CHO, I NERVIORUM

This translated as 'Julius, Son of Gaveronis, a soldier of the first cohort of the Nervii made this', thus giving the name of the garrison. The Nervii were considered to be the most warlike of the Belgic tribes living in what is now modern Belgium, and were recorded as being in Britain in AD 150. This appears to be the only surviving reference to the cohort. Only a few of these inscribed stones have been found in North Wales.

However, the inscription had been part of a larger decorative relief with only the legs of a man, those of a beast, and a wheel having survived the destruction. This surviving part of the stone was interpreted as being the carving of a man leading a beast pulling a cart. There had been another carving on the side of the stone which had featured a coiled serpent, but here, too, only part of the creature had survived the breakage. This historic stone is now preserved inside the Museum of Natural History and Archaeology at Chester.

In 1969 the timber-built barracks were found in the southern corner of the camp, which had been laid out in their usual pairs. Among the objects recovered there were many coins lost by the soldiers, among which was one of Domitian dated AD 81–96.

It was thought that the small fighting force garrisoned here was under the command of the 20th Legion.

LLANFOR

The Romans apparently favoured this part of North Wales, because as well as the fortress of Caer Gai they saturated this small area around Lake Bala with a series of military sites that were confirmed by aerial photography. With such a large number of military sites in the area, the Celtic population would have felt completely overpowered.

The first to be located was a small Roman fort measuring three acres which had been defended by two ditches but had only three gateways. Surprisingly, close-by at the village of Llanfor, on the outskirts of Bala, was a massive square-shaped enclosure measuring nearly 10 acres, which made it the largest in North Wales and equal in size to Llandeilo. And like Llandeilo, this fortress faced to the north-west.

The plan of the Roman Fort at Llanfor as revealed by a geophysical survey. It was first published in the Archaeologia Cambrensis. *(By kind permission of the Archaeologia Cambrensis.)*

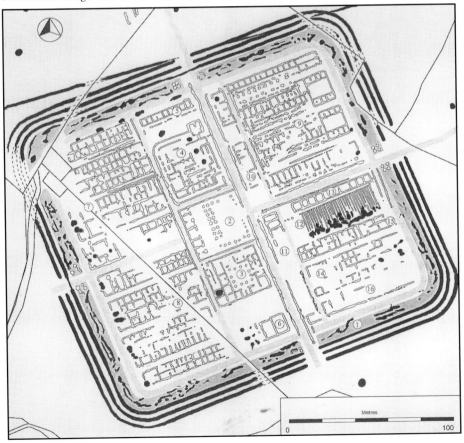

As the area in question was soon to become the site for the forthcoming National Eisteddfod in 1997, the Gwynedd Archaeological Trust decided to conduct a geophysical survey before building work took place, and this produced clear, almost photographic images of all the internal structures lying beneath the soil, and showed that every available space had been taken up with internal buildings, even to the edge of the *intervallum.*

There had been 22 barrack blocks, although they were much shorter than usual, and it was thought that they would have accommodated detachments of legionaries from the 20th Legion (Lego XX Valerie Victrix), the 14th Legion (Legio XIV Gemmia) or the Second Legion Adutrix, all of which were known to have been operating in the central and northern borderlands during the Neroian and Flavian period.

The images also made it clear that there had only been one building phase when the fortress had been constructed during the late Flavian period, with materials that were readily available like earth and timber, and signs were that the fortress had not been operating for long. An extra bonus were the images of multiple hearths, pits and walls attached to the site which indicated the location of a thriving *vicus* outside the ramparts, with its buildings flanking the roads leading into the north-west and north-east gates.

The military cemetery was located outside the north-eastern gates where a quantity of Flavian grey earthenware and cremation urns were found. Many of the urns had been decorated with simple designs.

The aerial reconnaissance also revealed a large marching camp with rounded corners a short distance from the fortress. It was twice the length of the fort and had a large compound attached to its south-west corner for drilling purposes. The entire area measured 28 acres.

CAER LLUGWY

This Roman fort lay in an open valley surrounded by tree-clad hills, between Capel Curig and Betws-y-Coed in the north-west corner of Wales, beside the River Llugwy, and it is regarded as being the most beautiful area in the district, dominated by the peak of Moel Siabod mountain rising 2,800ft above the valley. In the distance rises the great massif of Snowdonia.

The fort occupied a plateau only 1ft above the flood level. It was an important blocking post, admirably placed to control the beleaguered Ordovices.

Caer Llugwy was one of the smaller fortresses in Wales, enclosing nearly four acres, similar to Castell Collen after its reduction. Occupation began around AD 70 and ended approximately 50 years later, either during AD 120 or 140.

Roman remains were first noticed here in the 17th century, and Samuel Lysons, the antiquarian who first discovered the remains at Caerhun, outside Conway, visited the fort here and was quoted as saying that 'in all probability, the Romans favoured this part of Wales because of its slate quarries and lead mines.' He also went on to discover some of the buildings at Llugwy, which included what had been a grand building, measuring 660 x 20ft and a room 180ft square, in which were large square stone pillars that had supported a hypocaust. From the evidence of other excavations, this large building could only have been the bathhouse which was usually built on a grand scale.

A full-scale excavation was not carried out until 1920, when it was found that the fort was nearly square shaped with the usual rounded corners, all of which were exposed and each one found to have a radius of 21ft. The sides of the fort, though, had differing measurements: the north side was 39ft long, the south 378ft, the west 440ft, and the eastern side 425ft long, making a total area of approximately four acres.

The fort appeared to have been enclosed inside a stone wall 2ft thick, and judging by the amount of large stones found in the neighbouring fields the wall had originally been quite high. On the western side there was an annexe which was almost as large as the fort itself, and this extended for another 300ft. Its south wall was identified by the lines of the burnt and dried ground which made an obvious line along the surface, and raising it 2–3ft above the surrounding area to the same level as the fort. This had apparently been done to avert flooding when the river overflowed its banks to a height of 8ft. Had these measures not been taken, then the entire fort and annexe would have been completely swamped. Running water was found in one of the defensive ditches, and had probably been there since the fort was occupied.

Although the stone walls had been extensively robbed on its northern side, the remaining two-thirds appeared to be full of stone buildings extending to the south. No post holes were found, so it was unlikely that timber had been used initially as at some of the other forts.

Excavations continued in 1922, when three latrines were uncovered. Examination of the north rampart and the fort's north-west corner revealed the primitive materials used by the Roman builders and the way in which they worked.

In the north-west corner, the walls had been built with rough stones set in clay, which appeared as dark decaying vegetable matter and had survived to five courses high. In this corner, the base of a watch tower was uncovered. The road outside had been made up of river gravel which had been beaten down to form a hard surface. However, the rampart on the east, south and west appeared to have been built with roughly hammered dressed stones 5ft thick with a space of 5ft between them. The fort had been defended by two broad ditches, and outside the western rampart were the remains of much heavier masonry, which suggest that they had been crossed by a bridge.

The trenches yielded many fragments of pottery, including an *amphora* which was recovered whole. Other *amphorae* had not been so lucky, and many of their fragments revealed several curious graffiti marks. There was also an abundance of glass fragments from bottles, one of which had been coloured blue, and an abundance of nails.

Again, the lead mines in the area attracted the attention of the Roman invaders and were exploited to the full.

TOMEN-Y-MUR

The auxiliary fortress of Tomen-y-Mur was sited on the south-eastern slope of the mountain Mynydd Maentwrog and was chosen by the Romans for its extensive outlook in every direction. To the north there were uninterrupted views over the Vale of Ffestiniog, and southwards over the valley of Trawsfynydd, with the mountain of Cadair Idris in the distance, considered to be among the finest views in North Wales.

According to the *Antonine Itinerary*, the fortress was identified with Heriri Mons, the old name for the Snowdon mountain range, and was used for protecting the military road from Segontium (Caernarfon) to the other Roman fortress and town of Wroxeter on the eastern borders.

The Romans had also astutely chosen this site because it commanded the territory of the Ordovices in this part of Wales and was centrally located, with one road leading directly to the fortress of Caer Gai. The *Sarn Helen*, which had come up from the south to Dolgellau, also passed Tomen-y-Mur to reach the village of Trawsfynydd, and onwards to Conovium. This road, also known as the Great Watling Street, divided into two branches with both meeting at Segontium. Another road went on to connect with the fortresses beside Lake Bala.

While most of the forts were located on the banks of rivers, Tomen-y-Mur was the one exception, although a stream ran close to the site from which water was obtained. This stream, which still exists today, would have been constantly full of water from the mountains as, it is said, rain falls here 300 days a year.

The discovery of the fort was made from quantities of bricks that had appeared after ploughing, and during the construction of the farm gates when the farmer confessed to having cut through the fort's defences. Large quantities of roofing tiles had also surfaced. They were a lighter colour than the bricks and had been scored with evenly incised lines to make rectangular, square and diamond shapes. A number of querns had also surfaced.

When excavated in 1850, the entire area of the fort had been covered over with grass and was said to have had a curious rectangular shape that stretched across two fields. The site had already been levelled for cultivation, and ploughing had destroyed many vital areas. The northern part of the defences had also been levelled and their walls extensively robbed for building the retaining walls around the adjoining fields. There was a farmhouse to the north-east but, fortunately, the defences there were found to be intact and had been better preserved towards the western corner, despite ploughing in that area. There were no signs of any of the gateways to the fort, and it was probable that the north-eastern gate had been the first to disappear through cultivation since it was the nearest one to the farmhouse.

Outside the south-eastern side, the land sloped down towards the stream, and this, in part, had also been disturbed by the local farmers. However, on the sheltered side of the site were the remains of several buildings. These had been built on each side of the roadway running from the south-east gate in an almost straight line and were presumed to have been parts of the legionary bathhouse. Some 30ft from the stream was a ford, but as there were no signs of there having been a bridge, it was thought that the Romans had crossed this on foot. Traces of an ancient leat was found nearby which had channelled fresh water into the fort.

The interior was found to be in the region of 700 x 500ft, and when first built it was composed of earth and timber. It had a large inner bank, a ditch and an outer bank for its defences. The whole of its south-west side, though, had been levelled by ploughing. However, the surviving walls of the fort had been surrounded by an enormous ditch that was 50ft wide.

The south-east entrance was successfully uncovered, revealing a considerable portion of the masonry on its south side. This walling, 5 x 7ft, had flanked the gateway and had survived to a height of three or four courses. It had been built with squared masonry of a greenish-grey colour. This stone was identified as Cambrian grit, which was obtainable to the south-west over a large area, although the nearest outcrop was just 250 yards from the fort, providing the Roman builders with accessible building material of the highest quality. It was also observed that each stone had been precisely cut by the Roman masons and laid without the aid of cement. So expertly had the work been done, that it was impossible to insert even the finest blade between them. It was presumed from this enormous care that the Romans had intended to stay for a long while.

Inside, the fort was found to have undergone two stages of construction, having been built for the second time in stone during the early years of the second century, at about the same time as Castell Collen. It became apparent that it had been reduced to almost three-quarters of its original size when part of the garrison was transferred north and when it was considered too large and uneconomical to sustain it in its original form. Complete evacuation had taken place during AD 140.

Outside the defences was a rectangular area of level ground, which was identified as a large parade ground, but excavation revealed that this work had never been completed.

Also outside the defences was an oval-shaped amphitheatre, enclosed by high banks of earth. This was considered to be another important archaeological discovery, because this amphitheatre and the one found at Moridunum (Carmarthen) are the only two to have been found attached to auxiliary fortresses in Roman Britain. It had probably served as a theatre to entertain the garrison in this very remote region.

The banks of the amphitheatre had been so mutilated by disturbance that it was difficult to estimate its original size, but the remaining banks were 12ft high and 21–22.5ft wide, suggesting that it had been quite an imposing structure. The oval enclosure itself measured 81ft in diameter, but there were no signs of any seating plan. An old tramway from the disused Braich Ddu slate quarry had driven through its middle to make two artificial entrances situated opposite each other. Such was the ignorance of local farmers as to its historic value that a wall had been built across its southern side in which a sheep dip and pens had been installed. Even so, the remains are still an imposing feature upon the bleak landscape.

An engraving of the amphitheatre, first published in the Archaeologia Cambrensis. *(By kind permission of the Cambrian Archaeological Association.)*

On the brow of the hill, close to the fort, was a small enclosure about 34ft square, which had probably been an outpost covering the ground not visible from the fort. Between the parade ground and the north-west corner of the fort were two small rectangular areas next to each other with their own high enclosures. What purpose these served remains a mystery.

Also in the vicinity of the fort were at least eight mounds of earth of varying shapes and sizes. These were the burial places of the centurions. There were also the same corresponding number of inscribed stones, one of which was inscribed: I PERPETVI. P.XX. This referred to the centurion Julius Perpetius. A 'P' is a Latin contraction for *Passus* or paces, stating that the centurion in question had been responsible for building 20 paces of a wall. Another centurion thus remembered was Julius Mansuetus. There was a fragment of a ninth stone, but it offered no information as to why it was there. The stones are the largest number to have been found at the Welsh auxiliary fortresses. Six of the stones have now been retrieved from Harlech Castle, where they had been taken to be used in its walls.

The barrows themselves were of great interest. One, standing 8ft high, was found to have been robbed by digging right into it, and two others had been surrounded by low banks; one 17ft square and the other 20 x 22ft, both of which were almost touching each other. But the most striking and largest of all was located immediately east of the parade ground. It had been built up to form a pyramid with a flat top 22ft square and was flanked by two wings of terraces projecting along a ridge 100ft in each direction. The north-west face of this ridge had been scarped to give height and dignity to this curious and incredibly impressive monument, perhaps reflecting the importance of the person for whom it was built – perhaps the commandant himself.

A mile away, a reddish-brown urn 11in in diameter, was unearthed with a lattice pattern around its top band, and among the cremated bones was the blade of a bronze dagger, suggesting that the remains could have been those of a soldier who was interred with his weapon. Curiously, another cremation had contained a wooden bodkin, 6in long, intimating that the deceased had been a woman. When these urns had been committed into the ground, fragments of brick had been carefully placed around them in an effort to prevent crushing. It was thought that these urns had been manufactured at the fort as, during excavations, five similar urns were found in the kiln ready for firing, no doubt forgotten by the man in charge when the fort was evacuated.

Few objects were recovered from inside the fort, but it was understood that quantities of Roman objects had been taken from the site in the preceding years, mainly querns and Samian ware of the first century. No coins were found either, but a cornelian intaglio was recovered intact and is regarded as being of high-quality native workmanship.

Several practice camps were also known to have been in the area, with a group of five two miles away to the south-east and two much larger camps, over 1,100ft square, located a mile away. There was also one just 350ft away from the fort's defences.

PEN LLYSTYN

The auxiliary fortress of Pen Llystyn was built 12 miles south of Caernarfon, commanding the valleys of the Dwyfach and the Llynfni across the face of the Lleyn Peninsula, and was situated on the road leading to its neighbour at Tomen-y-Mur.

The fort was first discovered by chance while excavating for gravel from 1954–62, and was estimated to measure 448 x 356ft, giving a total of four and a half acres. An annexe of about three acres was also found to the south-west, and this was enclosed by a small ditch.

The defences of the fort measured approximately 54ft overall, and comprised two wide ditches and a rampart made of gravel, faced with turf. The gateway had double portals recessed between timber rectangular towers with turrets.

Excavations of the interior revealed such buildings as the headquarters, the commandant's house, a multi-roomed structure which was thought to have been a hospital and a complement of granaries, built entirely of timber and lying parallel with the *Via Principalis*. All buildings appeared to have had walls made from clay. In the southern half, two long buildings were discovered which were likely to have been stores and workshops. There was evidence that iron smelting had been carried out in one of them. There was also considerable evidence to support the theory that iron working had been carried out north-east of the *intervallum*. Six barrack blocks had been found altogether, with four positioned alongside the *Via Quintana*, and large post holes suggested that a timber gateway had stood across the *Via Decumana*, which had virtually separated the two parallel barrack blocks from each other.

The commandant's house had four ranges of rooms and, as was usual, they opened on to a central courtyard which had a colonnaded verandah, thus giving the rooms the benefit of quiet seclusion.

Objects recovered from the fort suggested that occupation began within a few years of AD 80 and continued for about a decade until the fort was evacuated and its buildings purposely destroyed by fire. After a short interval, a new defensive ditch had been dug across the north-eastern part of the *Via Principalis* in order to drastically reduce the size of the fort to about two and a half acres.

A smaller fort was then built over the northern quarter of the original defences, comprising a rampart made of clay and turf on a cobbled foundation and protected by one ditch only. One gateway was then made in the middle of the south-east wall and was surmounted by a wooden tower. This plan suggested that the fort had been converted into a storage depot, protected by a small body of men. It was found that water had been carried to the fort through wooden pipes which had been wrapped in clay for protection.

Decayed stumps of wood were all that remained of the earlier buildings, and, apart from the few surviving pieces of pottery confirming the commencement of occupation, there was nothing else to be found that dated later than AD 150 to suggest further activity at the fort.

BRYN GEFEILIAU

This fortress was sited in a central position in the Llugwy Valley on the Roman road running from Tomen-y-Mur to Caernarfon. Its name means the 'hill of smithies' and may indicate that ironsmiths of an Iron Age settlement may have operated in the locality.

The fort's ruins were found in a meadow within the broad loop of the river, just above the flood plain. However, it was a group of stone buildings of its annexe that led to the fort's discovery and identified it as a Roman military station. Its outline was clearly visible and was found to be almost square in shape with the usual rounded corners, and was estimated to measure 430 x 394ft along the ramparts, covering nearly four acres.

Trial excavations were begun in 1920–22, which revealed two defensive ditches; one measuring 6ft across and 6ft high, and the second 10ft wide and 4ft high. It was also found that the Romans had used very basic materials for building their ramparts, which were mainly composed of clay laid over a core of rubble and fronted with layers of turf on top of a stone kerb. Only three entrance gates were found, and while the east one was centrally placed within the rampart the southern gate was located abnormally close to the south-west corner, and the west gate was also curiously off centre.

The annexe was almost as large as the fortress. It measured 439 x 300ft and covered three acres, and it had a narrow stone wall running down its side with a wide bank which had been ploughed over on its western side. This suggested that a more substantial rampart, like that of the fort, may have run around its perimeter.

Inside the annexe, the foundations of a large stone building measuring 114 x 224ft were found, which had been divided into eight rooms with corridors interconnected with doors. The walls had been mortared with earth and cobble and the floors were made of clay, but in two rooms the floors had been made from earth. Tiles and short pillars within some rooms suggested that the building had benefitted from a hypocaust heating system. It was probable that this building may have been a boarding house, and that the annexe had sheltered a small community with traders stopping for the night.

CAERNARFON (SEGONTIUM)

With Agricola establishing auxiliary fortresses across the northern coastline of Wales, one here at a place we now know as Caernarfon was considered to be of great strategic importance since it gave the Roman fleet complete control of all shipping in the area and enabled their ships to deliver essential supplies to their troops without any undue opposition from the local tribe.

The fortress was established around AD 77, and it gave the Romans control of the Menai Straits and strengthened the military position of the conquered Lleyn Peninsula, leaving the way clear for them to conquer Anglesey. Across the area, Agricola had routed the Deceangli without mercy, as he had done with the Ordovices in central Wales, whom he had almost annihilated. However, even Agricola had succumbed to the constant warring. The ever informative Tacitus informs us that Agricola died 'not from battle, but from fatigue' in AD 193.

The Romans named their fort Segontium, which is thought to have derived from the name of the minor Celtic Segontii tribe who lived in the area. Or, it is possible that the Romans named it after the River Seigont, similar to their naming Caerleon Isca Siluria after the River Usk. The modern placename of Caernarfon literally means 'fort by/on the river'.

Llanbeblig Hill – looking down to the river with Caernarfon in the distance. The fort is behind the railings on the right of the picture.

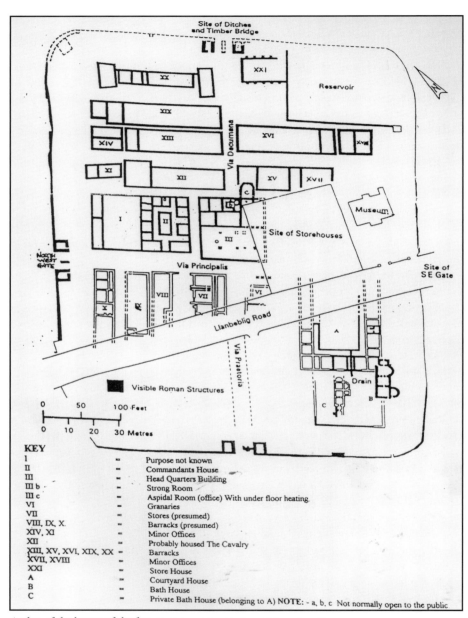

KEY

I	=	Purpose not known
II	=	Commandants House
III	=	Head Quarters Building
III b	=	Strong Room
III c	=	Aspidal Room (office) With under floor heating.
VI	=	Granaries
VII	=	Stores (presumed)
VIII, IX, X.	=	Barracks (presumed)
XIV, XI	=	Minor Offices
XII	=	Probably housed The Cavalry
XIII, XV, XVI, XIX, XX	=	Barracks
XVII, XVIII	=	Minor Offices
XXI	=	Store House
A	=	Courtyard House
B	=	Bath House
C	=	Private Bath House (belonging to A) NOTE: - a, b, c Not normally open to the public

A plan of the layout of the fort. (*By kind permission of the Gwynedd County Council.*)

Over the ages, modern Caernarfon has been one of the natural gateways into Britain from the west, and has offered safe anchorage to all sailing craft crossing the turbulent Irish Sea.

Segontium was listed as being on *Iter XI*, the 11th route in the *Antonine Itinerary*, which gave the distance of 'Segontio a Deva' (Segontium to Deva) as 74

Roman miles, i.e. 68–69 English miles, which is the actual present-day road mileage from Caernarfon to Chester.

Again, the Romans picked a commanding location for their fortress at the top of Llanbeblig Hill, a main road with a steep incline that overlooks the town of Caernarfon. There was another Roman station at the bottom of the hill, but this may have been a large works or a supplies depot. Being close to the sea and on a busy highway, the Romans had all the facilities they needed to run an efficient military station here, and it is thought that Segontium had also been the administrative centre for north-west Wales to include Anglesey, encompassing the tribal territories of the beleaguered Celts.

Early recorded evidence of the fort's existence also appeared in William Camden's fourth edition of his *Britannia* in 1594, following his visit to Wales in 1590. In it, he made the comment that 'there is a possible existence of a Roman station near to the church of Llanbeblig.' Roman artefacts found on or near to the site of the fort had also drawn people's attention to that possibility.

In 1845 a letter was addressed to the editor of the *Archaeologia Cambrensis* stating that there was a 'subterranean passage at the bottom of the hill' and that workmen had come across what they termed a 'Roman house'. As Wales did not have museums at that time, letters also expressed concern that historic artefacts were being lost to souvenir hunters. As a result of this awareness for preserving antiquities found in Wales, museums were finally established in the country.

In 1846, during the building of a new vicarage, workmen came across a well, 5ft square, which was excavated to a depth of 21ft. The sides of the well were composed of 5ft-long oblong blocks, which had been precisely chiselled and set in place without cement. Interestingly, they were found to be identical to the corner stones of Caernarfon Castle. It was suspected that stones robbed from the fort had also appeared in the castle's walls. Among the kitchen refuse in the well were the antlers of two red deer, three or four bucks' horns and a small boar's tusk. There was also an accumulation of large oyster shells, nails, some pottery, an oak bucket and a large key. A large semicircular piece of iron was also salvaged and was thought to have come from a barrel. A curious stone object about 2in high in the shape of an egg cup was also found. Sparking off interest was a flat piece of stone engraved with 2in-high letters, S and E. The stone had broken off after the letter E, but had revealed a portion of a third letter, thought to be a G, suggesting that the whole word could have been SEGONTIUM. This was the first real piece of evidence to name the fort.

Another significant discovery recovered near the vicarage at the end of the 19th century was a complete sword. The blade, slightly leaf shaped, had suffered damage through decay, and its hilt showed signs of repair. Its distinguishing feature was a rounded pommel made of ivory with bronze and copper bands beneath. The bands were regarded as being unusual. It was thought that this fine specimen could have belonged to a high-ranking officer. The original is now in the possession of the Bangor Museum, but a replica is on show at the Segontium Museum, situated on the site of the fort. Another valuable discovery was a gold cross-bow brooch, 2.5in long and 4in wide. It was

An exhibit of a sword on display at the fortress museum. (By kind permission of the National Museum of Wales, Cardiff. The original is in the Bangor Musuem.)

dated to the middle of the fourth century. Another relic was a square-shaped altar, 2ft high, which had been dumped in the churchyard until someone, realising its historic value, rescued it. The altar contained an alternate design in relief of a garland and a flagon around its four sides, but one had been defaced. The altar is also on display at the site museum.

In 1919 members of the Cambrian Archaeological Society purchased three and a half acres of land attached to the fort in order to stop modern developments from taking place so that excavations could continue without any hindrance. These took place during the summer of 1921 by the late Sir Mortimer Wheeler, then director of archaeology at the National Museum of Wales. Despite the close proximity of garden allotments, two acres of the fort were successfully excavated to reveal all the principal buildings, including two granaries, stores and the barrack blocks. The entire site is now open to the public. An excavated bathhouse, situated on the other side of the main road, can also be seen.

The fortress was said to measure 510 x 415ft, giving an area of approximately five and a half acres. Apart from Caerleon, it is the only other fortress to have provided such a wealth of information regarding its occupation.

The barracks in the north-east corner.

This photograph shows the excavated bathhouse, which is situated on the site of a villa opposite the fortress museum (the white building in background).

As with all of the other auxiliary fortresses, Segontium conformed to the usual military plan, and originally its defences and internal buildings were all made out of timber. The fort was well defended by an 18ft-wide clay rampart, a berm, varying in width between 3–7ft, and two identical ditches 17ft wide, which were separated by a gap of 15ft. The bank was composed of rammed boulder clay and was a little over 5ft high, but as the ground sloped away, it effectively added another foot to its height. Turrets had been placed along the defences but one showed that it had gone out of use by the end of the first century, and only the remains of the guardrooms flanking the gateways survived. Double roads leading into the fort had been laid with boulders and covered over with a thick layer of local slate, but these had been destroyed at some time. During the fort's long occupation of at least 300 years, it was no wonder that road surfacing had been carried out on numerous occasions.

The south-west gateway was found to be lying inside the existing vicarage grounds, and after obtaining permission from the vicar of Caernarfon to fell some trees obstructing the site, the necessary excavations were carried out. Two roadways were found to have entered the fort there and had been divided by a central pier. Their footings were remarkably still intact.

There was a space outside the north-west guardroom which had been occupied by some structure such as a large drain or aqueduct which had collapsed. Its repair was recorded on a broken inscription tablet found inside the fort. It read:

...[S]EPT. SEVERVS PIVS PER...MA AVREL ANTONI...S...AQ
VAEDVCTIVM VETVS...BS COH I SVNIC RESIT

It was translated as '[Under the Emperors] Septimius Severus Pius Pertinax and
Marcus Aurelius Antoninus, the First Cohort of Sunici restored this'. The names of
the Emperors indicate that the conduit was repaired either in AD 198 or 209. This
inscription provided an important clue that the soldiers responsible for repairing
the aqueduct had been part of the *Cohors Equitata Quingenaria*, a 500-strong unit
of mixed infantry and cavalry who had garrisoned the fort. The Sunici were a Belgic
tribe living on the shores of the Rhine and were known to have come to Britain
around AD 124.

Just inside the defences, a pair of bronze cupids surfaced, as did another lead figure
holding a cylindrical object which was a holder for a torch. Another unusual discovery
outside the fortress was a gold Gnostic talisman, 4in long and 1in wide and covered
with roughly inscribed lettering in Greek, thought to have come from a grave. The
opening lines contained the names of Adonai, Eloi and Sabaoth, and it also mentioned
four of the seven planets, namely the Sun, Jupiter, Mars and the Moon. The last three
lines read 'protect me Alphianos'. It appeared to be associated with the mystic belief
established in Syria during the third century and had obviously been a good luck
charm to its owner. The talisman proved interesting in that it highlighted the
cosmopolitan character of the culture enjoyed by the inhabitants of Segontium during
the third and fourth centuries.

During excavations of the fort's interior in 1921–23, surviving pottery shards
and coins suggested that there had been three periods of military occupation: AD
75–140, 210–290 and 355 or 365, spanning well over 200 years, during which time
several phases of rebuilding had taken place, notably in the headquarters and the
commandant's house.

Two main streets were also excavated: the *Via Principalis* and the *Via Decumana*, which
divided the barracks in the top half of the fort. The width of the first was 22ft, with one
end having been paved with cobbles and the other end gravelled. Here a coin of
Constantine II was found, (AD 320–324). The *Via Decumana* had been well cambered and
ran at right angles to the *Via Principalis* but was only 13.5ft wide. Some coins of
Valentinian I (AD 364–375) and of Valens (AD 364–378) were also recovered.

Excavation of the headquarters building proved interesting. It once had sculptured
archways over its entrance and a central courtyard surrounded by a verandah. The
courtyard itself had been laid with a mixture of broken roof tiles and other matter, and
had a well in its centre. At the rear of the building were a range of rooms flanking the
Sacellum. Between them was a long hall that appeared to have been divided by wooden
partitions. There was also a group of five rooms that had been the offices of the
administrative staff, and these had been screened off by curtains. The *Principia* had
been rebuilt in the third century when a small apsidal room, projecting from the back
wall and heated by a channelled hypocaust, was added to the plans that included a
sunken safe inside the *Sacellum*. Being the most important room in the building, the

The sunken safe in the Sacellum of the headquarters building.

Sacellum was the only one to have its walls decorated with painted plaster. This contained striped patterns in bright red, blue, yellow and green. Hidden underneath its floor, the sunken safe was entered by a flight of five stone steps and measured 10 x 9ft and was 5ft deep. Its original floor had been laid with large well-squared slabs of local stone, carefully grouted with pink cement and raised 7in above a clay floor. It was thought that the Roman builders had intended to lay this as a precaution against the dampness of a wet winter. A thick layer of salt had then been laid to ensure complete damp-proofing. During this work, one of the workers had dropped a *denarius* of Elagabalus (AD 218–222) which was found under a large slab on the original floor. Three silver *denarii* were also discovered under some slates: one from the time of Faustina the Elder (died AD 141), one of Severus Alexander (AD 222–235), and one belonging to the reign of Julia Mamaea (died AD 235), all of which were in almost mint condition when lost. *Denarii* were given to soldiers in their pay packets and, being small, were easily lost.

A surprising find in the cellar was a 16in-high altar dedicated to Minerva, goddess of wisdom. It read:

DEAE MINERVAE AR SABINANVS ACT. V. S. L. M.

Translated, it read: 'To the Goddess Minerva, Aurelius Sabinanus, Actarius, gratefully fulfils his vow.'

Minerva was also a goddess favoured by scribes, so it would appear that she had become the chosen goddess of the administrative and clerical division of the army, of

The shrine dedicated to Minerva.

which Sabinanus, the above mentioned Actarius, was part. An Actarius was a kind of quartermaster who was responsible for securing the necessary allotment of rations to the recruits and organised their distribution at the granaries and other store houses. As there was no rank of quartermaster in the Roman army before the beginning of the third century, it was reasonable to assume that the altar belonged to that period. The style of lettering was said to have been characteristic of the third century. Made from local sandstone, the mountings showed traces of plaster or cement which had been used to conceal the natural defects in the stone, and traces of the red paint used to highlight the letters was still visible in the grooves. It is more than likely that Sabinanus, in not being able to take the altar away when he left, had hidden it there to escape possible desecration from gangs who were known to invade Roman forts after they had been abandoned to steal their treasures. Also found in the cellar was a fragment of an iron box and a hoard of 114 coins, which had obviously been its contents. It is strange that this money should have been left behind when the fort was evacuated. The cellar had suffered neglect during the abandonment of the fort, during which its trap door had broken off and allowed soil to drift down from the surface to cover the floor with a layer 18in thick.

Third-century coins suggested that the *Sacellum* had been refloored not later than the time of Elagabalus (AD 218–222) and had continued in use until the middle of the third century. However, further evidence showed that it had been razed to the ground before the end of the fourth century. Coins from the reigns of Constans to Gratian (AD 367–383) were also found in abundance on the uppermost floors throughout the *Principia*, including over 200 from AD 290–350.

Next door was the commandant's house. It consisted of six rooms on one side of a courtyard with four on the other. One of the rooms was thought to have been a domestic shrine, as it contained a pedestal on which a statue or an altar had stood. This room had three doors, giving access to the courtyard with a verandah supported by timber posts. It had been completely redesigned when a new colonnade had been laid out with re-used base blocks, seven of which were still in place. However, the builders had resorted to makeshift methods when broken roofing tiles had been mixed with other materials to use as metalling for the courtyard.

The granaries were lying opposite the principal buildings on the other side of the

Via Principalis and had been divided into three storage compartments, but the Llanbeblig main road had cut through the end store on its south side.

Although the garrison was withdrawn in AD 290, evidence from the coins suggests that the fort was re-occupied again 60 years later, and that occupation came to an end around AD 380 or 390, soon after the reign of Carausus. At this time, there was a period of violence and unrest when invaders took possession of Segontium. This was also a time when Christians vented their hatred on the monuments and buildings they regarded as anti-Christ, either by defacing them or destroying them altogether. Taking this into consideration, it is therefore not surprising that only a few inscription slabs have survived inside the fort. During excavation, it was found that the arched entrance over the *Sacellum* had been wrecked, probably at this time, along with the stone sculptures which had appeared over the gateways. Much of the remaining stonework also disappeared when it was taken away for building purposes, and in the end very little of the fort remained. The only inscription of the second century to have survived is the one recording the restoration of the viaduct by a cohort of the garrison. Even the inscribed tombstones which had once lined the main roads had been uprooted by vengeful intruders.

The final days of the fort were undoubtedly after the Romans had left, indicated by a small room having been built within the south-eastern guardroom and occupying about two-thirds of its area. It had apparently been built after the main structure had fallen into ruin. Unlike the well-mortared work of the Roman era, the flimsy walls of this new structure had been roughly held together with clay, and it was regarded as belonging to the period we often refer to as the 'Dark Ages'. It was probably a make-shift shelter for some migrant family. Interestingly, beneath the lowest step of the entrance, a *styca*, a coin of the Northumbrian King Eaured (AD 808–840), was discovered. This seems to be the earliest of the very few Saxon coins to have been found in Wales. In fact, Northumbrian coins are rarely found outside Northumbria. A few coins from the reign of King Edgar (AD 959–975) were also found, but were then subsequently lost at Bangor.

It was during periods of unrest that people buried their life savings and treasured possessions as a safeguard against robbers and intruders in the area. Many hoards were left forgotten, either because their owners had suddenly died or because they had been forced to leave their homes, and had not told their families of their hiding places. Eighty-six such hoards are known to have been buried in Wales, and at least 36 of these had been buried within a few years of AD 300.

As a result of the discovery of so many coins at Segontium, archaeologists were able to date the fortress with more certainty. Among the last to be found were 22 belonging to the reign of Gratian (AD 367–383), thus providing evidence that the military occupation of Segontium lasted until the end of the fourth century.

However, Segontium had not fully revealed all its secrets. In April 1985, while workmen were digging trenches to take sewer pipes for the proposed housing estate on land beside the fort, they struck the foundations of a large structure, the discovery of which provided the modern world with one last glimpse into the Roman era, and particularly the religious life at Segontium from the first to the third century.

The Mithraeum

At once, the archaeologists recognised the layout of a *Mithraeum*, a temple dedicated to the mythological god Mithras. The Caernarfon Borough Council were instantly informed, and in response they agreed to halt further work so that the new structure could be investigated.

Mithras was, in reality, a mythological character of Persian origin, but was introduced and accepted into Roman culture in AD 68. As god of light, Mithras represented the power of goodness and promised his followers that they would be recompensed after death for the evil they had suffered in life. In mythology, too, Mithras was said to have killed the sacred bull from which all life sprung, and a bath in the blood of a bull was said to have formed part of the initiation ceremony of the Mithraic cult. One of the essential elements of a *Mithraeum* was a windowless sunken nave which represented the cave in which Mithras had killed the bull. These naves were lit by artificial light, mainly from burning torches, and it can be presumed that the torch bearer, found previously, had once been part of the lighting arrangements. No less than 12 candle-holders were found in the northern end of the building, where they had illuminated the sanctuary area of Phase III. At least six were found to have come from the same mould.

Excavations were carried out by the National Museum of Wales on behalf of the then Ministry of Works. They found that the *Mithraeum* measured 48ft by 21.5ft, and although much of the foundations had been destroyed long before the modern-day workmen had dug into them, much of the architectural plan was still recognisable.

Evidence showed that the temple had been functional during a period of great activity at the fort, and that the life of the temple continued into the third century in conjunction with the large civilian settlement which had established itself on all three sides of the fort.

As the excavations progressed, many aspects of the temple emerged, including an antechamber with an alcove. This was the shrine where images of the god were displayed. The shrine itself measured 35 x 18ft.

The nave was 35ft long and had a raised floor covered with fine gravel. Down each side would have been benches on which the participants sat and which would have been covered with fur or some kind of matting for comfort. On either side of the benches a sill was detected where ritual feasts would have been consumed. Cobbling laid on the natural soil beneath the nave's foundations revealed that there had been another building on the site long before the *Mithraeum* was built. This cobbling was covered by a layer of soil, 14in thick, and suggested that quite some time had elapsed between the erection of the two buildings. There was no way of knowing what the other building had been, only that it had not been for religious purposes. In the south wall of the nave was an entrance 5ft wide which had been finished with a sill of soft pink sandstone. The floor of the nave had been made of brick mortar 2in thick, but this had completely rotted. The step, too, leading down from the *narthex* or antechamber, had been destroyed by the modern trench work for the housing estate.

The foundations of the antechamber had been totally destroyed, and the original floor had almost vanished. Outside, though, was a patch of cobbling which suggested that some kind of shelter had been erected over it. The wall between the *narthex* and the nave had been built with much heavier stones, but the workmanship was considered poor for such a building and was similar to the poor contemporary work at the fort. The *Mithraeum* had been roofed in three phases in purple Cambrian slate which had been obtained locally. The individual slabs were thought to have weighed between 9 and 14lb each, and measured about 16 x 14in and half an inch thick. Cambrian slate was also exported to Chester. The insertion of timber colonnades inside the *Mithraeum* was the main feature of Phase II which was to render the roof of Phase I safe. Ten bases were found, with each one having a central, squared mortise to fit the base of the post. Only bases one, two, three and nine had remained in their original positions. Others had been moved and probably used as altar pedestals. In the foundations were two recognisable shards of first and second-century pottery, including a flagon and three *denarii* of Faustina, dating the temple to the third century. A complete beaker and a tin cup, presumably used in the rituals, were also found, including a chain made of fine links. Beneath an altar lay fragments of ironwork which included a bell only 1in high. Even its clapper had survived. Several of these fragments were then placed together to form a two-branched candle-holder, considered to be of an unusual type. The socket at the base suggested that the candelabrum had been fixed to a pole and carried as a standard during the ceremonies, and that the little bell, with others, had been suspended from it by the chain.

When the rubble filling in the nave was cleared, the brown soil changed into a layer of ash and charcoal in which were fragments of large, squared oak beams. Below this layer, a thin film of brown earth was found directly on top of the Phase III floor. There was little doubt that this represented a period of abandonment when the *Mithraeum* lost its roof and had been opened to the elements.

No Mithraic sculptures were anywhere to be found, apart from the altars. It is probable that they were destroyed by vengeful intruders. Only six Mithraic temples have been found in Britain so far. The others are located at Walbrook in south-east England, three on Hadrian's Wall, and the last one emerged in the City of London. While Mithraic sculptures have been found at Caerleon, Carmarthen, Chester, Carlisle and Castlesteads, suggesting that *Mithraea* were there, none of their buildings have yet been found.

Like the fortress, the *Mithraeum* fell into irreversible decline and had its walls robbed, almost down to the foundations, but through the good fortune of modern excavation its resurrection has given a good account of its past history.

HOLYHEAD (CAERGYBI)

Caergybi fortress, which was designed as a small coastguard unit as part of the Segontium–Deva defences, also served as a shelter for the coastal patrols waiting to intercept Irish invaders during the last days of Roman rule.

This little fort was an oblong enclosure, 230ft in length and 150ft broad, extending less than an acre in area. On investigation, it lay beneath the old church and churchyard at what is now Holyhead. The modern South Road also ran through the fort. The western end of the fort disappeared when the cliff was cut back to admit the railway and the modern harbour at its foot.

At the time of the Romans, the seashore came right up to the edge of the cliff, and as the fort commanded such a strategic position at the top of this 40ft rock face, any approaching enemy would have been rapidly repulsed. The rugged face of the cliff had been strengthened by the application of masonry and was supported at one place by a strongly constructed arch about 20ft in diameter. As part of their defences, on the three landward sides the Romans built curtain walls 5.5ft thick, made of cemented rubble with very roughly dressed stones set in a distinctive herringbone pattern. The lavish use of mortar on the walls suggest third or fourth century workmanship. On the

The surviving Roman walls and the impressive arch of the northern gateway. First published in the Archaeologia Cambrensis. *(By kind permission of the Cambrian Archaeological Association.)*

north and west sides, the adjacent ground varied according to the gentle upward slope of the hill, but on the eastern (seaward) side it had a high vantage point, which was all-important to the Roman defenders. They also had a strong bastion at each corner of the fort. Built into the junction of the north and west walls were the remains of the north-west tower, 15ft in diameter, which had survived to a height of 12ft. It was considered to be of an unusual construction, being a three-quarter round structure that was partly hollow. Although the northern part of the tower had been destroyed, a short length of its arc had survived with the rest of the walling, 2.5ft thick, standing only four courses high and extending another 14.5ft eastwards. Here again, the stonework had been constructed in the distinctive herringbone pattern. Modern buildings had, though, almost obliterated the south-west tower.

The discovery of a parapet, nearly 2ft wide, was probably part of a rampart walk and would originally have been 3.5ft wide. Here, the brow of the cliff was outlined by a low wall which had replaced an earlier parapet, and the careful strengthening of the cliff suggested that a similar parapet was intended as a rampart walk to complete the original seaward defences.

The north wall of the fort had an imposing arched entrance, and the entire wall was given some cosmetic treatment in 1951 to prevent further decay after centuries of weathering. On the whole, the excellence of the Roman workmanship had ensured its durability, and the repaired wall stands as a sturdy reminder of their expertise.

As the church and its churchyard dominate the site, no excavation has been possible.

CAERHUN (CANOVIUM)

T he auxiliary fortress of Canovium was established in the heart of the Deceangli territories, a few miles north of Bryn-y-Gefeiliau at the top end of the same Roman road that had come northwards from Llandovery. The fort was discovered in Caerhun Park, four miles from the town of Conway. Following excavations in the 1920s, the site reverted back to the farmland it had become.

Canovium was mentioned in the *Antonine Itinerary* as being on *Iter XI*, Route 11, and was also described as being on the road from 'Segontio a Deva'. The first stage of the journey was given as 'Conovio XXI a Segontio' (21 Roman miles) on a Roman milestone which was found buried alongside the Roman road at Llanfairfechan. In modern terms, Canovium is 24 miles to the east of Segontium (Caernarfon). This milestone was certainly instrumental in identifying the site as the long-lost fortress of Canovium listed in the *Itinerary*. The excavations revealed that the Romans established their fortress here around AD 70. It commanded a strategic position alongside the navigable and broad Conway river, which enabled the Roman fleet to sail directly in from the sea to the fortress's riverside entrance and deliver both men and supplies. The structure also commanded a high viewpoint on top of land which sloped steeply down to the river's edge, thus creating an awesome picture of power and strength.

In 1696 and 1697 the Welsh antiquarian Edward Lhwyd visited the site and identified the ruins as being of a military character from its rampart and surrounding ditches. He also discovered stonework in several places. Another antiquarian, Samuel Lysons, from London, came across the hypocaust of the bathhouse and excavated the whole building in 1801. The discovery of the bathhouse outside the eastern ramparts drew the attention of many visitors to the site in search of relics during the 18th and 19th centuries, and many valuable artefacts were taken away and remain in private hands. Coins in particular were easy bounty, and a member of a local family went on record as saying that they 'had played with hundreds in the nursery'.

One item of historic value to have been rescued was a circular shield with a covering of leather and a stump of iron at the back for a handle. This was identified as having been used by a native warrior and had probably been taken as a trophy after a battle by some victorious Roman soldier. A small iron shield was also discovered, 13–14in in diameter, which had been studded with brass beads for decoration. Tiles were also dug up in abundance. Many had been stamped LEG XX which implied that a cohort of the 20th Legion had been stationed there. Lead weights were also found in one of the cottage gardens, with one having an engraving of a human face.

Excavations began in July 1926, when it was found that the fort was in the form of a rough square with external measurements of 460ft, and 410ft internally, giving an area of nearly four acres. As at other forts, the Roman builders began by using the natural materials around them and built their defences with clay and timber. Later, the clay rampart, which was 24ft thick, was strengthened with a stone wall, and one ditch was divided in two by adding a midrib. Originally, the rampart had been resting on a layer of clay 3–4ins deep which had been thrown up from the ditch. On this foundation a pile of boulders had been laid, measuring nearly 10ft across and 2in thick. They were then covered over with a layer of clay which had been brought up from the river bed. An annexe, measuring just half an acre, was found attached to the southern rampart. A curious discovery in the filling of a well near the *intervallum* was a large tile bearing the imprint of a child's foot. The tile was similar to those used for the *pilae* of hypocausts, and its presence so deep in the well may have been the result of the well having become filled up during the time when the fort was being rebuilt, thus suggesting that the bathhouse had been built at the same time during the mid-first century. Also in the well were the remnants of a pointed oak stake, 6ft 5in tall, which had been a *vallus* or pointed stake used to form the *vallum* or palisade on the top of the rampart as an extra deterrent from attack. This stake had probably been thrown into the well when the palisade was dismantled in the second century in favour of a stone wall.

The east, west and southern gates were all excavated, but the northern gateway lay under a thick yew hedge. It was found that the church and its graveyard had been built over the north-east corner of the fort, thus obliterating all buildings in that quarter. The roots of the yew trees there also made excavation difficult. However, in spite of this, one-eighth of the fortress was excavated in that year, commencing with the east gate which lay immediately opposite the churchyard. The Roman road ran through this gateway and showed two levels of construction. The gateway itself also showed

The site of the fortress of Canovium on the banks of the River Conway.

two periods of construction; one of timber and the other when the fort had been rebuilt with well-squared blocks of stone during Trajan's reign, around AD 105–110. The stone gateway had previously been made of timber and had projected 7–8ft outwards from the wall, so that the back wall of the guardroom was in line with the summit of the rampart. Because of the steepness of the slope, it was thought that all doors facing the river opened outwards. Throughout the fort very little of its walls remained. Only their foundations had survived to about 3–4 courses high. Nevertheless, enough remained to enable the archaeologists to identify each building.

The buildings in the lower half of the fortress had also been extensively robbed, with most of the stone ending up in the walls of Caerhun Church. The stone robbing had also extended to the neighbouring farm cottages including their retaining walls. During the rebuilding in stone, it was discovered that the *Principia* had never been completed. Its walls and those of the east gate were found to have fallen in the order they had collapsed and had therefore escaped the stone robbers.

Ovens were located along the rampart roadway and close to the barrack blocks, which offered the soldiers easy access for cooking their meals.

The *Principia* occupied the centre of the fort where there was a distinct fall in the ground. It was a nearly square building, measuring 100ft east to west by 98ft north to south, with walls made from local stone nearly 3ft thick. A modern pathway cut across its southwest corner and this, along with two trees, made excavation a little difficult, although much of its floor plan was recovered. Along the back of the building was the usual range of five rooms, in front of which was a cross-hall with clay floors indicating that it had been roofed, otherwise the floors would have turned into a sea of mud

A detailed plan of the fortress at Caerhun, with the substantial buildings marked with Roman numerals.

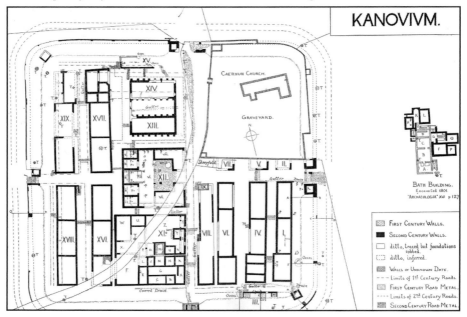

during wet weather. The area between two of the rooms was floored with gravel, and below this gravel was a thin layer of what looked like powdered sandstone. This may have resulted from the practice of sawing sandstone blocks to their required size. It was thought that this had been a courtyard that had been partially covered by a verandah roof supported by columns. Here, several large blocks of sandstone were found. Also there was a roughly circular depression, 2ft 4in in diameter, which was clearly intended to form the foundation for the circular base of a column. One such base was found close by. There was also a well in the courtyard. On the floor of room three, which was presumed to be the *Sacellum*, were fragments of painted plaster, and there was enough to show that it was cream-coloured and had a design of red and yellow stripes and was bordered with black and green. One particular fragment had a pattern of green leaves with yellow stalks. Unfortunately, the fragments were too small to restore the whole design. The debris also abounded fragments of roof tiles, as well as cockles, oyster and mussel shells, but only a few dozen potsherds, all of which were Samian, with one bearing an imperfect stamp marked EMI. The headquarters had not, however, been the only building on that spot. Two post holes sunk into the natural soil testified that a timber building had preceded it in which the *Sacellum* had been built in stone and elaborately decorated with painted plaster, but when general rebuilding had taken place the *Sacellum* had suffered the same fate as its wooden neighbours. A stone-built *Sacellum* in a timber building was considered unusual, although not uncommon, since an earlier fort at Newstead appeared to have had the same arrangement. The stone headquarters at Canovium was raised during the first years of the second century, although evidence for occupation in that century was meagre. No pottery was found, but a curious discovery was a letter 'D' made of lead, nearly 2in high and 1in thick. It had probably been used for inserting into stone for engraving purposes. Several *mortaria* rims were found and a piece of a well-decorated Samian bowl. Judging from its condition, it must have been exposed to the weather for a considerably long time. Along with these items was a halfpenny coin dated 1699. The sunken safe in the *Sacellum* showed that items had been thrown in when the fort was being dismantled. Included among them was a column and its base from the courtyard. It was noted that the floors in all the rooms were covered with considerable quantities of small pieces of lead sheeting and that roof tiles were noticeably absent. It was then conjectured that the Romans, having discovered the reliability of lead, which was plentiful in the neighbourhood, had begun using it on their roofs. There were also considerable traces of timber building, beneath the second-century structure, with post holes going in a straight line all through the rooms along its western side.

The commandant's house, building XI, standing adjacent to the headquarters building, was of a rectangular shape, measuring 112ft east to west, and 118ft north to south. The modern lane which had cut through the headquarters also ran through the interior of this one. Again, trees obstructed some of the excavations. In the northern part, the walls had been extensively robbed, but they had survived in the south to two courses high. Some of the rooms contained local stone, but when the building fell into disrepair, better quality red sandstone from Cheshire was used for rebuilding in the fourth century. In room I of the house, a pit was found lined with tiles, suggesting that it may have been used as a temporary regimental safe during the period before one was built in the headquarters. A number of Trajanic coins found in the foundations marked the construction of the commandant's house to that era, between AD 103 and 115. This number also included a *denarius* of Trajan in mint condition. A large piece of a Samian bowl was found right up against the south wall of one room. Its decoration was characteristic of the early east Gaulish work of the pottery of La Madelaine. A black *olla* with a ribbed trellis pattern and considerable fragments of at least eight vessels were also found. More personal items included a makeshift draughtboard which had been made out of a piece of slate and roughly marked into squares. Such boards have been found on many Roman sites. The overall plan of the commandant's house was totally different to the one at Segontium and was regarded as being abnormally large. Here, there were at least 12 rooms crammed in the south-east corner, one of which covered the area occupied by three of its neighbours. In the courtyard there were at least six timber uprights for a wooden verandah, and an outside fire had also been lit there at some time. The courtyard had also had its first-century surface re-laid at a later period, and a slate-lined gulley had carried off the excess rainwater, probably into the gutter lying between the house and the headquarters building.

Two complete barrack blocks built during the second century were excavated, and in barrack I, next to the *intervallum*, the centurion's quarters comprised one large area, while its neighbour, barrack IV, had been divided into three separate compartments with dividing walls. The centurion's quarters in the next block had also comprised one large living area. At Caerleon, the living quarters had been split up into at least 10–12 small compartments, but here the plan had been totally different. All the barracks in this small group showed three successive occupation levels and had been built at the same time as the other stone buildings in the fort.

Also in barrack I, occasional signs of burning suggested the presence of hearths, and its eastern wall showed signs that it had been subjected to intense heat. A layer of ash as much as 19in thick covered one floor. In the bottom barrack, barrack VIII, there were no dividing walls at all, presenting one long area. It was thought that this building may have been a stable, as there were only slight indications of occupation when a few pieces of pottery appeared. However, all the corresponding barracks, numbered II, V, and VII on the opposite side, lay beneath the churchyard, and only their outside walls, built in the second century, could be excavated.

Another group of barracks were located close to the riverside rampart. These were 168ft long and 32.5ft wide and had been divided into three rooms with 3ft-thick walls. The barracks produced an assortment of finds, including an arrowhead made from flint and a fair amount of pottery, mainly Samian. One barrack was found to have had stone slabs forming a threshold. Many of these slabs were still in place, and they too had shown a slight projection forward.

Two buttressed granaries were also excavated. These were buildings XIII and XIV, and were located just beyond the walls of the churchyard and faced down the hill

towards the river. Regrettably, these had also been extensively robbed, with the culprits having dug along the lines of their walls to remove all the larger stones and throw back the smaller ones. The buttresses, though, had escaped the plundering. There were eight in all, 2.5ft square and 7.5ft apart. Measurements of the buildings showed that each one was 74.5 x 29.5ft externally and 67.5 x 29.5ft internally. All of the foundations had been packed with blue puddled clay. Alongside the granaries was a road running east to west which enabled the grain to be delivered. In building IX there was a water tank which was merely a pit dug into the natural clay, 10.25ft x 16.5ft and only 1ft deep. It had been built with small stones set in cement containing a large quantity of brick dust. This mixture seems to have been common in Roman building when the cement was intended to be watertight. The only object found inside was the bottom of a Samian bowl, dated AD 75–85.

Building XV, situated alongside the *intervallum*, had probably been a cookhouse. There, a flanged *mortarium* was found under the occupation layers of the floor.

For a fort of this size, it was disappointing to find only one small fragment that had been part of an inscription. This contained only two letters and was separated with an oblique: 0 / A. It had been expertly cut in the style of second-century lettering and was thought to have been part of a dedicatory inscription that had hung over the east gate. What these letters represented, there is no way of knowing, and it remains one of Canovium's unsolved mysteries.

Canovium continued to be occupied until the early years of the fifth century, and it was thought that a Romanised township had existed here for 200 years without any military force in the neighbourhood.

After the archaeologists had completed their 1926 investigation, all the excavations were filled in. It was already approaching nightfall and consideration was given to the horses in the field.

PRESTATYN

This fort was discovered in the summer of 1933 by Gilbert Smith, who devoted the next three years to the exploration of the site at his own expense. A trial trench, excavated along the south side of the Ysgol Llys playing field, finally revealed the presence of the fort. Here, too, the fort was situated on high ground commanding the surrounding area at a place in North Wales regarded by the Romans as being of great importance in their military strategy to occupy the territory.

In 1934 three sections of the defences were explored, and a ditch was found in the north-western direction to a distance of 150ft. It was thought that the defensive ditch may have protected a civilian settlement of some kind outside the fort.

The regimental bathhouse was located where many fragments of roofing tiles were found with the usual triangular shape and stamped LEG XX V.V., which identified the garrison as the 20th Legion. The addition of the letters 'V.V.', meaning *Valeria Victrix*, referred to the battle honour conferred upon the legion by the reigning Emperor. The legion's emblem of a charging boar with its standard also appeared on the tiles. These were brownish-red in colour and had come from the legion's kilns at Holt. One ditch was found to have become filled with wood ashes, meat bones and fragments of pottery, which had formed a layer of charcoal sometime during the second century. The southern line of the defensive ditch was found to run almost continuously from the south-east corner to a distance of 150ft, and it was here that three buildings were found lying on the southern slope.

Building I was rectangular, 62.5 x 23ft, and was divided into three large compartments, with the western room measuring 18.5 x 17ft. It had a shallow hearth in which was a thin layer of charcoal. The central room measured 18.5 x 6ft, and it too had a shallow clay hearth. The eastern room was much larger at 32.5 x 18ft, and it had a small patch of flooring in the north-west corner consisting of a primary layer of sand on which a carefully selected layer of pebbles had been placed. While most of the walls consisted of irregular pieces of limestone set in clay, the northern wall had been built with quarry-faced blocks of Gwespyr sandstone. The whole had then been capped with a thin layer of fine gravel and clay. A bronze coin of Vespasian, dated AD 71, was found in the western room, with two fragments of a Samian platter. No tile fragments were found, and it was assumed that the building had been covered with a thatched roof, or similar. The finds suggested that it had been built during the late first to early second century. Its function, however, was not clear.

Building II was 36.5ft long and again Gwespyr sandstone had been used, and a large fragment of an *amphora* was found embedded in the floor foundations. There was a fairly thick deposit of charcoal along the north side of the building, which indicated that it had been destroyed by fire. No dateable material was found, but in the absence of broken roofing tiles and bricks this pointed to an early period of occupation.

It transpired that building III was the bathhouse. It was discovered several feet under the surface and comprised three large rooms with an overall measurement of

47 x 18ft. The cold plunge bath had a floor composed of a thick layer of brick cement, while the floor of the *caldarium* was made of fine gravel to a thickness of 3in. Only the bases of the two hypocausts remained, each one consisting of a central square brick set in mortar, and each one bearing the legion's insignia and stamp.

At a later date, the baths had been extended with a raised aqueduct and water towers built to supply water to the *frigidarium*. This portion of the building appeared to have been added as an annexe to the hypocaust-heated rooms, and was constructed entirely of undressed blocks of limestone set in puddled clay. All traces of its floor had been destroyed, but its primary foundation had survived. This consisted mainly of irregular blocks of limestone, many of which showed signs of having been worn away by water. Water from the bath was discharged via a timber-lined drain extending south of the cold plunge bath. Antefixes were also found, with most also showing the legion's insignia. Most of the examples were in the upper stratum, dated to the second century. The foundations of two buttresses were also found projecting 3.5ft away from the external wall. These had been placed on the downhill side of the building and had served as supports.

The cold water bath was approximately 8 x 5ft and had a floor composed of a thick layer of brick cement which might not have been comfortable on naked feet. Its sides had also been lined with the same material to make it watertight.

Looking from the west of the excavation of Building III (the bathhouse) at the Roman station at Prestatyn. It was first published in the Archaeologia Cambrensis. *(By kind permission of the Cambrian Archaeological Association.)*

The hypocaust room of the *tepidarium* measured 11.5 x 8.5ft, but only the bases of two hypocausts had remained, each one made up of single bricks 11in square, such as those made at Holt, and bearing the legion's stamp: LEG XX VV. Its floor was composed of broken limestone and boulders set in clay to a depth of 3ft.

The hypocaust room of the *caldarium* measured 12.25 x 12ft, and its floors showed a different method of construction. Here, the floor consisted of fine gravel with traces of mortar in many places.

The furnace was centrally placed at the west end of the building, and its floor had been flagged with two large blocks of purple sandstone which had come from the St Asaph district. Two short walls, composed of a single course of bricks, also 11in square, had probably supported a cauldron for the supply of hot water for washing. Some pottery was found beneath a layer of charcoal which included the rim fragments of Samian dishes, all attributable to the latter half of the second century. As there was another thin layer of charcoal beneath, the upper layer was thought to have represented the period when the bathhouse was demolished.

In all, 13 timber buildings were excavated inside the fort, dated AD 80–160. Three of these had been copper-alloy workshops producing brooches and probably harness fittings. The workshops were the same date as the first phase of the bathhouse, about the late first to early second century.

Ceramic remains revealed that the fort had been occupied from the second to the fourth century. Among the finds was the rim of a cooking pot of dark fumed grey with a rivet of lead still in place. This suggested that the utensil had been mended. Also found was a curious shield-shaped piece of lead weighing nearly 2lb, which was 10in high. It had a series of circular studs and iron staples creating an unusual design.

Unrelated to the fort, but curious nevertheless, was the discovery of an infant's burial in a fenced off enclosure. Radiocarbon dating revealed that the burial had taken place sometime during the last century BC. This would indicate that a late Iron Age settlement had occupied the site long before the arrival of the Romans.

CHESTER (DEVA)

The siting of a new fortress here on the eastern banks of such a wide and navigable river as the Dee was a great strategic decision on behalf of the Roman military, since it controlled the Dee's estuary and enabled ships to deliver supplies and men to its door. Inscriptions from the site, such as a length of lead water piping on which was stamped Vespasian's name, gave the construction date to around AD 78, the year Julius Agricola, Frontinus's successor, was appointed governor. Another interesting discovery of this period was a lead ingot with the name of Agricola stamped on one side and the name of the Deceangli on another. It is known that the lead mines of neighbouring Flintshire in Deceangli territory were in full operation by the year AD 74, and that they were fully exploited by the Romans. Over the years they transported vast quantities of the lead to the fortress for making water pipes.

With the fortress situated in this north-east corner of Wales, it enabled Agricola to launch his offensive across the Deceangli tribal lands and invade Anglesey where he eliminated the druids. Thereafter, the conquest of North Wales was complete.

The purpose of the fortress was also to impose a barrier between North Wales and the Pennines in order to prevent the tribes of those areas from meeting up and causing serious trouble during the latter stages of the conquest. Strategically, too, the fortress lay at the junction of several major roads leading to the fortresses of central Wales and westwards to Caernarfon. It was also connected to its other sister fortress at York. More importantly, it lay on Watling Street, which was one of the great arterial roads of Roman Britain, running north-west from London to Wroxeter where it met the military road going from Chester to Caerleon. Subsequently, the fortress became a focal point of communication both by land and by sea.

With the river running alongside the western defences, the Romans built a quay beside the west gate, thus allowing ships bringing in supplies to anchor there. The river also ran along its southern defences to provide a natural defence.

The Romans gave their new fortress the Celtic name of Deva, after the river and meaning 'goddess', arising from the fact that both the Celts and the Romans considered that all rivers possessed divine spirits. The name appeared several times among the 15 routes mentioned in the *Antonine Itinerary*, first as *Iter II* on the route from the 'Entrenchments' (Hadrian's Wall) to the port of Rutupiae (Richborough in Kent), the port of embarkation from the Continent. On this route, Deva was mentioned as Deva Leg XX Vict. Deva also featured on *Iter XI*, being the route from Segontium. Its subsequent name, Deva Victrix, appeared in the *Ravenna Cosmography* of the seventh century. The title *Victrix* was an honour given to those legions who had helped in the defeat of Boudicca's rebellion.

The construction of this great fortress in around AD 78 was assigned to the men of the Second Legion Adiutrix pia fidelis, shortened to Legio II Adiutrix, on the evidence of 11 tombstones recovered from the site, and a length of lead water piping bearing Vespasian's name. Legio II Adiutrix was eventually withdrawn from Britain in AD 86.

Prior to that, men of the 20th Legion, known as Legio XX Valeria Victrix, joined the Second Legion at the fortress, and thereafter became its permanent garrison to give the name of Deva Victrix to the fortress.

The fortress conformed to the usual playing-card shape with rounded corners, and it was originally 10 acres in extent. But when the 20th Legion arrived, the fortress had to be extensively enlarged, making it a massive 59.8 acres, measuring 1,930ft north to south and 1,340ft across. The extra space was also attributed to finding accommodation for the governor, his staff and bodyguard of 1,000 men. This subsequently required a massive workforce adept at building large structures, at which the Roman army was expert, and massive quantities of wood – perhaps an entire woodland – was required to build its defences and timber buildings. But, after the commencement of the second century, everything changed when, according to military practice, the fortress was reconstructed in stone. Again, the Romans used local materials, with the sandstone blocks being obtained from quarries lying to the south, just across the river.

Such a powerful fortress was substantially protected by deep ditches, 24ft wide in one place and 22ft in another, and a massive surrounding sandstone wall 22ft high. Initially, the defences had been constructed with banks of turf laid on a foundation of logs to prevent them from slipping. There was also a 5ft berm and a rampart 5ft thick, constructed with turf and clay. At the beginning of the second century the turf was replaced with the wall. In around AD 102, rectangular stone towers were added at each corner, including 26 along the sides of the fortress that were spaced at approximate intervals of 200ft. Six of these were successfully excavated, and the surviving remains of the south-east corner tower is now on public display. The overall dimensions of the towers were 21.5–22ft wide, and they projected 17ft back from the rear face of the fortress wall. All of them were solidly built with no interiors, suggesting that they had served as platforms for the heavy catapult machines, or *ballistae*, which the Romans used for hurling stone balls at the enemy. A large number of these balls were recovered in various places around the excavations. Internal turrets completed the defences. Contrary to the usual central siting of the main gates, the ones on the west and east sides were positioned about three-quarters of the way down the walls. Behind the ramparts along the *intervallum* were a line of narrow buildings, also built with sandstone and about 70ft long. These were thought to have been the cook-houses. Close by were traces of circular ovens. Fortunately, a large section of the north wall has survived to a height of 16ft and can be viewed from the bridge over the canal at the top end of Northgate Street. What had once been the deep defensive ditch at its foot was made into a canal. This stretch of the fortress wall is a permanent reminder of the Roman occupation, and it is the only surviving Roman wall in Europe to be in such a good state of preservation.

During 1883 and 1892, about 90 inscribed and sculptured tombstones were found built into a section of the wall, and this enclosed location certainly helped to preserve these unique memorials, the best of which are now on display at the Grosvenor Museum. One was the memorial stone of Gaius Lovesius Cadarus, a soldier of the

20th Legion. Another was dedicated to Gabinius Felix, a soldier of the Second Legion Augusta Antoniniana, which was actually garrisoned at Caerleon. What was he doing at Deva? It is thought that he was a member of the legion's unit which had helped with the reconstruction of the defences during the early third century. One of the exhibits was an altar inscribed:

GENIO SANCTO CENTVRIE AELIVS CLAVDIAN OPT V.S.

Which translates as 'Aelius Claudianus Optio fulfilled his vow to the sacred Genius of his century by setting up this altar.' An optio was a junior officer next in command to a centurion. He was responsible for book keeping. A Genius was a 'guardian spirit' (a statuette of one was found at Caerleon). On the side of the altar was a relief of an axe and a knife, with a jug and a saucepan on the other side. All of these items would have been used in the religious ceremonies held at the altar. Sometimes, an altar would be used as a marker for a grave.

The Romans believed that the soul lived on after death, and many of the sculptured tombstones reflected this belief. One tombstone in particular showed the deceased, Curatia Dinysia, reclining on a couch and drinking from a wineglass, presumably celebrating her life in paradise. Below the sculpture, an inscription told us that it had been erected by her heirs and that she was 40 years old when she died. Another showed a bearded man who was likewise celebrating with wine. These tombstones also had

A plan of the fortress at Deva, which also shows how the modern city of Chester has been built up over the site.

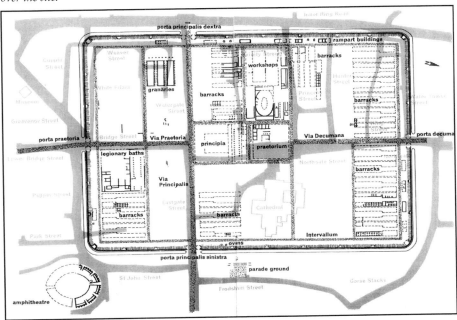

The tombstone of a 40-year-old woman which is now displayed in the Grosvenor Museum.

images of birds and various fruits incorporated into their designs, with the most popular icons being bunches of grapes. Other monuments just as interesting and telling a different story are all on view at the Grosvenor Museum. They are the largest collection of Roman tombstones in Britain.

While the city was built entirely over the fortress, excavations were successful in locating many of its main buildings. The first discovery was made in 1725, when the demolition of the Feathers Inn revealed the foundations of a vast rectangular area, 250ft long and 80ft wide. This was identified as the basilica of the fortress baths which lay in the southern area of the *praetentura*, close to the south gate. The structure, which functioned as an enormous covered exercise hall, was 34ft wide and had two rows of columns creating an aisle 18ft wide on either side. The basilica also contained an adequately sized swimming pool. An interesting discovery was a decorative mosaic with a pattern in blue, red and white. Unfortunately, in 1863 building works destroyed all traces of these remains, but a member of the Chester Archaeological Society had the foresight to take photographs and make a written record beforehand so the valuable details would not be lost. A small piece broken from an inscription was found in the basilica and firmly dated the baths to the reign of Vespasian.

Excavations to the east of the basilica were made between 1909–10 and 1926–27, exposing the massive columns supporting the basilica's enormous roof. Another beautiful mosaic was also found featuring sea creatures which had come from the floor of the *frigidarium*. Large scale excavations were then conducted under Pepper Street in 1964, during which the three main bathing areas – the *frigidarium*, the *tepidarium* and the *caldarium* – were exposed with their hypocausts found still intact, but again these valuable remains were tragically destroyed when building work commenced on the Grosvenor Shopping Centre in 1963–64. The inadequate archaeological examination of the baths was blamed on the lack of resources. Fortunately, the 'marine' mosaic survived, and the plan of the complex was recorded.

The excavations had revealed many of the delightful aspects of Roman architecture with exemplary workmanship, and again no expense appeared to have been spared by the military in providing luxurious facilities for its off-duty soldiers. In the *caldarium*

there had been semi-circular recesses containing communal wash basins as well as large bathing pools. The pool at the west end of the *caldarium* was about 33ft across and lay in an apsidal bay which projected from the main body of the building so as to receive the maximum amount of sunlight. There were several furnaces that supplied heat to the *caldarium's* pool and wash basins, and two large cold water reservoirs that fed an open-air swimming pool were located to the south-east of the complex. The main water reservoir had rested on a concrete base, 35ft long and 3ft thick, supported on 15 sandstone blocks arranged in three rows of five. The amount of water required to feed the individual baths, wash basins, fountains and swimming pools was extensive, and was estimated to have been in the region of 850,000 litres per day.

To maintain such a massively sophisticated and intensely used complex was a major undertaking. This is especially apparent when one takes into account the fact that maintenance could not be undertaken until the last bather had left, when each pool would have had to be drained and cleaned by morning since the water had been polluted with oil from the bathers' bodies. Also by the morning, there had to be an ample supply of hot water for washing, which required vast quantities of wood to feed the nine furnaces. This enterprise alone would have required several tonnes of wood to supply the minimum of 63,000 litres of hot water by the next morning. It was also estimated that the amount of cold water required to fill the swimming pools, fountains and the cold baths was in the region of 55,000 litres per day. Since water was another essential requirement for the latrines, drinking and cooking, another 15,000 litres was added to each day's requirements. The source for this enormous amount of water came from Broughton, a mile away to the east, and was channelled along an aqueduct to the fortress. Lead pipelines also transported the water into the fortress,

The remains of the south-east corner guardroom at Deva.

and these were found in three separate places along the route, including the one stamped with Vespasian's name. The baths functioned to the end of the fourth century.

As the general maintenance of the fortress's baths alone show, the garrison appeared to work all around the clock. Apart from being an efficient fighting force, the soldiers were also responsible for carrying out repairs to the buildings and looking after the roads, thus keeping their sawmills and workshops fully occupied throughout the day.

During the 1960s excavations, quantities of animal bone were found and a substantial quantity of charcoal, inferring that after the Romans had vacated the site civilians had squatted inside the baths, just like at Caerleon.

It is interesting to note that all the baths inside the fortresses and civilian settlements were the forerunners of the great imperial baths constructed in Rome from the late first century onwards.

Rebuilding in Eastgate in 1894 revealed part of the pipeline taking water into a central reservoir from where it would be distributed around the fortress. Waste water was generally routed along covered drains built in stone to discharge into the main channel running underground on the side of the roads.

Also during the 19th century, a portion of the *Principia* was exposed when five massive column bases, with spaces for two others, were found in the cellar lying beneath No.23 Northgate Street. These were identified as part of the north colonnade of the judgement hall lying behind the courtyard. One column base was left in situ. Further excavations in 1948–49 in nearby Goss Street uncovered the colonnaded west front which was estimated to have been 122ft long and 244ft or 250 Roman feet wide. It was also revealed that the Roman streets on either side of the *Principia* followed the natural slope of the ground downwards to the south, and that the headquarters had been built by terracing, to give the front courtyard a level surface to create a much more impressive façade.

The stone-built headquarters appear to have been erected during the rebuilding of the fortress early in the second century, when it replaced the one built with timber. There was a good indication that timber uprights had supported the north aisle of the cross-hall, and signs were that the timber *Principia* had been a modest building, but that it had evolved into a much grander structure when it was rebuilt in stone before the end of the second century.

After excavation, the site was built over with commercial buildings, leaving no trace of the excavated remains apart from the underfloor 'strongroom' or treasury of the *Sacellum*. This can be viewed through a glass window on the street outside one of the stores next to the indoor market. It is clear to see that this strongroom was quite a large one, about 6ft long and 5ft deep. Leading into it are large blocks of stone making a short flight of steps, but the grey stonework looks abandoned and trapped in its own time warp.

In the central area of the fort there would have been quarters for the governor and his personal staff, and adjoining the north side of the *Principia* was the commandant's own personal residence.

A short distance to the west, two extraordinarily large buildings were found, and there may have been a reason why extra space was required at the fortress. The first, measuring 480ft long and 180ft wide, also had a courtyard, an inner colonnaded portico and an outer range of rooms. Its unusual plan featured a long rectangular structure in its centre. This had been built with stone but, strangely, work had apparently stopped once it had reached ground level; however, after a lapse of about 10 years building work had recommenced, although its layout was changed to add smaller rooms with wide doors. The purpose of the building could not be determined and it remains a mystery.

The second additional building measured 180 x 100ft overall and was described as elliptical because it possessed an oval inner courtyard. This also had a surrounding colonnaded portico, behind which was an encircling range of 12 wedge-shaped rooms, all having enormous arched entrances that were 12ft wide. In the centre of the courtyard was the foundation for a sculptured fountain. It was here that the length of lead water piping was found running up to its base on which were stamped the names of Vespasian and his son Titus. This inscription dated the pipe's manufacture to the first half of AD 79. This lead piping is the only example to be found in Britain and is on show at the Grosvenor Museum.

Adjoining the courtyard, on its southern side, was a large bathing complex occupying more than half the width of the building. These baths were said to have required an estimated 80,000 litres of water per day. Despite the presence of the baths, there was no evidence that the elliptical building had been a residence, and neither was there evidence that it had any military features. In fact it is unique to Deva and has no equal in any other fortress. Like its neighbour, it was also a mystery. One wonders, therefore, if the building had not been built by command of the governor as a symbol of Roman power to impress the various dignitaries he would have entertained at the fortress. It has been suggested that the 12 rooms may have represented the 12 Roman deities or months of the year, but what is certain is that the purpose of such an elaborate building would have been to conduct certain rituals or celebrations at various times of the year, similar to a temple. Excavations revealed that partial rebuilding had taken place to the main building and to the baths, and that the building continued in use until the early fourth century. Like the *Principia* and its mysterious neighbour, these remains were also built over after excavation, and this once regal building is now buried under the Town Hall.

A large quantity of antefixes were found around the site, showing how well the eaves of these buildings had been decorated. One type showed the head of a lion and another the face of Jupiter in his guise as the horned god Jupiter Ammon. The lion was the zodiacal sign of Jupiter. Other antefixes displayed the legion's emblem of a charging boar.

The foundations of yet another extensive building came to light in the immediate area, and, interestingly, on two different occasions altars dedicated to Greek doctors were found, suggesting that the building had been the fortress's hospital. The altars dedicated to Greek doctors were not considered too unusual since the Romans favoured Greek physicians and recruited them from the Greek-speaking regions of their empire.

At Deva, the barracks occupied a major portion of the fortress, with blocks being found at many different places. Only when their siting had been agreed could the rest of the interior be planned. As was usual, they occupied the entire width across the top of the northern half, as at Caerleon, with the *Via Decumana* dividing each of the 12 blocks.

During the 1923 excavations of this area, one block was shown to have been sub-divided into centurion's quarters 85ft long and legionary quarters 165ft long, with a 5ft alleyway separating the two. The centurion's quarters had a suite of 10 rooms with an internal passage, and there was evidence that his walls had been plastered with a painted floral pattern. In the corner of two rooms was a makeshift latrine made from an upturned top of a storage jar which had stones placed inside. In comparison to the above, the legionary quarters were 28ft wide and were divided internally into 11 double rooms, with each set consisting of a large inner living-room with bunks for sleeping. Each pair also had a smaller outer room for storing equipment. On the evidence of pottery finds and various floor levels, it was found that the timber structures of these barracks had undergone alterations at the end of the first century, probably after the Second Legion had been withdrawn, and they were rebuilt entirely in stone at the beginning of the third century.

Legionary barracks were also discovered close to the eastern defences and were occupied by the First Cohort. In the centurion's quarters here, another upturned storage vessel had been used as a makeshift urinal. A separate block for auxiliary units was located on either side of the *Via Principia*. There were even barracks alongside the western defences next door to the *Principia*. Another large block occupied its usual position in the south-west corner of the fortress, and was found next to the excavated baths.

While the remains of the fortress baths had been mostly destroyed in 1863, the hypocaust of the *sudatorium* (the steam room) had fortunately been left intact and can be seen in the cellar of premises now occupied by Spud-U-Like in Bridge Street. Access is by a steep flight of stone steps at the back of the shop. In the cellar, the hypocaust is well lit and can be viewed through a cutting in the wall. As one can see, the pillars are high enough to enable a man to crouch inside.

Three granaries were discovered during modern building development in 1954, and they were found lying lengthways, side by side, and close to the west gate. Each one measured 159ft long, and all had been massively built with sandstone blocks during the early second century. None of their floors had survived, but the sleeper walls supporting them had. There were seven in each granary, 3ft apart, laid on grouted rubble foundations. Their siting close to the west gate suggested that the grain had been collected directly from the quayside, thus making delivery to each granary an easy process. Next to the granaries were the houses of the senior officers with stables and stores nearby.

Another integral part of the fortress was the parade ground. This was located immediately outside the east gate and occupied an area extending three-quarters of

A photograph showing the hypocaust of a bathing suite inside the fortress.

the way down the east wall. In the 10th century, Ethelflaed, King Alfred the Great's daughter and Queen of Mercia, was credited with strengthening the decaying walls and extending them down to the river to create a fortified town. The fortress's east and north walls are the only two to have survived. Inside the fortress there were signs that demolition work had taken place over a long period from about the middle of the third century to the early fourth century, with some barrack blocks being reduced to no more than their foundations. Broken roof tiles between the granaries also suggested that these too were demolished during that timescale. The western defences were also dismantled which might have meant that their stonework was required elsewhere.

Certainly, the stone was required to build the communities that were growing up outside the eastern, western and southern defences, and vast quantities of sandstone had already been used to build the fortress and others further afield. All this stone came from quarries lying to the south, on the opposite side of the river, now known as Handbridge. But as the quarries have been totally stripped, they have been transformed into a beautiful parkland called Edgar's Field.

The most enduring monument to those industrious times is the shrine to Minerva which the soldiers had carved into the rock face, and which is now preserved for all to see within the park. Minerva was the goddess of wisdom, handicraft and the arts. She was also the goddess of warriors and was adopted by the soldiers to protect them during their daily work in the quarries. They probably made an offering to her before starting work. The shrine, about 5ft high, is the only one to have survived in Britain. Over the centuries the figure of Minerva has almost withered away, but parts of it are just visible. Early woodcuts of the shrine showed the helmeted Minerva holding a spear in her right hand and having an owl sitting on her left shoulder.

This is the only surviving block of sandstone in the old Roman quarry (now Edgar's Field).

Close to the shrine is one surviving portion of red rock towering above the footpath running beneath it. Being located alongside the river bank, the park is a pleasant place to walk among the flowering elder trees where one can briefly glimpse a fleeting moment of Roman times. Pottery from the first century was found here when the large-scale Roman excavations were in progress.

The park is reached by the Old Dee Bridge. The Romans probably had a bridge here, although it would have been more convenient to transport the stone by barge to the dock right outside the fort's west gate. Since Roman times the Dee has changed its course and is now located further south, flowing east to west along the southern boundaries of the city.

In 2006 a sandstone quarry was found on land that had been stripped ready for development in the north-east corner of the city. Trenches cut by the visiting archaeological team found a solid layer of sandstone 3–4ft below the surface. Cut marks in the stone, as well as shards of pottery, confirmed that the Romans had already started to excavate the site.

The shrine to Minerva in the old sandstone quarry.

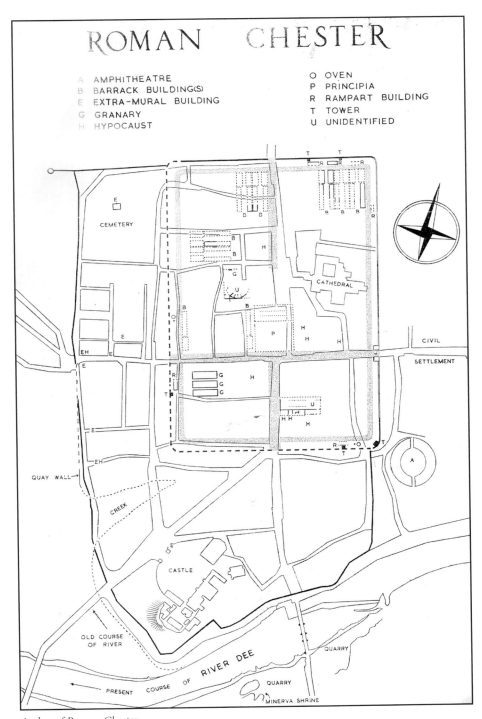

ROMAN CHESTER

A AMPHITHEATRE
B BARRACK BUILDING(S)
E EXTRA-MURAL BUILDING
G GRANARY
H HYPOCAUST

O OVEN
P PRINCIPIA
R RAMPART BUILDING
T TOWER
U UNIDENTIFIED

A plan of Roman Chester.

Outside the Fortress:

The civilian settlement which had established itself alongside the river outside the western defences flourished into a maritime trading centre with a large harbour, importing goods from Wales and the Continent. Excavation of the area revealed it to have been densely populated, with good quality masonry, and that most of the buildings were residential. There were also a number of warehouses in the vicinity. To the north were the workshops and the settlement's cemetery. In the centre of the community were the public baths. They covered an area of over 300ft square, a third larger than the fortress's baths. At excavation, both concrete and herringbone tiled floors were found as well as mosaic. The baths were probably as luxurious as those at Caerleon. Some of the earliest features of this building suggested that it was built not long after the fortress and that the legion had been involved in its construction. The early provision of extramural baths to a neighbouring civilian population would suggest that the military were keen to offer those who came into contact with their soldiers the same high standards of hygiene and cleanliness.

Civilians had also begun to settle on the available plots of land around the parade ground. This settlement eventually met those which had been established in the south, and had extended their dwellings down to the river's edge.

In the southern area, a series of large, well-built and imposing buildings existed from the late first century down to at least the fourth century, most notable of which was the amphitheatre, the largest in Roman Britain, which was sited outside the south-east corner of the fortress as a symbol of power to impress those coming into the area. In fact, the amphitheatre was discovered 'just across the road' from the excavated south-east corner tower.

The Amphitheatre

This exciting discovery was made by accident by a schoolmaster who had come across its outer wall in the cellar of the Ursuline Convent School in 1927 while heating was being installed there. At once he recognised the walling to be Roman and immediately alerted the authorities. At the time, there were plans to straighten the road between New Gate and St John's Church, which would have meant it cutting across the amphitheatre's area, but as a result of a public appeal by the Chester Archaeological Society the plans were amended, and sufficient money was raised to commence excavations of the site. This decision was greatly encouraged by the news that work was commencing on the amphitheatre at Caerleon, and it was considered a matter of civic pride that the one at Chester should also be quickly excavated. But owing to buildings still occupying the site, only the northern half of the amphitheatre could be excavated. (At the time of writing, its southern half is still partly covered by a clump of trees and the gardens of the Old Bishops Palace, but may be excavated at a later date.)

In 1930 the face of the existing arena wall was exposed in a number of places, as was the arena itself, which was found to be 14ft below the ground, measuring 190 x 162ft overall. The wall was standing to a height of 9.5ft and had originally been

The excavated northern part of the amphitheatre, with the passageway to the VIP's seats in the foreground.

covered with primary coats of white lime plaster and then painted a dark reddish-brown. At a later date the wall was covered with a thicker plaster to hide any cracks or imperfections.

The visiting VIP's private 'box' in the centre of the amphitheatre.

It was found that St John's House, an old ecclesiastical building associated with the Church of St John, was encroaching upon the site, so it was bought by the Chester Archaeological Society and demolished in 1958 to make way for further excavation. In August 1972 the site, albeit with excavations still going on, was opened for public viewing, and a walkway was provided across the bottom end of the excavations.

After clearance of the arena in 1967, it was found that its natural surface had been covered with a layer of yellow-brown sand, 6in thick, and a few isolated slabs set in sand were thought to have been the scattered remnants of the original floor.

At each end of the long axis were the main entrances leading to the arena. The north entrance was investigated in 1960–61 and was seen to be 18ft wide at the door end, narrowing to 12ft where it entered the arena. Around the periphery were subsidiary entrances with flights of steps leading up to the seating terraces and the separate areas reserved for the legion's senior officers and visiting dignitaries. One such enclosure, a square-shaped chamber with its walls still intact, was found at the edge of the eastern side of the arena.

As a result of the 1960 excavations, the most noteworthy discovery was the revelation that there were TWO amphitheatres on the site, the Romans having extended the outer walls by approximately 8ft to create a larger interior. The second amphitheatre was also capable of seating more spectators, 7,000 as opposed to 5,000, and its walls had been raised from 15 to 30ft.

The other difference was that the first amphitheatre had a staircase leading to the seats outside the walls, while in the second there was an internal staircase to reach the terraces. The only other amphitheatre with an external staircase is at Pompeii.

Two outer walls can be seen in this photograph taken during the archaeological excavations.

A quantity of Flavian-dated pottery, and a little worn coin of Vespasian, dated the first amphitheatre to around AD 71. There is reason to believe that work on the second amphitheatre may have started as early as AD 80, giving the first one a life of only a few years.

Recent and on-going excavations into the seating banks in the northern half have produced some interesting results with the recovery of animal bones to suggest that food vendors were in attendance to supply the spectators with a variety of snacks which included chicken legs and beef ribs.

It has been proved that gladiatorial contests took place in the arena. A gladiatorial scene was found sketched on a piece of Welsh slate in 1737, showing a combatant who fought with a trident in one hand and a net in the other, known as *retiarius*. Included is a perfect sketch of a *gladius*, or short sword, giving valuable information as to the weapons used. Such fights were popular and were often the highlight of a Roman's day out. Also found was a miniature Samian bowl with a decorated gladiatorial scene. It is thought that these little bowls were sold wholesale as souvenirs to the public. A piece that had come off the bone handle of a *gladius*, possibly broken in combat, was also recovered. After the combats, the arena sand was raked up, particularly if it was bloodstained, and dumped outside the amphitheatre walls. Curiously, examination of this sand revealed a human tooth.

Another significant discovery by the wall of the first amphitheatre was a painted shrine dedicated to the goddess Nemesis, the patron goddess of the gladiatorial games. She was also the goddess of retribution, on whom the Romans called if they wanted a particular favour – namely, to curse or seek vengeance on someone. The *Nemeseum*

was discovered close to the main north entrance and consisted of a small stone-built chamber measuring 12 x 14ft. Centrally placed at the rear of the room were two bases which had served as plinths for altars or cult figures, but no such figures were present. The missing altar dedicated to Nemesis was found a little distance away, and its inscription read:

DEAE NEMESI .
SEXT MARCI >.
ANNVS . EXVIS

This is translated as 'To the goddess Nemesis, Sextius Marcianus, the Centurion, set this up after a vision'.

An altar dedicated to Nemesis, found in the amphitheatre, which is now on display in the Grosvenor Museum.

183

Another small altar was found lying in front of it, and it is possible that the two were moved from their original positions so they could be incorporated into the new amphitheatre.

The altar to Nemesis measured 19 x 13.5ins and was 10ins deep. It had been carved in hard red sandstone with a six-petalled rosette design at the top. The altar is now on display at the Grosvenor Museum, Chester.

Under the Romans, the amphitheatre continued in use for 200 years, although it fell into disuse for a short period. However, after the Romans had left during the late fourth century it continued to be used to some degree, with people of the post-Roman period and beyond making use of the building. Late Saxon pottery from around AD 800 was found on the site, and the remains of a timber structure were found within the arena, which were thought to have come from the mediaeval period. Cesspits were also dug in the arena floor during that period, and one contained a decorative comb. A mediaeval coin also surfaced. Another pit produced a complete, late 13th-century jug. It was found that two of the amphitheatre's main entrances had been deliberately walled up, which may indicate that it was later intended to be used for defence only. This may possibly have been during the Civil War, a theory which was strengthened when lead musket and pistol balls were found at the site. Gaming dice from the 18th century were also found there.

As time went by, the area surrounding the amphitheatre was much sought after by the wealthy, who built their mansions here. The church, too, was attracted to the site, and many ecclesiastical buildings were constructed, including St John's Church, which became Chester's first cathedral and was attended by King Edgar in 973. There were also chapels and houses for vicars and cannons. This, in effect, stopped the over-development of the site.

Excavations were still proceeding in 2006, with daily finds being sent to the nearby visitors' centre for recording and storage. Conservation of such unique and often delicate items is a painstaking process that requires patience and dedication. Most bulk materials such as pottery shards are bagged in self-sealing polythene bags with labels indicating the site code and they are then stored in cardboard boxes. Later, attempts are made to match up the individual pieces to rebuild the original object. Metal objects are routinely x-rayed and kept in conditions of constant temperature and low humidity in perforated polythene bags. At each excavation preservation is the main concern, and a conservator will be on hand to advise on the lifting or handling of problematic finds.

Just south of the amphitheatre was a temple, and it was thought that a *Mithreum* might also have been in the vicinity. For such a prestigious Roman centre such as Deva, there is no doubt that one would have been erected here, and as it would have been well attended by the expanding population.

Close by was a large *Mansio*, built in the first century. It had a long and chequered history, having been rebuilt several times, and it burnt down during the third century to be rebuilt again. Some of the debris and rubble from the fire was found dumped down its two wells, including the body of a young man aged between 18–23 who had

died in the fire. His skeleton showed that he had sustained a broken leg during his lifetime, and had probably walked with a limp, which perhaps had impeded his escape. His skeletal remains are also at the Grosvenor Museum. A rectangular blue-green glass bottle of the second century was also recovered. The *Mansio* was finally demolished in the fourth century.

The incoming civilian population even settled two miles south-west of Deva at the places we now know as Saltney and Heronbridge.

At Heronbridge there was evidence that it had been an industrial site, with finds of bronze slag, clay crucibles and clay moulds, suggesting the production of bronze objects. The site was also similar to Holt in that it was situated on the left bank of the Dee, with the ground sloping gently down to the river's edge. The earliest occupation was probably around AD 90.

The buildings included substantial structures partitioned internally into rooms of over 30–40ft wide and more than 100ft in length. These 'strip' buildings were thought to have been repositories for goods, and the rooms at their ends used as living quarters. In addition, four buildings about 5ft square showed signs of intense heat having been achieved there, and the presence of grain in one of the stoke-holes implied that they had been grain-drying kilns. It is possible that some of the grain was supplied to the fortress.

It was thought that pottery from Holt may have been unloaded at Heronbridge and transported by road to the fortress as the river was no longer navigable here.

At Saltney, the community had been much poorer, living in flimsily constructed homes surrounded by fenced and ditched enclosures. And despite the poor quality of the soil, the presence of querns suggested that the people had managed to glean a meagre existence from agriculture. The discovery of a high proportion of third and fourth-century pottery suggested that the community went on to occupy the site until at least the end of the fourth century.

Around Deva itself, the communities continued to grow in size and importance, until they finally evolved into modern-day Chester.

HOLT: THE 20TH LEGION'S TILE & POTTERY WORKS

Holt, also known as Castle Lyons, was a branch of the works depot of the 20th Roman Legion based at Chester, which manufactured and transported tiles and pottery to the army. The site is situated on the left bank of the River Dee, in the present county of Clwyd, and occupies the north-eastern corner of North Wales in close proximity to the English border. Opposite the site, and located across the river, is the modern village of Farndon.

From a location point of view, the Romans had selected a convenient place for transporting the pottery to the designated forts, not only by the river but also by the well-planned roads they had created throughout the country. One such road actually ran through the centre of the site and connected with the auxiliary fort at Caersws. It also connected to Wroxeter. The location of the site ensured the plentiful supply of raw materials for manufacturing the pottery: the clay was obtained from the site itself and fuel came from the surrounding forests. As well as oak, ash, hazel and cherry, verified from samples of charcoal taken from the kilns, gorse had also been used in large quantities, no doubt having been gathered from the surrounding areas where the plant grew in abundance. Lastly, stone for the various buildings came from the local outcrops of the red Bunter sandstone obtained from both Farndon and Holt.

Roman remains were first recorded at Holt in the early 17th century when a local landowner unearthed some of the site's foundations.

The site was excavated by Mr W.F. Grimes, assistant keeper of archaeology at the National Museum of Wales in 1927, who found that the site covered some 20 acres. At the extreme top end of the complex was a Bronze Age burial ground. Following a lapse of some 18 centuries, the site was found lying under two large fields called Wall Lock and Hilly Field. The ground was also seen to slope gradually down to the river, where alluvial meadows extended some 100–150 yards along the river bank. Between the site and the meadows, large hollows were very much apparent as much as 9ft deep, and it was from these pits that the Romans had extracted the clay for making their pottery.

Excavations showed that the site had been a well-planned industrial settlement, with an efficient kiln plant and various workshops for the preparation and manufacture of the tiles and pottery. The kilns were located close to the clay pits, and the proximity of the river provided the much-needed supply of water. The Dee was also conveniently placed for the discharge of all the drains from the site.

One of the buildings, identified as a workshop, was 100ft long and had a range of rooms in which the manufacturing processes had taken place, such as the washing and preparation of the clay for the potters' wheels. Large quantities of pottery fragments littered the floors, together with potters' tools and the stamps used for creating patterns and 'branding' the tiles with the 20th Legion's insignia. Quantities

An example of a Samian bowl of the type produced at Holt, with a potter's stamp used for making the bottom designs displayed alongside it. It is now displayed at the National Museum of Wales, Cardiff.

of clay in its raw state, which had been ready for working, was also found. One floor was even covered with the clay to a depth of 2ft. Large stones thought to have been used for pounding the clay were among the artefacts taken away to Wrexham Museum.

A second workshop, 42ft long, was found with a separate room and a hypocaust attached. This was thought to have been where warm air circulated for drying the finished articles. The upper floor of the hypocaust had been destroyed, but the pillars had remained intact. As usual, 8in tiles had been used, with many bearing the stamp of the charging boar. The adjoining workshop, which was 18ft long by 13.5ft wide, had fragments of pottery strewn across the floor and may have been used as a storeroom before despatching the finished articles to their respective destinations.

Adjacent to the drying shed was a double-flue kiln, which had been built in a pit dug out in such a way as to take advantage of the sloping ground to retain maximum heat. The kiln measured almost 30ft square and was built with red sandstone lined with tiles. The height of the main flue openings were 4ft and showed that great care and attention had gone into building them, with voussoir-shaped tiles forming archways over the entrances. The flue tiles had vent holes 9 x 5in wide, through which the heat was conveyed to the pottery. An interesting find were finger marks still legible on the clay, which had been left by the person who had made the pots. The kiln was in an excellent condition when excavated. Close to the double-flue kiln was the wood store with the main complex of kilns close by. These had oven floors built 8ft below the surface, again to give maximum heat. Their structure, though, was considered to be unlike any others found. The floors had been made up of rectangular tiles with

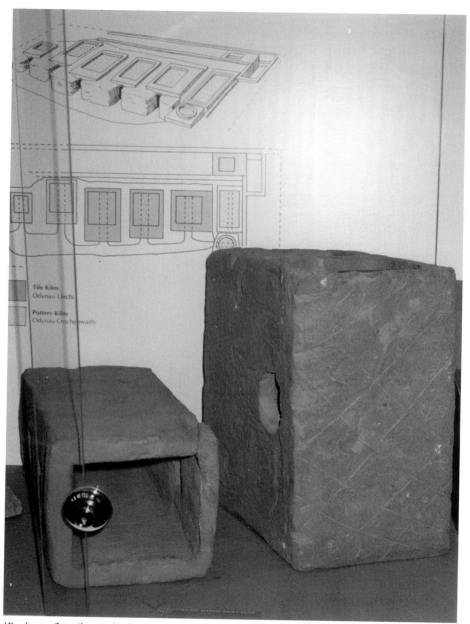

'Box' type flue tiles on display at the National Museum of Wales, Cardiff.

semi-circular holes. Other tiles had then been placed across them so that the holes formed a full circle when placed together. These had been daubed ready for firing. The pit of this kiln had also been robustly built with tiled walls 2ft thick. Its floor, however, was on the natural rock, and access was by means of a small set of steps.

The potters and their assistants had certainly been given accommodation befitting this well-run establishment. They had their own enclosure which benefitted from an efficient heating system. They also had their own bathing complex comprising the usual suite of rooms built to the highest standards. As at all the military establishments, a hypocaust system had heated the waters of the *tepidarium* and *caldarium*. Excavation of the bath building proved interesting. It lay 100ft to the north-west of the barracks at the top of the riverside meadows and was conveniently placed for discharging waste water into the Dee. The structure was recovered practically complete, except in the north-west where some destruction had occurred. The building had an overall length of 81ft, which was in keeping with the size of the settlement. The baths were entered by way of a large rectangular entrance hall or anteroom, 39 x 12ft wide, and led to the cold plunge bath, dressing rooms and the usual suite of bathing rooms. All the rooms were floored with concrete. The drainage system of the cold plunge bath was found to be in an excellent state of preservation. At the farthest end of the suite were the two sets of rooms, each heated by a hypocaust, one just over 20ft long, with the fire hole of each room excavated out of the natural rock. It was found that the structure of the hypocausts were more elaborate than that of any other building, and the system was considered rare. This had been fed from one furnace with the heat being transported through a gap in the party walls. Attached to the anteroom was a latrine which comprised a simple 3ft pit made of tiles and concrete. The drain of the latrine consisted of box tiles, no doubt having all been made on the site. The entire bathing complex had, apparently, remained unaltered during its lifetime.

A display at the National Museum showing how mortaria were separated in the kilns.

Another large building, identified as a 'dwelling', was discovered within a few feet
of the baths. This measured more than 85ft overall and overlooked the riverside
meadows. It was excavated in its entirety to show that it had a range of rooms going
off a corridor with remains of *pilae*, or brick pillars, which had supported the
hypocaust. Another hypocaust system was found extending across two other rooms,
with the heat again being transferred through a gap in the party walls. As only a few
of the *pilae* supporting the floors had survived, it was felt that the bulk had been
destroyed when efforts to excavate the house were made in 1600, following comments
that a 'Romane monument' existed on the site. This remark had enticed many curious
people to the ruins, and, consquently, their efforts to excavate had unfortunately
destroyed valuable evidence of habitation and other stratified remains.

The workmen's barracks were recovered under Hilly Field and consisted of an
enclosure 384ft x 198ft wide with rounded corners. It was a well-structured building,
with 7ft boundary walls, and had five ranges of rooms. Three of these ran the whole

length of the enclosure, with the most northerly having rooms 17ft wide connecting to a 7ft-wide corridor. The third range was not in a good state of preservation but had faced inwards towards a similar corridor. Blocks four and five each had rooms 90ft long by 22.5ft wide and set 6ft apart towards the eastern end of the enclosure. These could have been the dormitories. In block five, a line of water pipes were found which had conveyed water to the latrines situated in the eastern corner. These buildings had also suffered damage by intensive cultivation of the land and also from continuous stone robbing.

Close to the barracks were two rubbish pits, into which the men had thrown the remains of their meals, such as animal bones of various kinds and oyster shells which appeared to be a delicacy enjoyed by all the Romans soldiers. The pits also contained fragments of pottery, including large numbers of broken *amphorae* that had stored their wine.

A selection of pottery manufactured at the depot and displayed at the National Museum of Wales, Cardiff.

The other buildings at the eastern end of the enclosure were latrines, but many of these had also suffered some destruction in the past.

A 'centurial stone' was found, built upside-down in one of the walls, but as it was not in its original position its exact purpose could not be identified, although it was probably the tombstone of one of the centurions. However, it identified the military character of the site. Iron nails were found in large numbers over the whole area, which had survived past the timbers into which they had been hammered, and much window glass was discovered. Roofing tiles were also in abundance, as were the patterned triangular atefixes which had decorated the eaves. All the building material throughout had been of the red Bunter sandstone, which had been cut into fairly large blocks.

During excavations, there were no traces that any of the buildings had been modified or rebuilt in any way, suggesting that they had remained unaltered throughout their history.

There was no doubt that this had been an extremely productive branch of the Roman Army, producing vast quantities of pottery in a well-planned and orderly manner with strict military precision.

A quantity of personal items had been lost while the depot was in operation. These included many bronze brooches of various types, including penannular, trumpet and T-shaped, one of which showed traces of enamel. Very personal items, such as tweezers, a nail-pick and ear-pick, were found lying together near No.2 kiln, with the loop and pick of the last two items having been hammered out of one piece of metal, perhaps handmade by the owner. Several intaglios from rings were also found, including two Carnelians, one of which was engraved with the draped figure of Minerva wearing a plumed helmet. Another had the figure of Demeter or Ceres holding a basket of fruit. Domestic items included several spoons, iron keys and vast quantities of sandal-nails. It is said that a Roman soldier had as many as 100 nails tapped into each sandal. Someone had even put a large supply of them into a leaden lamp holder for safe keeping, probably one of the depot's cobblers. Curiously, some of these items were found in the bath building. Apparently, the losing of ring settings was one of the hazards of bathing in hot water, as often the heat melted the glue fixing the stone in the ring. Coins were represented by 16 examples from the reigns of Trajan and Hadrian, and 19 from the reign of Domitian in the late first to early second century, but the latter were too badly corroded to indicate the length of their circulation. There was a pre-dominance of the late first to the early second-century forms of coarse pottery, but a cooking-pot and a pie dish carried the occupation into the third century.